ASK
JOHN

STRAIGHT-TALKING, COMMON SENSE FROM THE FRONT LINE OF MANAGEMENT

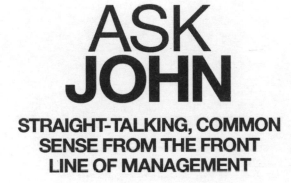

JOHN
TIMPSON

The Daily Telegraph

ICON

Published in the UK in 2014 by
Icon Books Ltd, Omnibus Business Centre,
39–41 North Road, London N7 9DP
email: info@iconbooks.com
www.iconbooks.com

Sold in the UK, Europe and Asia
by Faber & Faber Ltd, Bloomsbury House,
74–77 Great Russell Street,
London WC1B 3DA or their agents

Distributed in the UK, Europe and Asia
by TBS Ltd, TBS Distribution Centre, Colchester Road,
Frating Green, Colchester CO7 7DW

Distributed in the USA by
Consortium Book Sales & Distribution
34 13th Avenue NE, Suite 101
Minneapolis, MN 55413

Distributed in Australia and New Zealand
by Allen & Unwin Pty Ltd,
PO Box 8500, 83 Alexander Street,
Crows Nest, NSW 2065

Distributed in South Africa by
Jonathan Ball, Office B4, The District,
41 Sir Lowry Road, Woodstock 7925

Distributed in Canada by Publishers Group Canada,
76 Stafford Street, Unit 300
Toronto, Ontario M6J 2S1

ISBN: 978-184831-789-5

Typeset in Epic by Marie Doherty

Printed and bound in the UK
by Clays Ltd, St Ives plc

To Alex, who is the ultimate source
of common sense

ABOUT THE AUTHOR

John Timpson CBE was born in 1943 and educated at Oundle and Nottingham University. In 1975 he became Managing Director of William Timpson Ltd, the business that had borne his family name since 1865, and he is now sole owner of the company, which has a turnover in the UK of £200m per year. His last book, *Upside Down Management* (Wiley, 2010) was described by the *Financial Times* as 'a practical and inspirational manual for anyone who runs a business'. Timpson and his wife Alex have been foster carers for 31 years, during which time they have fostered 90 children. He lives in Cheshire.

Contents

Disclaimer

The advice in this book is given with the best intentions but the author and publisher disclaim responsibility for any loss or damage resulting from following any tip – big or small.

We do not intend to provide smart lawyers with the chance to make a quick buck at our expense!

Introduction

When some *Daily Telegraph* readers suggested I should put a collection of 'Ask John' columns into a book I was amazed to discover I've written over 250,000 words since starting to answer their questions in 2009 – and that's after subeditors cropped my carefully crafted columns to fit the space available.

I started writing about business in 1997, driven to pick up a pen by my long-time corporate communications advisor Michael McAvoy. 'We manage our business in an innovative way but never seem to get the recognition we deserve', I complained. 'No one ever gives much credit to a cobbler – we are seen as a third-rate business by prospective employees, property people and probably the rest of the business world.' Michael had a simple answer: 'Let's get someone to write a book about the Timpson story and your maverick method of management.'

I liked the idea of a book but didn't fancy the thought of it being written by an outsider – if anyone was going to tell the Timpson tale I would write it myself. I was worried that my set of management tips would appear arrogant until I came up with the title: *Dear James.* There is nothing arrogant about a father who wants to pass on advice to his son. The manuscript took me nine months, then I discovered it is much easier to write a book than get it published. I got excited when one publisher was keen enough to buy me lunch but then her phone went dead. The only person to show a genuine interest was Stuart Rock from Caspian who wanted to use my manuscript to write an article for their magazine *Real Business*.

The book stayed unpublished but I was asked to come up with a couple of 850-word pieces for *Real Business* – that was the start of a column I wrote every month for over ten years. After another fruitless year chasing publishers, Stuart Rock came to the rescue and *Dear James* was finally produced as a joint venture between myself and Caspian. To boost the circulation I handed out signed copies to Timpson colleagues who attended our senior management training course. Some years later one of the delegates at a conference where I was speaking gave me the copy of *Dear James* that he'd bought on eBay. In my handwriting, on the inside cover, I saw 'To Ray – Best Wishes for your Future at Timpson – John'.

I'd been writing in *Real Business* for about seven years when they asked me to add an agony column. Their preferred contributor had turned them down so I was the substitute selected to serve up light-hearted but controversial advice in correspondence that appeared on the last page of the magazine. A couple of years later *The Daily Telegraph* asked if I would do a bit of the same for them.

At first I was in an Appointments supplement, hidden at the back of the Business section about once a fortnight, alongside a couple of panellists from *Dragons' Den*. In December 2009 I was moved to the main business section where my column has appeared every Monday ever since.

I suppose anyone who writes an agony column can be expected to have all the answers. I confess to knowing little about the detail in Timpson but I've lots of colleagues who between them know the business inside out and have been happy to give me sound advice. As a result, by answering their questions I have probably learnt more than any of my readers.

Writing the column has never been boring; each question has presented a challenge. I faced a tricky task in deciding which questions and answers I should include in this book and in what order. Originally I was going to make it easy by picking all the ones I most enjoyed writing and putting them in chronological order. That was before I realised how much I'd learnt by finding an answer to every question. As a result I've divided the book into themes to cover a catalogue of management ideas, problems and hopefully a few solutions. To some the result may be an unusual, but hopefully amusing trip through the trials and tribulations of an entrepreneur. To others I am hopeful it will prove to be a unique business book with loads of ideas to help solve large and small everyday problems. The column claims to talk common sense but not everyone will agree. I try to be blunt – too many managers fail to face up to facts, which is why businesses spend over 80% of their time dealing with those colleagues who are pretty useless at the job – and when possible I hope my answers have a hint of humour: business should also be fun.

I'm grateful to the team at *The Daily Telegraph* for giving me space in the Business section every Monday and particularly to Richard Tyler, James Hurley and most recently Rebecca Burn-Callendar who have, as my link with the paper, always picked up my phone calls and replied promptly to every email.

Christine Hickman, my PA, has been the vital communication link making sure we never missed a deadline.

Thanks are due to all the people who put the questions

and keep finding new corners of business life for me to explore, especially my competitive friend Brian Thompson who has made it a personal mission to pose particularly tricky and quirky questions.

I would not have been able to cope with some of the queries without the help of a number of expert colleagues on the Timpson team. Gouy Hamilton-Fisher, our People Support Director, has helped me with most of the people problems; I have also pestered Paresh our Finance Director, Property Director Tricia, Computer Controller Paul Churchill and of course son and Chief Executive James who is now teaching me much more than I ever taught him.

My most prolific helper is my wife Alex, who not only often features in the column as my quiet superstar but also supplies most of the common sense and puts up with me breaking her home BlackBerry ban whenever I type the answers.

I have had great fun answering the questions – please keep sending them in.

The Importance of People

I suppose it isn't surprising that my biggest category of questions is about people problems and problem people. Situations and solutions that should be simple and obvious are misunderstood and made unnecessarily complicated.

Our modern world of best practice seldom creates the best result. It is wrong to assume all people are alike and that everyone in the same job should be paid at the same rate. Modern management is being hampered by putting people into a process that is policed by HR professionals, whatever you call them (we prefer People Support). Personnel departments have a vital role to play but they should not be allowed to determine how the business is run. As a result we have a generation of managers who are terrified of being at the wrong end of an employment tribunal. Their lives are ruled by employment legislation and they follow guidelines that go way beyond the law, created by experts to keep the record so straight they could answer every detail if called to give evidence at the dreaded tribunal. Day-to-day business decisions are now dominated by the system and few managers risk following their instinct.

When I started in business it was trade unions that prevented management from tackling people problems properly. Today we are held back by the lawyers who give safety-first advice to HR departments (where there are twenty times as many 'professionals' compared with the 1970s). As a result 5% of our employees (the poorest performers) take over

80% of management time. Bosses are constantly involved in back-to-work interviews and performance management programmes designed to improve employees who are probably not interested in getting better. The time would be better spent telling the poor performer: 'Your best will never be good enough for us and it's time to find your happiness elsewhere.' A vital part of people management is to say 'Goodbye' to the poorest performers as quickly, nicely and generously as possible. As soon as they have gone, all your good people will cheer and the business will be better for their departure. This hard-nosed attitude to problem people is even more important when it comes to bad bosses. One poor manager can ruin a business.

It isn't all bad. During my career I've seen many changes for the better. Today there is a lot less 'them and us' in business. Not many companies still have executive loos, dedicated parking bays or a directors' dining room. The role of women in business has changed dramatically – equal pay, maternity leave and a different company culture is leading to more women getting senior roles and appearing in the boardroom. Very few employees now have to clock in for a standard 40-hour week; flexible working is becoming more popular every year.

But with all the obstacles put up by the 'employment police' it isn't surprising that middle and senior managers are reluctant to tackle the day-to-day problems like office romance, expense fiddles, bad timekeeping, bullying and body odour.

Years of HR dominance has turned people management into a chore, a series of box-ticking exercises that include warning letters, appraisals, recruitment and exit interviews that all have to follow the system and be carefully filed for future reference.

Too many managers have handed over the recruitment role to the HR department and their consultants, who take a lot of notice of the applicant's qualifications, their CV, the application form and perhaps the added guidance of psychometric testing. We have discovered a simpler system. We pick people purely on their personality. Our interview assessment form is a series of pictures including Mr Keen, Mrs Slow, Miss Happy, and Mr Dull. We ask the interviewer to tick the boxes that most fit the applicant. That way we make sure they concentrate on personality. It works. Our aim is to have a business full of colleagues who rate 9 or 10 out of 10. We believe that the way to create a great business is to employ great people.

*

What are the most common causes of headaches at the moment in your HR department?

To find the answer I had a long chat to Gouy, our People Support Director, and learnt a lot from his surprising comments.

'We honestly don't have any headaches', said Gouy. 'It's eight years since we had a redundancy programme, we have a waiting list of good applicants for every vacancy and with salaries handled individually we never have a problematic pay round.'

'The day-to-day difficulties with long-term sick, poor performance, and terrible timekeeping fill a lot of our week – it is fair to say that the weakest colleagues take up a lot of our time, but we still have the chance to pursue our priority. We prefer to help colleagues WITH a problem instead of dealing with people WHO ARE a problem.'

I asked Gouy the obvious question: 'Why are you headache-free when most HR departments seem knee-deep in aggravation?'

'We are guided by instinct rather than process. I call my department "People Support" instead of "HR", because we find the formal approach driven by employment law far too confrontational. I prefer a management style that relies on trust and respect.'

I pressed Gouy further. 'Be honest, there must be some situations that give you grief.' After a bit of thought he admitted: 'Acquisitions create a colossal amount of work – we take on a lot of people who don't understand our culture and some casualties try to take us to a tribunal.'

'But my biggest nightmares come from outsiders who find it difficult to accept our "Part as Friends" approach to terminating employment. When filling in forms for the Department of Work and Pensions we can't tick a box labelled "Parted as Friends".'

Recently I was shocked to discover that in 1953 there were only 20,000 'HR professionals' in the UK. Today there are 400,000. I guess I am lucky to have a department of only six people caring for the personnel affairs of our 2,700 colleagues. I am sure it is because Gouy follows his instinct in preference to a process.

The last few years has seen a mushroom-like growth of 'HR' and (what I consider) the malignant and unnecessary spread of appraisals as a tool of measuring employee ability. Are these methods a clinical means of avoiding 'hands on' management?

Sometimes you wonder who really runs UK companies. Too often the agenda is dictated by HR, health and safety, the accountants and the lawyers, none of whom are engaged in the sharp end of affairs where you make the money.

I am embarrassed to admit that I carried out a few appraisals in the 1970s, when business schools and consultants started to push the idea that running a business is about best practice and process rather than flair and experience. Using a standard list of topics I found something to praise about people who were useless and for the sake of balance pointed out some shortcomings in our superstars. Fortunately I eventually realised that appraisals took up weeks of management time so scrapped the scheme and nearly everyone cheered.

Today our managers don't store up important conversations for a formal meeting. They have a continual dialogue with their team, issuing plenty of praise where it is due, and having a frank face-to-face chat with anyone who is failing to impress.

I am pleased to report that, at Timpson, the function that others label HR is called People Support – their job is to help, not to lay down rules. It is important to remember that it is people, not a process, that produce the profit.

Are we doing enough to provide our future leaders with career opportunities and guidance from a young age?

The straight answer to your question is definitely 'No!' We can never do enough to prepare young people for the world of work and probably never have done. I don't know whether things have got worse but thankfully I'm pretty certain that even a poor education won't put off a budding entrepreneur.

We should always look for ways to improve business links with schools and universities but I'm wary of think-tanks and councils producing guidelines and codes of practice – a lot of talking and official reports may tick political boxes but they make little difference.

Thankfully plenty of people are making the right moves. There are lots of teachers who get first-hand experience of business and many schools teach students interview techniques. More businessmen than you perhaps think visit universities to talk to students. Work experience schemes really work when the organisers become more worried about giving young people a real feel for business and less concerned with filling in the risk assessment forms. An encouraging recent trend is company involvement in Academies and Free Schools, thus creating a natural and direct link between young people and a local business.

We should never forget that it is our job to teach recruits about business – that is what apprenticeships are for. Schools that teach business studies are a bonus, but it is more important for school leavers to be equipped with a basic understanding of maths, English and day-to-day discipline.

We, in turn, must have the courage to give our young

people the responsibility and experience needed to become confident managers.

Despite the prophets of doom, I am optimistic. At Timpson we find a constant stream of enthusiastic recruits who will clearly be capable of running the business well beyond the day when I have to hang up my cobbler's hammer.

Don't be put off by teenagers who spend too much time on Twitter and Facebook. Give them a challenging job and you are likely to find that they are as bright as a button.

Do you ever use interns in your office? I'm tempted by the free, or perhaps only cheap, labour but worried about running foul of employment legislation.

You've got the wrong attitude. This isn't about cheap labour: interns turn up for work experience, not to be a dogsbody. If they do a useful job they should receive a proper pay packet.

I had to reveal my age by checking the precise definition of internship, which I now know is white collar apprenticeship or work experience in an office. I still have the old-fashioned view that trainees learn a lot more in a factory or a shop rather than sitting behind a desk or feeding the photocopier.

The first few days in a business can make a major impression on a newcomer. It could be a big turn-off or inspire the start of a dream career. It may give you the chance to meet a future superstar.

It's hard work having a raw trainee hanging around. Far from finding a cheap pair of hands, you need to pay for a proper training plan to make any apprenticeship worthwhile. If you have a good reputation on the intern circuit you should attract good candidates who will enhance their CV while giving you the perfect chance to decide whether to offer them a full-time job.

If you only care about getting cheap labour without breaking the employment law, interns are not for you, and you are certainly not right for them.

When you hire graduates, do you ever narrow the CVs down based on what degree they got? I saw a report recently saying some employers ignore anyone who doesn't have a first. Seems a bit extreme to me, what do you think?

In June 1964, I was having a drink at Wollaton Park Golf Club to celebrate the end of exams. I was lucky, as a player on the Nottingham University golf team I was able to be a club member for £3 a year (of which the University Union paid half!). I was chatting to one of the committee members about my chances of a decent degree, when he took off the pressure. 'Hope you get a 2.2', he said. 'It shows you're not just a swot. 2.2s are the sort of chaps I want in my business.'

I remembered his words a few days later when the results were posted on the noticeboard and revealed that I did indeed (like almost everyone else) get a 2.2. No one was awarded a first.

Today there are a lot more first-class degrees so I guess the country has more brains to choose from, but they don't always come with a guarantee of common sense. Boffins at university and prefects at school seldom develop into captains of industry. Perhaps common sense sits in a different part of the brain to the bit that helps you pass exams.

During my three years at Nottingham, I am sure I learnt much more from running the Students' Union laundry, dry cleaning and shoe repair service than I did by attending lectures on industrial economics.

At Timpson, we don't set out to recruit graduates. Everyone who joins us starts as an apprentice and we appoint our managers from within the business. However, without looking for them, a number of graduates have become Timpson colleagues. When they apply to join our apprentice scheme we are not bothered about their degree, we simply want to know what they did with the rest of their life at university. Intelligence helps but personality is vital.

I am happy to let the high-flying academics go and work for the big lawyers, multinational accountants and the civil service at Whitehall. I will stick to the advice I was given in the golf club bar. A 2.2 may not be good enough for everybody but as long as it comes with personality it is certainly good enough for me.

My PA is leaving after fourteen years and I feel lost. I've done everything I can to keep her but she just wants a change. I'm now starting to recruit her replacement but can't work out if I'm trying to find another 'Pam', with the same work ethic and patience, or if I should also consider someone with a different personality and skillset? Help.

Before starting the search for her successor it is wise to find out what Pam actually does. Be prepared for a shock – she almost certainly organises much more of your life than you ever imagined. After working with you for fourteen years Pam probably knows you so well she can take most of the day-to-day decisions on your behalf.

Don't be tempted, however, to look for her identical twin. There is no need to pick someone just like her but make sure you find someone you really like.

Look for attitude rather than secretarial skills. You don't need someone with shorthand and typing training but you do need a character who can use their initiative. Good PAs don't need to be told, they already know what you want to do next. And when action is needed they 'do it now'.

Personal skills are more valuable than efficiency and meticulous filing – your PA needs to command respect in the office and find it easy to get on with colleagues throughout the organisation. They also need the patience to deal with your most difficult moods. It won't be easy to find someone who can mix all these skills with tact and discretion, but the ideal candidate could be staring you in the face.

Why risk recruiting an unknown candidate from elsewhere when there may be someone already on your payroll who has the potential to do the job? Do you have anyone standing in while Pam is on holiday? Is there a bright person in Personnel who would like to move to your office? Your life will be a lot easier if you can find an internal candidate who has already caught your corporate culture.

Finally I must draw your attention to an important part of PA selection.

I sincerely trust that my own PA, Christine, has no

plans to move on, but if she did I would never dream of appointing a replacement without taking advice from my wife Alex.

I hear it's going to be illegal to ask people about their health before I consider offering them a job. I ask all candidates to fill out a health questionnaire so I can have an idea about their reliability – this is just one more thing to put me off hiring in the first place. Do you see any way around it – perhaps looking at their tongue or saying they can have the job if they beat me to the fire exit?

Never mind whether it is legal, your health questionnaire is a complete waste of time. If they are desperate for the job, few unhealthy candidates will tell the truth about their medical history. If health is a safety issue in your workplace, e.g. it is not a safe place for asthmatics, then you should make that clear but even then the candidate could lie.

By discriminating on health grounds you may be missing some positive personalities that could do your business a power of good.

The real problems that make people unfit for work – suffering from sickies, laziness and lateness – are not revealed by a BUPA medical. If you want to find out whether the candidate is fit for your business, get him to do a trial day. The colleagues who work with him will soon know if he is up to the job.

Forget the questionnaire. To decide what the candidate is really like, just look him in the eye and follow your instinct.

I've hired some excellent young people over the years and continue to do so. Sadly, I'm frequently amazed at their poor level of spelling, grammar and basic arithmetic. Have you encountered this problem? How do you tackle it?

Sat nav, calculators, emails and the lack of handwritten letters have created a generation who can't spell, don't bother to add up and think Glasgow is somewhere near Leeds. But if you ever want to solve a problem with your computer or iPad, ask someone under sixteen – they are word perfect.

Some failed at school or perhaps their school failed them, but even the academic elite with a good degree can be pretty bad at spelling if they can't use Spellcheck.

While we moan about traditional standards our children are developing a language of their own. You won't find too many examples of good grammar on Facebook.

I wonder how many over-60s would understand this message: 'cu 4121 2nite at *$ b49 coz lm bz l8r bfn.' If you struggle as much with this stuff as I do, perhaps you are 2o2l (too old to learn).

Some jobs need people who are good at geography, writing or arithmetic. It helps if a journalist can spell and a travel agent is able to read a map, and one hopes that accountants can add up. But you don't have to spell the word 'cobbler' to be good at repairing shoes.

When recruiting we are not bothered about sums or spelling, we want people with personality, but they need the ability to learn a lot of new skills in a short time. We expect our apprentices to reach a basic level in key cutting, watch repairs, engraving and shoe repairing within sixteen weeks.

Our skill tests are mainly based on practical exercises, so the testers aren't interested in spelling and numeracy and they make allowance for anyone who is dyslexic, but when it comes to cutting a key it has to work.

The media is suggesting there will be a large influx of Bulgarians and Romanians into the UK. Where will they find work? Did you recruit any Poles, when a similar situation arose from Poland joining the EU in 2004?

We discriminate in two ways. We have pledged to recruit 10% of our workforce from prison and we only choose applicants who 'get it'. You could say we discriminate against weaker candidates.

We always try to pick people with personality, and they come in all shapes and sizes. As a result the men and women who join us include Geordies, Poles, Cockneys, Somalians, Italians, Scousers, Scots, West Indians, Irish, Romanians, Welsh and Chinese – lots of nationalities with a wide range of accents who all speak our language.

Everyone starts as an apprentice so it is much easier for us to teach people with good English. Consequently, British-born applicants have a built-in advantage but I bet some Bulgarians and Romanians will become Timpson colleagues in the near future.

We need to freshen up our board. We're considering appointing a talented, enthusiastic, loyal, sometimes chaotic woman, who will head up an important section of the business. She has so much in her favour, how would you ensure that those failings are mitigated (aside from training) and that she really can step up?

She sounds great – don't hesitate, put her on the board.

In a world increasingly driven by 'process', quirky characters are just what you need. Don't think of eccentricity as a failing. Businesses grow by pursuing new ideas and having the courage to make bold decisions. The go-getting culture you need can only come from people with a creative character. Your lady sounds like someone who has 'got it'.

Most boards are dominated by professional managers who are determined to ensure their company keeps to convention. These 'safe hands' seldom make a difference – your chaotic woman could create the ideas that put you ahead of your competitors.

Don't give her any training – it might teach her some bad, risk-averse, boring habits. Your biggest danger is that the promotion will stop her being herself – you don't want this talented woman to become like the rest of the board!

I hope she accepts your job offer – you are very lucky to have her on your team.

I'm hiring some new staff in my business. We've seen some good people but some of the weaker candidates have thrown up some gems during the interview process. When I asked one candidate where he saw himself in

five years, he said 'in a rock band', while another started telling me where I was going wrong with the business before she'd even sat down. Maybe I'm asking the wrong questions. What's the strangest answer a candidate has given to you during the hiring process?

I passed your question on to our Area Managers who have been sending me lots of stories about comical candidates.

In the Midlands our Area Manager Paul asked a young man what interested him about Timpson. He replied: 'Nothing, my mum told me I had to come.' At least he managed it on his own. Les saw a guy in Scunthorpe who insisted that his mother sat in on the interview. When asked what he thought his strengths were, he lifted up his arms, flexed both his biceps and said, 'These babies!'

A young man in the north-east said he wanted a job 'until something better turns up', and a lad in Birmingham said he had to 'go out to work because Mum and Dad don't want me round the house'.

Some interviewees are unbelievably frank. Andy, our Area Manager in Northern Ireland, posed the question, 'What is your greatest weakness?' 'Timekeeping' was the reply. When asked to describe his personality, a man in Derby replied: 'I hate people, I get wound up easily and if someone looks at me in the wrong way I smack them in the mouth.' A young lady in the Beverley Job Centre started her interview by asking: 'How long will this take? I need to sign on, then meet my mate in the pub.'

Tony was interviewing a girl in Sheffield with the right sort of bubbly personality and carefully manicured nails.

'I think I should point out', said Tony, 'it can be a dirty job at times, especially in shoe repairs.' She winked as she replied: 'Don't worry, I can be a very dirty girl.'

At some point most interviewers ask whether the candidate has any queries. Sid in the south-east has had a couple of odd replies in the last few weeks. 'I'm thinking of buying a pet', said one. 'I'm not sure what it will be yet, but can I bring it to work?' 'Can you tell me the way home?' said another. 'I can't remember how I got here!'

Geoff explained our employee benefits to a jobseeker in Reading, who asked: 'Could you put me down for a company loan as soon as I start work? I'm in a spot of financial bother.'

Jackie, interviewing a guy in Shrewsbury, asked: 'Have you got any questions for me?' 'Yes', he replied, 'would you like to go out with me for a drink later?'

These anecdotes made me smile, but they also made me think. Who is going to employ these people? It doesn't matter how many grants are on offer, no business should give a job to Mr Careless, Mrs Dull, and Miss Can't be Bothered.

If any of these characters appear on your payroll they will irritate their colleagues and soak up management time. I would happily pay them to go and work elsewhere or do nothing. Which, come to think of it, is what happens if they go back on benefits.

What makes a good bonus scheme? I am keen to reward and motivate my colleagues by giving them a contribution from the company's profits. Should it be paid monthly or annually? Should it be for individual

performance or for group performance? What are the risks I must try to avoid?

Bonus schemes are a brilliant way to put buzz into your business but if you get them wrong they can cost money and demolish morale.

Find a system that works and stick with it. Good incentives keep running for years.

The bonus that operates in our branches has hardly changed since 1990. We make the same calculation in every shop every week. The wage bill is multiplied by 4.5 to set the turnover target. All turnover over target attracts a 15% bonus split between the colleagues in the shop according to the hours worked and their skill level. Prompt payment is made the following week.

We base the calculation on sales because people in our shops have little influence on profit margins. It is different for Area Managers, whose profit-based incentive has a key influence on keeping costs down.

Don't invent a different scheme for every department. If every manager has a custom-built incentive you will lose control. It is better to reward all your executives with a percentage of salary based on group profits. Keep the calculations simple.

I worry whenever we bring in a new scheme. I have seen so many incentives introduced with a great fanfare only to be quietly buried eighteen months later. To provide peace of mind we usually guarantee a minimum payment, but if that is all they earn, the scheme has failed. I don't like setting a maximum but if earnings are incredibly high we have almost certainly set a soft target. Either way it is prudent to launch anything new on a trial basis, and have the courage to change the rules as soon as you are unhappy.

Bonus schemes work best if you pick the right people in the first place.

Should the pay of directors be linked to the pay of other employees?

It may sound sensible for the highest paid director to get no more than twenty times the minimum wage but no system can solve the problems caused by jealousy and greed. Rigid salary scales pay poor performers too much, while great managers get less than they deserve.

To compensate for the few directors who pick up inappropriate pay packages and unwarranted bonuses, business is in danger of playing politics instead of paying people what they are worth.

You wouldn't expect Agüero or Suárez to turn up for twenty times the pay of a ball boy. Nor would you give Arsène Wenger twenty times an Arsenal steward's salary. Top managers deserve top money – and not just in football.

Whatever process is put in place, people will still feel underpaid while they think the rest of the world is paid too much. You will never make everyone happy.

We've had a remarkable spate of departures lately, including some key staff. Sales seem to be holding up and I'm pretty happy with the replacements we've brought in, but hiring is expensive and I'm worried that

company morale is suffering. How should I investigate – would exit interviews do the trick?

I wouldn't bother with exit interviews – we don't. They seldom tell you anything that you don't already know – and leavers often lie about the real reason for their departure. The more useful interviews take place well before a colleague has decided to leave (when it is not too late to do something) or a long time after they have gone (when they are more likely to reveal the truth).

You say you are recruiting some good replacements and probably console yourself by saying 'a regular turnover of staff is no bad thing' but, at a time when most people are thankful to have a job, you clearly have a problem. More serious, you don't appear to have a clue what is causing your workforce to be so fickle.

Is there an obvious trend? Is there a mass exodus to a competitor? Have most of the leavers been working in the same department?

If they are being poached by an aggressive competitor, what is he offering to tempt them away? If he is paying much bigger salaries there may be little you can do. Assuming you pay well above the minimum rate for the job, there is no point in paying fancy salaries to get people back – all you will do is increase costs and upset your loyal colleagues in the process.

People are more likely to leave a boss than leave a business. If you have a high proportion disappearing from a particular department, look at its leader. You probably have a management problem.

Whatever you discover, use the current spate of

departures as a spur to improve the way you care for your colleagues. You can never do enough to look after your star performers. We have pinched a lot of ideas from other good employers, like our free holiday homes and an extra day's holiday on your birthday – but we are constantly on the lookout for new ways to amaze our people.

With luck this big block of leavers will help you become a better boss.

Why do employees who have a job that pays well, provides a future pension and many other employee benefits, put everything at risk by stealing from their employers? Can you explain why they do it and, if you have the problem, how you manage it in your business?

It is a sad but certain fact that someone somewhere is pinching the company's money. Many start for what they think is a good reason – they need the money to settle a debt or pay for a purchase that they think they desperately need. Having successfully stolen they try it again and dishonesty soon becomes a habit. Other characters don't need a motive: they are career criminals who seize any opportunity to steal.

There is no excuse for dishonesty in any business, certainly not in ours. We have a Hardship Fund available to help colleagues in financial difficulty. We lend money to solve just the type of household debt that could otherwise tempt colleagues to take from the till. That is one of many employee benefits at Timpson, but being nice to your workforce doesn't always stop them taking your cash.

Don't spend a fortune turning your business into a

fortress. Take sensible steps but never let security become an obsession that gets in the way of doing business. Strict systems can make life difficult for the 95%+ honest colleagues, but your crooks will still find a way round the rules.

We spot most culprits by common sense observation. An obviously unusual sales performance, excess use of raw materials or simply the failure to look you straight in the eye can be enough to alert us to a possible problem. If suspicious we put in a covert camera.

Our team of tape watchers are so experienced they know from the body language when our suspect is at the point of putting his or her fingers in the till.

When we have the evidence we let the scoundrels see the film – then dismiss them for gross misconduct. It's an unpleasant but essential part of managing a business.

I've got an overachiever in my sales team who consistently delivers great revenues and earns good commission as a result. But a number of employees across the business can't stand working with him and we have had perennial disciplinary problems with him in the past. I don't want to lose him for obvious reasons but at the same time I don't want to be seen as a soft touch just because he's bringing the cash in. How do you manage mavericks and difficult people in your business?

You have to decide whether your blue-eyed boy is an asset or a liability.

It is possible that the others are simply jealous of his success. They will certainly be conscious that his spectacular performance has raised the bar, making their results poor in comparison. But personalities who can charm big orders out of customers tend to be arrogant extroverts, whose brash manner is best experienced in small doses.

You mention his disciplinary record, but don't reveal the causes for complaint. What has he done? Has he been fiddling his expenses, been abusive to colleagues or taken unauthorised leave? If you have been too lenient and let him get away with gross misconduct that was a sackable offence, don't be surprised if the rest of the team are hacked off.

In the USA, such a high achiever would probably be seen as a hero, but in Britain blatant bonus chasers may not be so welcome. Look at the situation from the team's point of view. Here is this irritating toad who is allowed to get away with breaking the rules and is still held up as an example for others to follow. He might be bringing in lots of business but he isn't helping morale.

The next time he breaks the rules I wouldn't bother sending another letter – I would give him the sack. It is only then that you will see the damage he has done. The rest of the team will jump for joy when they hear of his departure, and with renewed enthusiasm will probably make up for the sales you think have been put at risk.

For some considerable time I have been verbally promised a promotion involving taking over the management of a major subsidiary of my company. This assurance has been made by two chief execs. I was on the verge of being appointed when a new MD arrived and

has appointed an old school friend of his to the position. I understand the chief exec is highly embarrassed about this, but has not overruled the MD. What can I do?

You have my sympathy. One of the biggest bugbears of middle and senior management is being let down by your boss, and it happens a lot, especially following an acquisition or boardroom reshuffle.

Although you were offered promotion it didn't amount to much more than a nod and a wink. You haven't secured the job until you are sitting behind the desk and your name is on the office door. With nothing in writing I can't see any point in pursuing legal action. You are very unlikely to succeed at a tribunal.

Your new Managing Director has already brought in an old school chum and you can expect his previous PA, plus some more of his mates, to appear before too long.

Stay put but start looking elsewhere. They don't deserve your loyalty. It is time to take your talent (and your PA) to a company where you can be appreciated.

I'm increasingly buying into the idea that I should let the 10% poorest performers in my company go each year to keep everyone on their toes. It sounds tough but actively managing people out of the business who are not contributing as much has to be the right thing – doesn't it?

I first came across this idea in Jack Welch's book about General Electric. I thought his approach was pretty draconian (I still do) but understand what he was saying.

Every company should seek continuous improvement, and the better their people the better the business becomes. Try a simple exercise. Rate all your colleagues out of 10. If you have some 3s, 4s and 5s they should be encouraged to leave. If you repeat the exercise in twelve months when the low scorers have gone, you will look closely at the 6s and 7s. Perhaps Jack Welch wasn't as radical as I first thought.

Take this tough line and don't be tempted to replace all the leavers. Use some of the savings to pay your superstars more money, leaving a bit to boost your bottom line.

Most managers opt for the easy life. Spurred on by HR managers who point out the problems of making people redundant, they leave colleagues in the wrong job for far too long. Every business has a nettle to grasp. Beware of the bloke who has been over-promoted and the long-service colleague who has failed to develop with the business.

A payroll full of great people is a passport to excellence. Keeping up standards is a big part of your job and whenever you say goodbye to drongos the rest of your workforce will be delighted to see them go!

I've got a bunch of older workers all in their early sixties and nearing retirement. They've been with the business for years and are very loyal. I've read you can't forcibly retire them when they reach 65 anymore – even though that has been our way of doing things for over two decades. I'm worried they won't want to leave. How should I approach this?

I was as confused as you clearly are, until I had a chat with

Gouy, our People Support Director. Employment law has a wonderful way of building up myths that gullible managers assume to be the law.

You can set a retirement age as long as you go about it in the right way. In fact a recent UK Supreme Court ruling dismissed an appeal by a solicitor who had been told by his employer he had to retire after his 65th birthday.

Although you should no longer assume that 65 is the appropriate retirement age, forced retirements will still be accepted if they are part of a legitimate policy for workforce planning. This is where common sense is the winner.

If employers have no say on retirement, in twenty years we could find a payroll full of workers in their 80s and no jobs to offer to young people leaving education. Instead of careers ending with a dignified retirement dinner, long-serving colleagues will be pushed out on poor performance grounds.

You should set out a carefully considered workforce planning policy that doesn't just state your normal retirement age but also lays out your reasons. These will include succession planning and equalising opportunities through the age groups, giving younger people a realistic timeframe to reach their potential.

Whatever retirement age you set, there should always be exceptions (I am 71!).

Through the wonders of the internet I recently discovered that you are a member of the Women's Business Council, a government advisory group set up to help women play a full part in business. I was

wondering why you agreed to be involved and what you think you have achieved.

I'd never been asked to do anything like it before and was intrigued to see what happens when you come that close to government. Council membership turned out to be a testing experience for a maverick who loves breaking rules. Inevitably, I was surrounded by women, who probably saw me as a bit of a challenge, keen to recruit me to the feminine cause. Alex, my wife, has shown me the wisdom of a woman's viewpoint, so I listened a lot and said very little.

My fellow council members were on a mission to get a more equal share of the boardroom and produce plenty of publicity praising women at work. We launched a report, they tweeted on Twitter and networked on Facebook but it was mostly women talking to women. Not many men got the message. I didn't agree with all they said but did appreciate how giving women their rightful place at work can benefit us all.

There was a lot of debate about the cost and availability of childcare, but we must also make sure the kids come first. The EU has a childcare target that would mean young children spending less time with their parents. That worries me. We should find more ways to help the parents of pre-school children fit their job around lots of family contact. We also need a company culture that doesn't mean career breaks are a bar to reaching the boardroom.

New laws designed to make business more inclusive can have the opposite effect. Sensible ideas can get buried in rules, process and gender prejudice. Systems designed to avoid discrimination produce the sort of box-ticking that sits more happily in big business but smaller companies find hard to handle.

If you dig deep enough there is evidence to show that giving women a bigger role in business will increase our GDP, and common sense leads to the same conclusion. Put simply, if you employ the best people you get the best result. A good way to attract great people is to fit work around their lives. Thanks to being a member of the Women's Business Council I realised the fundamental importance of flexible working.

People come in all shapes and sizes and do their work in many different ways. No matter where, how or when they do their job, the only thing that really matters is the end result. In 25 years' time the world will wonder why everyone clocked in from 9 till 5.

There is no doubt women will benefit from a flexible job culture, but so will men. There will shortly be legislation giving most employees the right to request flexible working. Some bosses think this will make their life more difficult. I disagree. Flexible working makes the business easier to run and less stressful to work for, it attracts the best people and makes more money.

By pushing for more flexible working, women are doing all of us a favour.

I've got a lot of quite young staff, many of whom are keen on 'working from home'. I've always resisted it but my business partner thinks I should be more flexible. My suspicion is that not much work gets done when people are out of the office. Obviously your shop staff can't

serve customers from home, but do you allow office workers to 'work flexibly'?

It is a pity that most of the recent interest has centred on employees' new right to request flexible working, with lawyers working out how HR departments can create a process that follows the law without making much difference to the way employees actually work.

Not enough people are saying that flexible working is a fantastic way to run a business.

Research has shown that the classic 9 to 5 working day is inefficient. The human body operates in activity cycles that last about 90 minutes to two hours, from bright-eyed and ready for anything first thing in the morning to downbeat and downright uninterested by lunchtime. While the rest of the world has a siesta, an Englishman is still behind his desk staring into the middle distance.

I can tell from your question that your mind is a long way away from embracing the world of flexible working. It all depends on trust. If you are suspicious unless you can see your team at work in the office, flexible working simply isn't for you. Consequently you may well miss out on employing some potential superstars.

People work best if they are trusted to be themselves. The security that comes from having the freedom to fit work alongside the rest of your life reduces stress and increases commitment to the organisation. By working at a time and place that suits them, most colleagues will do a better job and feel a lot better about doing it. Clocking in, attending every meeting and following a proper process is not particularly important. What matters is getting the right result.

That does not mean that every colleague should have the right to work wherever and whenever they please. Flexible working should start with a conversation with both employer and employee seeking ways to help each other.

As you rightly observe, the scope for flexible working in our shops is somewhat limited. Each branch needs colleagues in attendance whenever it is trading. But many shops, particularly those open seven days a week, operate a rota organised by the colleagues themselves to suit their circumstances.

It is different in our office, where flexible working plays an important part. In our Finance department some mostly work from home, others come early and leave early, while a small group work well into the evening. We have mums and dads who arrange the week so they can drop off or pick up their children from school, and one keen table tennis player takes an extra 30 minutes at lunchtime.

Although it is particularly helpful to women, flexible working is for everyone. But as with every other part of employment, one golden rule applies – make sure you pick the right personalities in the first place. Flexible working will be a disaster with Mr Skive, Mrs Lazy and Miss Dishonest.

During the next few years some of the brightest and best people will work in a flexible way. If you think they are second-class citizens when it comes to promotion, you will miss some of the best potential candidates for senior management and the boardroom. It is this sort of stigma that could stand in the way of our future leaders, especially women.

It is time for you to think again and discover that a flexible workplace brings a better workforce and a happier team, and makes more money.

The women on boards issue isn't going away. Why do you think we've got so few female executives in the biggest listed businesses? Is the picture any different in family-owned businesses like yours? And how long will it be until we see a woman running Timpson?!

There is a strong lobby in favour of more women on boards but it is easy to forget how much things have changed already. In 1960, when I started work, there were no women on our management team, women had lower rates of pay and when they left to have a baby instead of receiving maternity pay they got their P45.

My great-grandfather had twelve children but only the boys went into the business; more able sisters were expected to stay at home.

Although we have seen a massive change in the last 50 years there is still a stigma that stops some highly suitable women getting the top jobs. It is a pity that this has created so much pressure on mothers to rapidly return to work at the time when they are most needed by their young children. (We are starting to hear reports that routine reliance on childminders can lead to attachment problems as the children grow up.)

The most successful companies are those that practise flexible working, allowing the job to fit in with a growing family. Perceptive Chief Executives don't see a career break as a barrier that stops talented women rising to the top.

We don't need targets to catapult a lot of token women into the boardroom simply to satisfy a politically correct Key Performance Indicator. Women can only play their full role in a business when the Chief Executive believes they have been appointed for all the right reasons.

Today, nearly 50% of the executive directors at Timpson are women but we have yet to have a woman on our Group board. I am, however, well aware that the best 'man' for the job is often a woman – not being on the board hasn't stopped my wife, Alex, playing a critical part in our success.

I am the only senior woman at my legal firm. I was recently told that I am in line for a further promotion – I am to join the board. The problem is that I was about to start trying for a baby. Should I put my family plans on hold? Be honest and possibly lose the promotion? Or keep quiet until it's too late?

You've put your finger on the key battle for women who want to make their mark as senior managers. Quotas for women on boards and more childcare subsidies won't make a level playing field. It is company cultures that need to change and although women are leading the campaign, the support of men will determine how quickly change takes place.

Anyone who fails to promote a star performer for fear they might get pregnant is missing the chance to create the best top team. Old-fashioned thinkers still fail to recognise that women are just as likely as men to be the best people in the boardroom, and a break to rear children doesn't dent their ability.

During my working life I have seen a dramatic shift in the role of businesswomen but company cultures still have a long way to go. You don't sound confident that senior colleagues in your law firm have got the message.

There are no guarantees in the baby-making business so I see no reason why you should tell anyone about your family planning until a pregnancy is abundantly clear. In the meantime take the directorship with a clear conscience and show that they picked the right person for the job.

I can't help thinking that I'm influenced – if only subconsciously – against recruiting a woman who may, in the next year or two, choose to start a family. I know it's the wrong way to think and I realise the government funds most of the maternity pay, but I still have the extra hassle of finding a replacement and with things being so tight I could well do without the extra cost. Your thoughts, please?

This is not just a matter of discrimination – it is also a question of good business. By turning your back on women recruits you could be ignoring some of the most talented people on the job market.

It might come as a surprise to you, but not all women are the same. You seem to imagine that they would all use you to help fund their, as yet unplanned, maternity leave. But a lot of them won't get pregnant and if they do conceive, the right characters will do all they can to make sure the job is properly covered during their absence.

Don't look at gender, look at the candidate. Make sure

you recruit personalities with talent. There is no law to stop you discriminating against selfish women with the wrong attitude.

Forget your secret fears – extended leave, whether due to sickness or time off to have a baby, is part of employment. If you are not prepared to take risks you are not equipped to run a business.

With paternity leave probably soon set to match time off on maternity, you will face the same dilemma with men as well as women. Stop trying to guess who is going to have a baby, and concentrate on finding the best person for the job.

Although statutory maternity leave is now an accepted part of corporate life, how do you manage the effects, particularly in those small but important departments where the paid absence of a key colleague for up to 39 weeks must be most difficult and costly to organise?

Maternity leave can cost extra money and certainly takes time to organise but at least you get a few months' notice to get things organised. I quite understand the problems this brings to small businesses and specialist departments, but it pays to be positive. See it as an opportunity to create a great workplace for talented women that others may be less keen to employ.

Although the rules are rigid, personal circumstances vary, so be prepared to take a flexible approach. If you need temporary cover, use the chance to provide work experience to a possible future superstar – but limit their contract to less than twelve months to avoid giving a long-term commitment to an extra name on the payroll.

Find out how you can helpfully support the expect-
ant mum while she is on maternity leave. Does she want
to receive the company newsletters to keep in touch with
progress? Does she want to phase her return on a part-time
basis? Would a change to her working week help her with
childcare? You may find many ways you can help her, while
also helping the business.

It is often wrong to stick to the statutory period – in nine
months some people can get so out of touch they find returning
to work very stressful. For others it can be too tough to leave a
twelve-month baby behind. It is much better to work out what
best suits both the new mum and the business, instead of reli-
giously sticking to the timetable set by the maternity benefit.

Maternity benefits are here to stay but they still influence
recruitment. I was talking to a talented businesswoman last
week who openly admitted that the prospect of pregnancy
had such disruptive implications she tends to recruit older
women. As long as businesses feel that maternity comes at a
cost, plenty of managers will do the same.

But despite the extra cost, most maternity leave works
out much better than expected. By the time the new baby is
brought in to the office for other colleagues to admire, you
can be pretty sure it won't be long before mum will happily
return to work.

**One of my really good workers is threatening to leave
to a competitor who is willing to pay more money. I just
can't afford to pay them more. Have I lost them or is it
worth me fighting for them to stay?**

Let him go, but do your best to ensure you part company on good terms. Although exit interviews seldom reveal the truth, it is worth having a frank discussion to see if you can detect whether money really is behind his decision or if there is another reason to do with your organisation or his own career plans. Whatever you discover, don't be tempted to offer more money. The chances are that he has been bribed by a massive increase; if you match your competitor you are likely to scupper your salary structure and upset the rest of your workforce. If it only takes a paltry £25 to persuade him to stay, before long he will be back for more. You can't buy loyalty simply by writing a bigger cheque.

All is not lost. Keep in touch (I make a point of popping in to see ex-colleagues who are working in someone else's shop). Over half of the good colleagues who decide to seek their fortune elsewhere return to resume their career with Timpson within three years.

Surveys show that overweight employees have twelve times the level of sickness absenteeism as their colleagues who maintain a healthy weight. What action do you take if one of your staff becomes unacceptably obese? Is it a breach of employment law to give them an ultimatum: 'Either you lose weight or you risk dismissal'?

As far as I'm concerned, as long as colleagues do a great job, it doesn't matter whether they are thin, fat, short or tall. An ultimatum saying 'lose weight or lose your job' may be appropriate for a professional footballer or ballet dancer but in most cases it is totally unacceptable and could lead to an expensive employment tribunal.

It is fine to help a colleague who wants to lose weight – offer free health checks, provide moral support, or even start a company slimming club. But no one should be blackballed just because they tip the scales over a company target.

Your question raises another issue. My iPad says the UK sickness level averages 4.5 days a year, although it is 9.5 in the NHS and 14.7 days a year for ambulance drivers. If I also believe the survey you quote, which suggests that overweight people take twelve times as many sickies, I can expect a fat ambulance driver to be off sick for 176 days. With 28 days holiday and 52 weekends he would only be at work 57 days a year. Some may consider this worrying. I just think it shows the danger of believing statistics in somewhat suspect surveys (produced for PR purposes) that the media sometimes publish as front page news.

How can I get rid of my boss? He has gone as far as he can go in the company and is blocking my progress. He is taking the credit for my work and is certainly not opening doors for my future progression. What can I do?

This isn't just a question of how to deal with your boss – it's about your career.

Lots of bosses block talented members of their team, mainly for selfish reasons – not wanting to lose an excellent colleague, or fearing that a rising star could compete for their own position.

The only person who can solve your problem is your boss's boss – it's time to have a talk.

There are obvious risks. Once you have declared your frustration and announced your ambition, your line manager will not be pleased, but as he has already lost your respect there is little to lose. If senior management doesn't recognise your talent or acknowledge that your boss has shortcomings it is time to pursue a career elsewhere.

Before making a move, have a big think – are you totally confident in your own ability and are you sure about your line manager? If so, knock on the big boss's door and explain your position.

Your approach may be very welcome – you could be providing precisely the confirmation management needs to take action – but be prepared for a frosty reception.

Your days with your present employer are probably coming to an end, but don't hand in your notice until you have found a new job.

I've got a hot-headed co-director who's making my life a misery. He overreacts to everything – he even threw a computer monitor across the room when it broke down last week, and has visited customers personally to deliver some colourful language when they've been late paying us. I want him out of the business, but fear he'll try to sabotage us anyway if I get my wish. What would you do?

I am wondering whether your co-director has always been so impossible, or is this a recent change in his behaviour? Have some serious problems cropped up in your business? Have things deteriorated recently? Is he suffering from stress? Has something happened in his private life?

Whatever the problem, you must not put up with his antics for a moment longer. Forget your fears of sabotage – the damage he might do as an outsider (which I think will be minimal) will be nothing compared to the harm he could do if he continues to throw his foul temper at all and sundry.

You sound frightened of him, but it is time to take charge. Meet up and make your position clear (if possible make sure another senior colleague is present). Start with a sympathetic chat but be blunt. Explain that his manner is harming the business and see if there are any ways you can help. The conversation can go two ways. Either he will accept there is a problem and talk about the cause of his stress (in which case you can start to help) or you will find another monitor flying towards your face.

Before the big conversation think through your legal position. Prepare the severance payment you are willing to offer to get him to go, and if he is a shareholder be ready to buy out his share of the company.

For the sake of yourself and the business it is time to show some leadership.

One of my employees has been with me for two years. For the first eighteen months, her performance was exemplary but recently she seems frequently tired and distracted and has started making mistakes. I don't want

to lose her but I'm worried about the decline in her work. How do I raise the issue delicately?

Even the best employees can go off the boil, especially when they work alongside the wrong people or if something serious is upsetting their life outside work.

Plenty of events can push work down the personal pecking order – breaking up from the boyfriend, a big payday loan, a period of stress, terminally ill mum or kids being bullied at school all have the potential to put a great performer off her stride.

You must find a way that lets you into the rest of her life. Look for the signs, listen out for comments that could be coded calls for help. Sometimes when I'm visiting shops a colleague will say, 'Can I have a word with you?' It can lead to a frank description of their overwhelming worry.

If she doesn't offer to talk, take her for a coffee and a chat and ask a critical question: 'I'm worried. I guess you know you've been below your excellent best recently – is there something in or outside work that is on your mind?'

Hopefully that will get her talking. You may be able to come to the rescue by arranging some time off, lending some money or pointing her in the direction of professional help.

Giving her the chance to talk may be all she needs. A vital part of management is to be a good listener.

A salesman at my company recently submitted an expenses request for a sizeable amount, spent at a well-known strip club on a Saturday night. He claims that he took a client of ours, who does spend a lot with the

company. I don't want to call this client to check. Equally, I don't want to fork out hundreds for a jolly that may have had nothing to do with the company. I also don't approve of this kind of socialising. What should I do?

If your salesman wants to go to strip clubs he should do it in his own time and use his own money. By using your expenses to fund his loose living he is putting the company reputation at risk and could be accused of breaking the Bribery Act. This behaviour may make you wonder whether your salesman is the sort of guy you want on the payroll and if his client is the sort of customer you should be cultivating. But, from bitter experience, I think it may be wise, on this occasion, to reimburse his extravagant expenses.

Some years ago we spotted a similar claim (this was a pole dancing club) from a manager who had already been reprimanded for previous brash behaviour. We dismissed him for gross misconduct and he took us to an employment tribunal. We lost and he got £40,000 because our expense guidelines didn't make it clear that our colleagues can't claim back the cost of pole dancers.

I suggest you immediately change your guidelines and make it clear to your sales guy that he won't be claiming for any more strip clubs. Then talk to your client and explain why he won't be getting any more titillating invitations.

You may lose a key customer and a good salesman but your action will make a much better business.

I've seen a great candidate, but they have a problem with body odour. How on earth do we raise this issue? I fear

it's something he suffers from constantly, but he's got so much going for him otherwise.

I have never had to interview anyone with BO but it would probably be enough to stop me asking them back for a second interview. Most people make sure that they're at their best when going for a new job. Sweaty nerves are no excuse. Even though you see a star employee in the making, I still advise caution: you might be able to live with it, but will your colleagues cope? And your clients?

You must have the courage to offer much-needed advice. Gentle hints about deodorant may seem the most tactful way to help, but, in the end, you will have to tell him he smells. A second interview is absolutely essential. If you have the slightest sniff of doubt, don't take him on. If he passes the test, though, you may not only have found a future superstar, you will probably also improve the lives of his close friends and relations.

I am a manager of a medium-sized department in a fairly large corporation. There are around fifteen people in my team. A few months ago, a rather unpleasant nickname for me began circulating. I'm trying not to let it upset me but it does. How can I shake off this horrible new moniker?

Without knowing the nasty name being used behind your back, it's difficult to offer specific advice, but I can't help wondering why you attract such negative attention. Judging by your level of concern, I guess the nickname is more offensive than just Big Ears or Fatso.

People can be pretty cruel, but there is usually a trigger that starts the name calling. It could be prompted by a reputation for being grumpy, lazy or sexually over-active, or even having body odour.

If there's a hidden message, take the hint. That may be enough to stop the insults. If your team persists in talking behind your back, tackle them face-to-face – let them know you know about the insults and ask them why. At the same time talk to your boss, who shouldn't be standing by while you are being bullied.

The last resort is to move on and find a happier job elsewhere. But make sure you don't deserve to be given the same nickname by your new colleagues.

I sense an office affair brewing between two of my staff – one of whom I regard as very important to the business. We only have about 50 staff and my biggest concern is actually disruption, awkwardness and gossip. I feel powerless to stop it – but can I at least take steps to minimise the damage?

It depends what you mean by an affair. I consulted Wikipedia, where I found details of romantic, extramarital and online affairs – but they had nothing to say about office affairs.

Your concern suggests that this isn't simply a starstruck couple who look lovingly into each other's eyes over lunch in the canteen. I guess the people involved are cheating on their permanent partners and it sounds as if they are pretty blatant about their relationship.

Today we are a lot more tolerant than previous

generations. An affair then would often lead to dismissal. Many years ago I remember one couple who cleverly coordinated their business travel so they always finished in the same hotel – we were paying for two rooms when they only used one. They were both dismissed.

Office gossips can create a major drama out of a minor incident so proceed with caution. Hanky panky in the office doesn't mean a red card. Even if there are cuddles behind the filing cabinet it can't be construed as gross misconduct. But if this alliance has become the top topic of conversation you can't ignore it. It's time to talk.

Have a chat with both the central characters, seeing them one at a time. Don't be critical or sit in judgement, start the conversation by saying something like, 'A number of people are talking about your relationship, and although it is up to you what happens outside the office, what happens here is my business ...' Get them to tell you the truth and ask how they would like you to handle the office gossip.

You will have done some good just by having a chat and you never know where the conversations will lead. The rumours may be exaggerated, or the affair could be causing such serious personal anguish it is affecting their performance at work.

The couple could ask for advice on how they should balance work and their new love life, and as a result you may become more of a mentor than a manager. By all means give advice but it is not your job to control their lives.

This affair may be a passing fancy that doesn't last long or they may have found a lasting relationship. Whatever the outcome, the gossip mongers will soon get bored and move on to the next rumour.

We have one member of staff who is turning up late in the morning and it is beginning to become a problem. How do you tackle such issues?

You say in your letter this guy's lateness is becoming a problem – turning up late is a problem the first day it happens. Stamp it out straight away with a blunt face-to-face chat. You must not let poor timekeeping become part of your culture.

A lot of our people are on flexitime so they have chosen their working week, but we expect everyone to turn up early – i.e. ready to start work at their chosen time.

If you let a colleague swan in several minutes late without saying anything, you are asking for trouble. When you eventually decide to clamp down they will complain with some justification, 'You never said anything before!'

We apply the same zero tolerance approach to sickies – with us, sick leave is not an entitlement, it is only available for people who are too ill to work.

To bring home the seriousness of lateness or regular sickies, Gouy, our People Support Director, always draws an analogy with employing a decorator: 'If you hire a decorator and he goes off sick with the room half-finished, how long would it be before you bring in someone else to finish the job?'

We are pretty lenient employers but there is only so long you can sit in a half-decorated room. If your guy keeps turning up late he will have to go.

We have been in business nine years and employ 45 staff. A long-standing employee has physical and mental health problems, is often away from work, and doesn't

come in at the last minute, letting us and her colleagues down. We have always subscribed to Mentor, the RBS/ NatWest employment law advisors. We need to let this person go – she is a total liability – but we are advised that we are just not able to. We have tried interviews, job assessments, health assessments, etc. Please, do you know a way that will not end us up in court with a bill we can't afford to pay?

I can understand your frustration but fear I may not be able to provide the perfect way out of your predicament. You are caught in a nightmare and the situation is fraught with legal danger. Through no fault of your own you may finish in an employment tribunal that could cost you a lot of money. I can't give a definitive answer; much depends on whether your colleague will cooperate or if she simply wants her day in court.

Following your employment law advisor's guidance you seem to have done everything possible to help this worker keep her job. You have tried meaningful consultation, obtained medical records for the experts' view and thoroughly explored how you can make reasonable adjustments to the workplace and to her role. But you still haven't solved the problem. Her absence is disrupting the business and getting up the nose of each and every colleague.

Your advisors may well suggest that you set a performance management programme and issue a series of capability warning letters to prove this colleague is incapable of doing the job on health grounds. But the red tape approach may well lead to a period of long-term sickness on the way to a tribunal. It is not always wise to follow the procedure prescribed by an employment lawyer.

Look at the whole thing calmly and logically. It is better to spend money on a compensation package that will persuade your sick colleague to go than to log up a lot of legal fees and still risk an expensive tribunal.

It is time for a heart-to-heart chat. Explain your situation and listen to hers. With luck she will see the advantage of an immediate settlement so you can all get on with the rest of your lives.

Don't let your frustration get the better of you. Although you feel she has already cost enough time and money, don't be mean. Look at things from her point of view and be generous enough to secure her agreement.

The sooner you get it sorted the quicker you can concentrate on running the rest of the business.

Customers and staff seem to be dropping a lot of hints lately that suggest one of my best workers likes a few too many drinks at lunchtime. I've got no proof, but am obviously concerned about the damage this could do to the business. How should I approach this tricky subject?

Don't let the situation drift any longer. It's time for you or your HR Director to meet him face-to-face for an open and frank chat. So far you only have other people's word – they may be setting him up. So, without warning, ask to see him after lunch. If he has had a drink that day you will soon know about it. Regardless of whether his breath smells, ask him about the rumours. If he denies the allegations, leave it there for the moment and dig deeper. If he accepts there is some truth in the suggestion, it is time for you to give him help.

Lunchtime drinking shows there is a real problem that might involve much more than alcohol. He may well have started drowning his sorrows to escape from difficulties at home – the habit could be caused by debt, gambling, relationship breakdown or many other difficulties preying on his mind.

You say he is one of your best workers but he won't be the pick of the bunch much longer unless he can get the rest of his life back on track.

It is worth checking the guidelines you give your colleagues. I don't like rules but other people do, especially the lawyers. Drink and business don't mix, so give your team zero tolerance: the liquid lunch went out of fashion decades ago.

Recently I was talking to a harassed boss who came out with the comment: 'Some people expect that I should provide a social service', to which I replied: 'That's exactly what a good boss does. Your job is to support your team.'

It's been impossible to ignore the fact that one of our senior salespeople has recently had her cleavage 'cosmetically advanced'. I see no problem with this but she's suddenly taken to wearing very low-cut tops which I've overheard female colleagues complain are distracting and unprofessional. How do I broach the subject without offending her, or worse, end up being accused of sexual discrimination? So far I've just

ignored it in the hope it will sort itself out – at least temporarily once winter arrives and she has to cover up.

As only the women in your team are complaining, I consulted my wife, Alex, to get the feminine perspective. 'I expect they're jealous', she said. 'The girl with the cleavage is clearly proud of what her surgeon has produced and as she has spent a small fortune on getting a bigger bust it would be a shame not to flaunt it.'

You talk about her bosom but you have missed out her most vital statistics – how good are her sales figures? Is she the star of your sales force? Has the drop in neckline produced an uplift in turnover? If so, her colleagues may envy the way she attracts sales as well as the extra attention.

However good she is at pulling in the business, you can't ignore the problem. Behind-the-scenes bickering is bad news. You might disagree with them but other people's opinions matter. A tiny bit of cleavage to one person could be a provocative plunging neckline to another.

Draw up a dress code to help your colleagues feel comfortable and look professional. Make the guidelines clear by using pictures of unacceptably tatty jeans, excessive jewellery and, of course, too much flesh.

Don't be tempted to get involved yourself. When it is time to act, leave the action to your HR department. Let them issue the dress guidelines but before they are published, persuade a friendly woman from HR to talk to your newly buxom sales executive and explain exactly why customer-facing colleagues must dress appropriately.

I am pretty sure she will quickly take the point, cover up

more of her cosmetic surgery and find another way to express her confident personality.

One member of my team is lippy and I feel he is undermining me as the manager in front of my team. I can't fault his work but he is influencing the others. I hate confrontations but feel I need to lay down the law. What would you do?

There are two people in the business you need to worry about: the guy who is talking behind your back, and, of much more significance, yourself. If you are so reluctant to face up to a confrontation I wonder whether you are in the right job.

Perhaps this is your big chance to take a practical course in assertiveness by tackling the problem head on. It is time to meet him face-to-face and pose the pertinent question: 'Please tell me what you've been saying about me to the rest of the world.' Don't see him on your own – have your HR chief at your side, partly for moral support but mainly to make sure you don't cop out at the last minute.

The longer you wait the worse things will become, so see him today (there is no point in having any more sleepless nights thinking about your options). The meeting will be good for the business and great for your self-respect.

Maybe his disloyal remarks were making a valid point. If the criticism is well founded, take his advice but make sure that, in future, all such comments must be made directly to you – tell him that any further backbiting will lead to his dismissal.

You might think he is a good worker but without loyalty and respect you are better off without him. There will be plenty of possible replacements who are just as good at the job but also know how to behave.

As soon as the interview is over you will already be on the way to becoming a much better manager.

One of my young managers made an honest but rather stupid mistake that's cost us a big bit of business. It's not the first time he's dropped the ball so I felt I had to give him a formal warning in the hope he'll pay more attention. What's the worst mistake someone in your business has made, and what did you do?

No one is perfect. We all make a few 'genuine' mistakes and I have made more than most, but some people are just too accident-prone to put it down to bad luck.

I can look back and smile at some of our most memorable cock-ups. In the 1970s we had a concession within Whiteleys the department store, then in Bayswater. The store was part of United Drapery Stores whose Chairman Bernard Lyons sent in his favourite pair of crocodile shoes for repair – we lost them!

In the 1990s we were asked to put a temporary engraving unit into Harrods for a trial run for a few weeks up to Christmas. Mohammed Al Fayed's daughter had won a sports trophy that she brought to us for engraving – we spelt her name wrongly! It was seventeen years before we got another chance to trade in Harrods.

Some mistakes are much more serious – when failure to

follow our simple safety precautions started a fire that totally destroyed a shop, I reckon we were pretty kind to the culprit by demanding demotion rather than dismissal. But we were not so lenient when a buyer added an extra '0' to an already big order, filling our warehouse with ten times as much stock as we needed.

Most people learn their biggest lessons by making mistakes, but it is worth emphasising the experience by showing a yellow card. Some make too many expensive errors before they get the message – issue a red card before their incompetence does real damage to your business.

I've heard some unsettling rumours about one of the senior managers in my construction law firm. The talk is of some jokes in very poor taste, sexist comments, that sort of thing. I've had a word with him and he says it's all blown out of proportion, but I'm worried he's making people uncomfortable – and of course I fear a tribunal. He's a talented worker so I don't want to lose him. How do I impress the seriousness of this on him without doing more harm than good?

You need to take a much tougher line and get a grip of a potentially dangerous situation. This is a tricky problem but there is an easy answer.

The words you exchanged with your indiscreet superstar haven't done the trick. He thinks you've been fobbed off by suggesting it's all blown out of proportion so it is time to use a more direct approach.

Tell him straight and tell him straight away but don't do

the job yourself. Get your HR chief to take on the task. People who work in Personnel are often held in awe, with some justification. They deal with difficult people problems and carry out tricky conversations on a daily basis – take advantage of their expertise. You might be the Chief Executive but a face-to-face with HR will be seen as being much more serious.

The message will be simple. 'It has come to my attention that you have been making inappropriate remarks that make your colleagues feel extremely uncomfortable. I thought better of you, but if you can't cut it out you are in danger of losing your job.'

If he is as good as you suggest, those words from HR should give him the message. It would be a pity to lose such a talented member of your team but if he can't toe the line he will have to go.

Day-to-Day Detail

Questions about the little things in business life have been the most interesting to tackle and the trickiest to answer. I've answered queries about company cars, staff uniform, Facebook, smoking, scantily dressed receptionists and interfering husbands. These are the bits of doing business that give it character, can make it fun and sometimes become very irritating.

The joy of running a company is never really revealed in the annual accounts. By being part of an active business you have a leading role in your own soap opera and never know what is going to happen next.

Perhaps some bosses think I shouldn't devote so much time to the detail, but if you don't know the day-to-day gossip you can't know what is going on in your business. We think trivia is so important that every manager has to tackle our 'Know Your People' quiz. We pick a member of their team, whom they should know well, and pose a series of questions about them: name their children – what football team do they support? – where was their last holiday? – what car do they drive? The best bosses really know the people on their team.

Nearly every company comes across problems caused by company conferences, car park spaces, an office move or changing office hours, and every manager has to cope with the highs and lows of Christmas. These situations occur week in week out but are never taught at business school and seldom appear in a management book.

I am often asked how I know all of our shops. 'Simple', I reply, 'I visit them all.' Then they ask: 'What do you do when you get there?'

I don't go round the country to give orders or catch colleagues breaking any rules, I'm there to have a chat, keep up to date with business and, with luck, spot some ideas that work so well they can be used elsewhere. Most of all I visit shops to meet our people. I am never bored – every day is different. Not much of the conversation is to do with shoe repairs, key cutting or photos. In a typical day I find myself talking about football, holidays, children, the dog that has just died and the latest news on their rock band. Most other companies use a marketing department to discover what sells and HR to talk to the people. I find that spending at least two days a week going round shops makes a massive difference. I keep in touch with the detail and all our colleagues get to meet the boss.

This section concentrates on the mundane things we are all doing most of the time – cost-cutting, bonus schemes, board meetings and mobile phones. You can't manage a business without them. It's the day-to-day problems that make business such fascinating fun.

*

My business partner is on a cost-cutting drive. All well and good in that we've saved money on things like newspaper subscriptions and employee expenses, but now he's talking about stopping the milk. Please tell me

you support me in saying this is bonkers and will make us look like skinflints in the eyes of staff – we all need a cup of tea.

My real worry is that you and your partner seem to be facing in opposite directions. When the top team are in conflict it is bad for business.

It is right to keep a firm grip on costs. Cancelling the trade magazines and putting 'switch off the lights' stickers round the office will not turn the business round, but it could make your colleagues much more economy-conscious.

But I have to agree that your partner's nit-picking cost campaign is in danger of going too far.

I knew we had lost our sense of proportion when, during a tough trading time several years ago, we started studying the office usage rate of loo paper – a clear example of that phrase about rearranging deckchairs on the *Titanic*.

From time to time every business needs an austerity campaign, but there is a danger that the cost-cutters can lose sight of where their priorities should lie.

At the first sign that trading is falling below budget, most Finance Directors offer to lead the campaign to cut costs (although they seldom suggest any savings in the Finance department!). Head offices usually propose reductions out in the field – the bean counters cutting out people that actually create the profit.

Economy drives have a part to play but they won't put a sick business back on track. Make peace with your partner over a cup of tea, give him a hug, and concentrate on things that really matter.

After months of putting it off, I have decided I need to cut some roles from the business. I have tried everything to avoid this, including shorter working weeks, but I'm just not getting the orders I thought I would and I have to let some people go. How do you approach redundancies and consultation periods?

Before getting into the detail I have two general comments.

If you take advice from professionals don't let them dictate the way you run the business. To a lawyer your employees are just numbers on the payroll; you know them as individuals. As a boss you have a moral duty to show decency with common sense and be totally honest.

You probably feel disappointed with the way your business is going. The current situation certainly wasn't in your five-year plan but try not to get depressed. Of course, you would prefer an agenda full of good news but every business has the occasional setback. Don't spend your life hidden in the office or stuck in meetings – however downhearted you might feel, be positive: your leadership is needed most when times are tough.

Waste no time before pulling all your colleagues together to describe your present problems and say what you have already done to put the business back on track. Outline the situation and ask your colleagues for their suggestions. Some may have good ideas, others could volunteer for short time or redundancy.

Stop recruiting – you can't take on someone new when you are about to face a round of redundancies. Then ditch the temporary staff – not just because they haven't got a contract but also to show loyalty to your long-serving colleagues.

When tackling redundancies, standalone roles are relatively straightforward and less painful. It is more of a problem when you have to select from a pool of people. This is when you need to take control – don't let your employment lawyer run the process.

Some years ago I let our team send out letters telling the whole of our Finance department that they were at risk of redundancy – it was a lie! There was no way we were going to say goodbye to Karina, Gail or Sharon, who are fantastic and have all been with us for over 25 years. We were advised to put everyone at risk but I should never have caused such distress to key employees. Sometimes it is right to take the risk of losing at a future tribunal.

We are looking for a non-executive chairman. We've got a few candidates in mind but we're not sure how best to approach them. Have you taken this post at any companies before? If so, what won you over in the companies' pitches? Is there anything we should avoid asking them for, like a specific time commitment?

I guess you want a non-exec who brings experience, useful contacts and strategic thinking. It would help if they can keep meetings short and to the point but the right candidate will probably bring the biggest benefit outside the meeting room.

If you know who you want, don't dictate what you want them to do, tell them why you think they are perfect for the job. Flattery will work much better than a job description.

Simply say: 'We want you to be our Chairman because we have always admired what you do and feel your help would make a big difference. You are just the person to help us grow to another level and we would enjoy working with you.'

The right person will know how to do the job so let them decide on how many days a week to work and how many meetings to chair.

I would almost certainly be put off by an approach that specified a meeting schedule and stressed the importance of governance and the salary committee. But the main reason I haven't taken on a non-executive role is because I've never been asked.

A recent board meeting I attended concentrated on financial figures. This seemed to give the executive directors an opportunity to snipe at each other. How are Timpson board meetings structured?

My first board meeting was in 1969. Since then, if you include all the charities and governing bodies, I must have been to more than 1,000 formal meetings, some dramatic, many humdrum, some surprisingly short and others unbelievably long.

I don't think I was ever suited to sit in a succession of meetings. During the last 44 years I've compiled a catalogue of pet hates that make me wary of any role that involves a compulsory rota of committees.

I experience a recurring nightmare that involves some of my worst fears. In my dreams I spend the night trapped in pointless debate forever discussing matters arising from the minutes of the last meeting. People who like the sound of their own voice make the same points they argued at length the last time we met and at many more meetings before that. Luckily my nightmare misses the middle of the meeting but jumps to a torrent of trivia raised under 'any other business'. I wake up thankful it was only a dream but I know, sadly, that it can be very close to reality.

Painful meetings are usually caused by weak chairmen, egocentric directors and poor papers. I like to receive our board pack at least five days in advance – not by email but an old-fashioned hard copy that is easy to read. You can't scribble comments on an iPad.

Our board papers are brief and to the point – background detail is available in the appendices, including our management accounts (these are seldom given much more than a passing glance). Past performance is covered in detail by our operational boards so there is no need for us to nit-pick.

We always put 'future growth' at the top of our agenda. At least half the meeting is spent discussing innovation and wondering where the business will be in ten years' time. We don't make any decisions. I witnessed one disastrous vote at a board meeting in 1972 and never want to see another. Our purpose is to focus on what matters most, share ideas and keep everyone fully informed.

Whenever I am due to chair a meeting I read the papers at least twice – noting those items worthy of discussion. This homework helps to politely make sure people stick to the point. It works because we have a small number (six) of the right directors. They all know the business, get the culture and have an unselfish interest in the company. Thanks to the cooperation of my fellow directors our bi-monthly board meeting covers the ground in little more than two hours – and there's even time for a ten-minute tea break.

You say you look at Timpson's cash position every week (or was it every day?) but what do you do with the information? What are you watching for and how do you respond when you see something? I'm swamped with analytics and data and can't see the wood for the trees.

I look at our cash balance every day (but not Saturdays or Sundays). It is the best way to test the financial temperature of our business. The trick is to compare with the same day last year, thus showing the last twelve months' cash flow.

It is not perfect (never forget that your Finance department may secretly massage the cash by paying suppliers sooner or later), but daily cash is more transparent than management accounts that are full of provisions and only appear once a month.

You claim to be swamped by figures – most managers have the same problem. Finance and IT take a delight in producing a deluge of data, but having too many statistics is counterproductive.

This daily cash report will help to clear the clutter created by computers. A simple report that helps you pose the right questions: Why have things suddenly got worse? Are we in danger of breaking our bank borrowing limit? Why does the cash look so much better than in the management accounts?

This cash report gives an early warning of changing circumstances. It came to my rescue in 2004 when, through a major acquisition, the business doubled in size overnight and was going through a lot of change. Our financial control suffered but I didn't realise how bad things were until I was waiting to board a plane to go on a Caribbean holiday. A quick look at my BlackBerry (when Alex wasn't looking) showed an unexpected £500k deterioration in our overdraft. It wasn't a great start to the holiday and Alex was upset when I spent the first day on the telephone, but we were able to tackle the problem six weeks before it would have been revealed in the management accounts.

This year feels like it's flying past already, the days are just not long enough to get everything done. Do you have any time management tips? Do you find it easy? And what things do you always make sure you do each day before you clock off?

Don't worry, you are not on your own. Most of us struggle to tick off every task and are envious of others who appear to breeze through life without any hassle.

I have always been keen on making lists of everything that needs to be done (an essential memory-jogger as I get older) but don't be too ambitious. There is a limit to the number of things you can do in a day.

Lists help but the really unflappable achievers are seldom obsessive list-makers – their secret is to 'do it now'. They deal with every problem as soon as it occurs. They get a lot done because they are decisive and they delegate. They don't waste time agonising over every small decision and they trust their team to use their initiative.

It is better to avoid spending too much time in meetings

or hours buried in paperwork. We can easily be diverted by trivia and find home time is approaching with little having been achieved.

But it is good to spend part of each day chatting to people round the office – even if you are just talking gossip. Time spent with your team is seldom a waste of time.

Be realistic: even the role models who are good at making quick decisions and delegate whenever possible have the occasional bad day. It is comforting to know that almost everyone wishes they were better at managing their time.

I have a core of about a third of my staff who have really stepped up to the mark in the last twelve months and now I'm wondering how I can reward them sufficiently without breaking the bank. What are the best options?

You can't give your good-performing colleagues a salary increase and ignore the rest. It is expensive and will cause trouble – someone is bound to claim discrimination.

The best way to make the good guys feel valued will take a lot of your time but will be well worth the bother. Treat them individually. Spring a few surprises and do things that make them feel special – here are a few examples:

1. Pay for them to take their partner on their ideal night out. Whatever they want – movies, restaurant, theatre, night club – and foot the bill.
2. Provide tickets for their dream Premier League football match or celebrity concert.

3. Provide an extra week's holiday – and give them some spending money.
4. Have an awards dinner for your key colleagues and invite their partners to help them celebrate success. Don't economise – make it a night to remember organised by a professional events company with a budget big enough to put on a cabaret.
5. Simply send a personal letter to their home address and enclose a worthwhile cheque.

The better you know your people the more possible it is to surprise them with your praise. There's always a perfect way to amaze each colleague and make them feel special.

But praising your good performers is only part of the story. What about the majority who are not pulling their weight? It is time you started saying 'Goodbye' to your drongos! With two thirds of your workforce performing below par you have no chance of being a winner.

What's on your business and non-business Christmas present wish list this year?

Dear Santa

I am writing to ask you for a special favour this Christmas.

Could you please get the government to bring in a new law?

<u>'The Common Sense and Simplification Act, 2014'</u>
The objective of this legislation is to reduce red tape and increase trust in the individual. This is bigger than 'The Big

Society'. It will lead to a lot less government, with today's blind belief in process giving way to a philosophy focused on results.

Headline measures within the Act will include:

Less legislation
Every week while Parliament is in session the government must repeal a minimum of five laws, including two that were introduced to comply with EU regulations.

No meaningless targets
The government will replace all existing Key Performance Indicators with two targets:
a) Eliminate government debt.
b) Keep the public sector below 30% of the UK economy.

20% tax
Income tax, VAT, corporation tax, capital gains and inheritance tax will all be fixed for the next twenty years at 20%.

The Budget
The Chancellor's annual Budget speech cannot last longer than half an hour and his measures must fill no more than five pages of A4 paper, with no small print.

Benefits for all
Every UK citizen will, whatever their age, receive £400 a month and £200 on their birthday. No forms to fill and no tax to pay. (This measure, at a stroke, replaces all existing benefits and the old age pension.)

And Santa, if there are any wishes left, could you also arrange for Manchester City to win the Premiership and Alex to be a winning owner at the Cheltenham Festival in March?

With Christmas behind us, are there any decent ways of boosting staff morale to get us through the next couple of months with a smile on our faces? I hate coming in to work and seeing miserable faces, but based on previous years I'm wondering if it's an inevitability in January and February.

Many years ago when I was area chairman of our local Citizens Advice Bureau I learnt that people store up their problems for the New Year. In the weeks up to Christmas our volunteers were relatively quiet but as soon as they opened after the holiday there was a queue of customers, mainly coming with debt or family relationship problems.

January can be depressing, the traffic jams are back and colleagues bring their frustrations and their flu to the office.

You could take a risk and try to lift the mood by launching your latest initiative that captures the imagination by promising an exciting year ahead. On the other hand it might be better to find a few new ways to amaze your colleagues. Buy everyone lunch, man the switchboard yourself on Friday afternoon and let everyone else go home early. Book a block of seats so your team can take their family to a pantomime or the cinema. Invent a special milestone and put £500 behind a local bar so everyone can celebrate.

Any of these things might make a difference but the post-Christmas period has always been downbeat. In the 1930s my grandfather spent the whole of February in the Caribbean, leaving strict instructions to be left in peace: 'I know sales will be poor so don't send me the figures!'

I will be following my grandfather's example. Next week I leave for a fortnight on Mustique.

Do you ever speak to former staff who have set up in competition to you to find out why?

Compared with most other retailers, we have a very low percentage of voluntary leavers but every year a few decide to set up their own shop.

We encourage our field team to stay in touch and when in the area I make a point of popping in to their new business to say 'Hello'. Many tell me, 'I felt I owed myself the chance to prove I could go it alone'. Some have been successful and I am still calling to see them as much as twenty years later. For others a year is enough to prove that life as an independent retailer can be quite tough and we are happy to welcome them back as a Timpson colleague. That is why, whenever we lose a star performer, we prefer to part as friends.

Ten years ago I visited our shop at Swinton near Manchester where the manager, Denise, told me she was about to leave to set up shop in Garstang with her husband Ian, who managed another of our Manchester branches. I tried to dissuade her, but their minds were made up and they had already exchanged contracts on retail premises with a flat upstairs. I knew I couldn't stand in their way but I was worried that they were taking on a big financial burden, so I offered to help. We paid for their refit and still supply stock from our warehouse at much lower than the normal wholesale prices. Denise responded by putting the Timpson name on the fascia.

Every year I call to see Ian and Denise and am delighted to report the shop is doing well. Although they now have their own business I still feel they are part of the Timpson family.

You hear about all sorts of big name companies banning their employees from using the likes of Twitter and Facebook. I've always been pretty relaxed about internet use, but I have become aware over the last year or so of more and more workers quickly minimising Facebook pages as I walk around the office. Do you think I should ban social media use – or at least make some sort of fair use policy clear?

Don't bother writing a regulation about Facebook – there is no point introducing a rule that colleagues are bound to break. Employees have always spent a significant chunk of the working day chatting to workmates; the difference today is that the internet now enables them to gossip in the company's time with friends right round the world.

What matters is whether the work gets done. As far as I am concerned a superstar can Tweet for most of the day as long as he is good at his job.

I am more concerned about the evil side of Facebook and the abuse of Twitter. They are both becoming a common form of bullying. Unkind personal remarks posted on the web can cause serious stress and misery – a flippant but thoughtless phrase could send a sensitive colleague into the depths of despair.

Facebook has its faults but it also gives you a hidden benefit. With employees constantly posting their opinions for all to see, you have a good way of checking out the backstage gossip. It is a rare opportunity to find out what your team members really think about the business.

So don't start drafting rules about social media. Let them log on during the working day but watch what they are writing about the company and their colleagues.

Do you supply a company car to your Area Managers, and if so, what influences the options you offer them?

Although I, myself, am not particularly interested in cars I recognise most of our Area Managers are. Their motor is priority number two after owning a nice house, and they want the keys to a car they can be proud of, especially if it is the envy of their neighbours. It is well worth trying to fulfil their dreams, but there is no need to buy everyone a Bentley!

We don't force them all to drive the identical model in the same colour. They can have pretty much what they fancy as long as it doesn't have a soft top and the leasing cost is in our price band.

That gives them a wide menu of cars to choose from, and, if they want to add their favourite gizmos like surround sound or flamboyant wheels that's fine by us, as long as they fund the extra cost.

The extras are an important part of the deal – they help make the car more personal and add a stronger feeling of ownership. Even I am paranoid about one extra. If I'm searching for possible new sites, especially in supermarkets, I need a sat nav that recognises the last bit of every postcode. That is why I had to abandon BMW.

We don't put our people in boxes. By letting them have the vehicle of their choice, everyone drives a car that suits their character, and we avoid a potent source of office politics.

If our Area Managers are happy with their car, they are more likely to look after it, and will be that little bit happier in their job.

Are you a uniforms man? What benefits, if any, do corporate uniforms convey?

In 1979 during a trip round our shops I suddenly realised that cobblers were a scruffy bunch. But we were no better or worse than our competitors, all of us were guilty of hopeless housekeeping and poor personal appearance. It was not unusual to see a high street cobbler who was unshaven, smoking a cigarette, reading a newspaper and wearing a sweatshirt under a filthy apron.

These appallingly low standards gave us a major opportunity. If we could up our housekeeping game and persuade colleagues that it is smart to look smart, we would stand out from the rest of the trade. It seemed obvious – if we couldn't look after our branches, why should customers expect us to look after their shoes? Well turned-out shop staff are much more likely to provide good quality jobs and friendly service.

To launch my housekeeping and customer care campaign I changed the uniform and got everyone to wear a tie. 'But', I was told by the diehards, 'no cobbler has ever worn a tie.' 'That's the point', I replied. 'The tie is a symbol that says we are different.' (At around the same time Eddie Stobart came to the same conclusion.) Despite a lot of resistance I won the battle and 32 years later the tie is still a significant part of our culture.

Recently we redesigned the uniform at Max Spielmann, our photo chain, to communicate a change in the business. After purchasing the shops from the administrator two years ago, we have just about altered everything to concentrate on portraits, photo ID, digital prints and photo frames. The new uniform has helped to get the message across to both customers and colleagues, who now feel part of a successful team.

With a management style based on individual freedom we give our people lots of leeway, but to be a member of our club you have to look the part and that means wearing the Timpson uniform.

Is it worthwhile taking top executives for a weekend to throw paint at each other or go on a treetop walk?

I'm sceptical. It depends on what you hope your outward bound trip will achieve.

If you are sending them away to stiffen up a few weak personalities or mould a dysfunctional team you are probably wasting your money. Whatever challenge they have to face they will remain the wrong people in the wrong company.

But I do believe that orienteering, go-karting, abseiling, and white water rafting can strengthen an already strong team.

The key players in our business are the Area Managers, 28 home-grown executives each responsible for about 25 shops. It is a lonely job with most located many miles from our office.

To help them keep in touch we hold half-yearly conferences. Each central department manager used to proudly produce his latest plan while the Area Managers yawned through the PowerPoint presentations. The only bit of the conference they enjoyed was swapping stories and banter round the bar late into the night. They learnt a lot more about the business over a beer than they ever found out in our formal sessions.

We still have a half-yearly conference but now there is very little talking. James and I go through the latest strategy (in half an hour) and we listen to their problems and complaints. The PowerPoint has been replaced by active enjoyment – anything from camping to tank driving – our Area Managers now look forward to the next conference.

Away days work well when they help good teams celebrate success by having some fun.

I'm a director of our business and I smoke. Not a lot, but a few a day. I'm totally aware that lines of people puffing away outside the front doors looks terrible to observers and clients. We don't have an obvious green space nearby. Discriminating against smokers is really unfair and, in truth, some good stuff happens in 'smokers' corner' – i.e., relationship-building, new ideas etc. I'm flummoxed on this one. Help please.

Don't worry about the smokers – we have all got used to seeing them being banished to the back yard in all weathers at break time. If you haven't got a place to convert into a luxury smoking den, then so be it – at least you have tapped into their gossip.

The nicotine clique have become a powerful social group on the business scene – the source of many rumours and a sounding board for business politics. You have done well to infiltrate such an influential crowd.

Doesn't it make you wonder whether you can create the same sort of dialogue with the non-smokers – people who don't have the same compelling excuse to get together every day?

You may well find that many self-righteous non-smokers complain that the addicted sinners are getting extra time off while the good guys continue working. Perhaps you should ban hot drinks at the desk and force them to get their caffeine fix in the kitchen or canteen.

The smoking clique are sending you a simple message: always set part of your day aside for an informal walk round the office to chat to as many colleagues as possible. They will tell you more about your business than you will ever discover from the management accounts.

The car park outside our offices is getting full, forcing workers and guests to park on the adjoining road which is now monitored by aggressive wardens. How do I best establish a hierarchy of need in our car park – first come, first served? Does it look bad having spaces for the directors right next to the door? What about my PA? She doesn't get in until late because she has to drop off her child at childcare. I fear a hornet's nest ...

Some people may think this is a trivial matter but it is an important indicator of your company culture.

In the 1960s all our senior executives had a designated parking space – the most senior were nearest the front door. This led to arrogance among the management and bad feeling from the workforce.

One day a young shop supervisor who had driven from Wolverhampton for an early meeting innocently parked in bay no. 2. The proud possessor of that parking space arrived an hour later and blocked in the poor visitor who had to stay for the rest of the day.

I have never forgotten that incident. Today we only reserve parking places for visitors and the disabled, plus one designated space for 'The Colleague of the Month'.

Assuming your crowded car park is not a sign of over-staffing (a redundancy programme would be an effective but draconian remedy!), talk to your team about practical solutions – car sharing, free bicycle hire or a shower and changing room so that keen colleagues can run to work. If all else fails, look for an overflow car park or move office.

Whatever you do, never make parking a privilege for the top brass. Spaces should be available on a first come basis – even for you.

My star divisional MD has been caught having a fling with my Financial Director's wife just weeks before completing the biggest deal of his life which could make our company a fortune. My FD says he should be fired (he says it is either him or me). What should I do?

Don't be too hasty – find out the true facts before you react. There is seldom such a thing as a quick fling. Speak to your

FD and your superstar MD and pick up the company gossip to see if there is a hidden agenda – is this affair just the tip of an iceberg?

It is advisable to keep people's personal life well away from work, but (especially in a family business!) there is always the danger that marital and extramarital problems can blow your company off course.

You probably have sympathy for the aggrieved FD, but you can't allow this personal problem to get in the way of good business. It would be foolish to lose a key executive when he is just about to deliver the deal of the decade.

As far as I am aware you can't fire someone for adultery or fornication, so you have no grounds to ask the divisional MD to leave.

If your FD really can't continue to work with his indiscreet colleague, let him go. You may need to look for another accountant but no one is irreplaceable.

I was recently asked to tell a joke as an icebreaker at a networking event. I was left completely redfaced – I could only think of very crass ones! What's a polite, PC joke I can tell if I ever find myself in the same situation?

I have lost count of the times I have cringed with embarrassment when a mediocre speaker tries to tell a mildly amusing story. It is bad enough listening to the best man at a wedding, but at a business function jokes are often totally inappropriate.

Here's a way to save yourself any embarrassment. 'I've been asked to tell you a joke. Fortunately, I heard three good ones at the golf club last weekend – one about two

Irish bricklayers, another about a meeting of the Women's Institute, and my favourite, one about a Russian girl who went windsurfing.

'I went home and tried them all out on Alex, who sat expressionless until I'd finished all three. She said: "The first story is racist and will upset any Irish people in the audience, the second is sexist and will offend women."

'"What about my favourite – the one about the Russian girl?" I interrupted. "The joke was okay", said Alex, "but you forgot half the words and messed up the punchline – that proves you should never tell a story in public."

'My two minutes are up so I've no time to talk about the Russian girl who went windsurfing.'

Recently I have been feeling overwhelmed by technology. I have two mobile phones, a tablet, plus several laptops that seem to be taking over my life. Do you ever 'unplug'? If so, how do you do it? I feel like my world will come crashing down if I miss a single email.

I certainly can't match your collection of kit. There isn't a computer on my desk, I'm not on Facebook and don't go near Twitter. But I do have an iPad and a BlackBerry, which I think are fantastic.

They let me spend most of my time out of the office but always keep me in touch. I reckon the constant flow of information reduces stress, but Alex disagrees. 'You're married to your BlackBerry – put it away and give your brain a rest. Who thinks they need to bother you at the weekend?'

My response is to set the BlackBerry to silent and put it

out of sight – I can't help picking it up if I see the flashing red light. Despite Alex's advice, my life has changed. We live in a world of instant communication and the only way to escape is to find somewhere that can't get the internet (there are times when we struggle to find a signal in some parts of Cheshire!).

You may think today's world is dominated by technology but I wonder what it will be like in twenty years' time. Will the children who already spend every waking hour tapping messages into their hand-held device finish up in a fantasy world full of virtual dinner parties and online weddings, or will they rediscover the pleasures of eating as a family and handwritten letters?

Whatever the future holds, I have come in for less criticism since I bought Alex a BlackBerry. It is well used and stays by her side but Alex never allows emails and text messages to take over her life – I will try to follow her example.

A lot of the meetings my staff hold are just exercises in glorified time-wasting. How can I make them more productive?

You are right. Lots of your meetings are probably a waste of time. You are paying several executives, some on high salaries, to sit round a table doodling on an A4 pad and secretly searching through their BlackBerrys.

Meetings are the most unproductive activity on the business calendar. Attendance is often based on office politics and most committee decisions would be better taken by individuals sitting in the bath.

Try to dramatically cut down on meetings but don't ban

them altogether. Some meetings are worthwhile – board meetings that monitor progress and discuss strategy, general monthly get-togethers to tell everyone the news, and expert think-tanks that brainstorm your latest problem.

Eliminate useless meetings by using eccentric tactics:

Make it abundantly clear you hate meetings. Write about them, speak about them and put a notice on your office wall saying: 'Most meetings are a waste of time – even when I am invited.'

Insist on receiving the minutes of every meeting. There is no need to read them – a quick glance will tell you all you need to know.

Gatecrash. Drop in on a whim and ask awkward questions.

If all this fails, copy the Asda example: take away the chairs and make your meeting room standing room only with a time limit of 30 minutes.

My sales people always file huge expenses. They claim that the boozy lunches are central to deal-making. Is this the case, or should I be curtailing the non-stop socialising?

Plying clients with caviar and Cristal is unlikely to increase sales. Good salesmen don't need the help of alcohol to sell their product. Boozy lunches belong to days before the BlackBerry and the breathalyser.

First find out the facts. Check whether the person claiming the most expenses is your superstar or a poor performer. If a person with high expenses sits in the bottom half of your sales league, you have an easy way to destroy their theory about corporate entertainment.

Even if there is a hint that lavish treats encourage more business, you should still put a stop to such extravagance. Don't allow your company to be associated with a laddish lifestyle, which can sometimes lead to backhanders and blackmail.

Launch a campaign to curb big expense claimants and get to know everyone's entertaining habits in detail. In the process you will learn a lot about your salesmen.

Try limiting expenses to a defined percentage of sales, with any overspend deducted from your rep's bonus payments. Or, use a more direct approach by pinning the rep's claim forms on your office noticeboard.

I'm getting some company business cards printed. I've been told that it's useful to include a photograph so that the recipient can put a face to a name. Do you have any other tips for being memorable? Or is simple and classy the best way to go?

For years I got by without exchanging business cards. They weren't an essential part of doing business until I went to Japan, where presenting a card was the polite form of greeting. Cards now come at me from all directions. When fund managers make a presentation they start their pitch by dealing their business cards round the table. After giving a conference talk I'm often approached by card-holding consultants keen to sell me advice on the very topic I've been talking about.

I'm too polite to refuse their cards but presume they realise where they finish up. Some people may keep them in their office where they are filed and forgotten. If I find a card in my pocket, unless it was picked up in a good restaurant, I simply put it in the bin.

Your card doesn't just need to be noticeable – it also must be one people will keep. It won't make much difference how much attention you give to the wording, although I've been intrigued by some of the bizarre job titles like Head of Global Change, Assistant Risk Director, and my favourite, for a UK subsidiary of a small American bank – Resident Vice President.

My son James has the answer. His card, in the shape of a shoe, is more memorable than most, but despite including a photo it would still be thrown away if it wasn't for a special feature. It doubles up as a 20% discount card.

One of my pet hates is trying to have a conversation with someone who is glued to their iPhone (and I am not just talking about teenagers catching up on Facebook, it happens to me at the office – even in board meetings). Do you find any features of the internet irritating?

At first I was irritated to find that I had to ask a ten year-old what to do, but now I'm used to kids being the experts. My present embarrassment is to find that older members of the golf club know so much more than I do about IT.

But even so I spend a fair bit of time online (Alex says it has taken over my life) and recognise what a big difference it has made, giving us the chance to run the business while we are on the move. It is just a pity that O2 doesn't get much of a signal on my route between home and the office. With mobile phones it doesn't always help if you are mobile – if you find a decent signal it is best to stop moving. I am told life will be better when we get 4G, or perhaps we will need to wait for 5G or more.

I wish our spam filter could keep up with the intrusive salesmen who talk to me in such familiar terms: 'Hi John, just checking in to see if I can book a 15 minute window to talk through the way our dynamic market evaluation matrix will revolutionise your bottom line.' Or: 'Bob here, I am in your area Tuesday to talk about ...' Thank goodness for the delete button.

But my pet hate is 'Reply to all'. Some people like the world to know what they are saying. They are probably similar characters to the compulsive memo writers who in the days of typewriters and carbon paper sent copies to the whole management team listed in order of seniority.

If I am on a committee it is not necessary to include me in everyone else's email. I don't want to know why Sheila can't attend the meeting, where she is going on holiday or why it would be more convenient to send the details to her husband's email address. Last week a member of one of my committees had her 50th birthday and everyone sent some cheerful birthday greetings, with a copy to all the other members. I received sixteen messages of goodwill and it wasn't even my birthday.

Perhaps I am old-fashioned and slightly anti-social. I don't follow Twitter, I don't chat to strangers on the train, I am not keen on shaking hands with the man in the pew behind at church, and I wish the people who use the 'Reply to all' button would keep the information to themselves.

Management Problems

A few years ago I was quite offended to be classified as an SME (Small or Medium Enterprise) but now I want to be one for ever. I felt like a second-class citizen, sitting near the bottom of the company pecking order while FTSE 100 companies looked down on us with a distinct air of arrogance. We were seen as amateurs playing for a non-league team in a game designed for professionals.

Like most other 'SMEs' I didn't realise how good we are. It's a mistake to confuse big with best; the amateurs can often play better than the professionals. Smaller companies mustn't try to copy what big corporations call best practice – they should have the confidence to use the freedom and flexibility that's only available when the management team can sit together round a small table.

Although it is normal to talk about economies of scale and buying power, big companies can become inefficient and waste a lot of money simply because they are big. FTSE 250 companies have whole departments doing things we don't bother with. We employ only one person in our Health and Safety department but no one at Timpson specialises in Governance, Public Relations or Marketing. As soon as you have a big management team, decision making gets complicated – everyone has to follow company policy, meetings are called to join up thinking and the decision has to be approved by a management committee before being signed off by the Chief Executive. All performance is measured against budget and a series of key performance indicators which have been set following three months of budget bids and budget meetings. Add to that appraisals, away days, sub-committees and a few think-tanks, and it's not surprising there is a big Finance and HR team to hold the thing together.

I was saved from building a big management structure by a merchant banker who had just bought our major competitor, Mr Minit. When I asked whether he would sell the shops to me, he replied: 'We are experts at buying family businesses and putting in professional management.' That remark led me to create our Upside Down Management, with trust and authority given to the people who work in our shops – management's role is to help and support the people who serve our customers. It wasn't long before we started to ask, 'Does everyone do something that helps the people in our shops to make more money?' It's a good question for any business, particularly those with several tiers of management where politics become paramount and the main executive aim is to be promoted to the next pay grade.

Big business with policies, process and company rules can get too complicated to run. SMEs have the flexibility to keep it simple. We should all aim to act like a small business and ignore sophisticated management tools devised by experts who know nothing about the people who serve our customers.

Management is an art, not a science.

*

As a man of many years' experience in business, you must have picked up hundreds of different but simple ways to make money. Do you keep a list in your desk drawer?

Last year I compiled a list of 60 simple things that have helped us make money. My idea was to make them into a book but so far I haven't got round to putting pen to paper. Your question has prompted me to make a start, so here is the first on the list.

Only pick 9s and 10s.

We try to discriminate in favour of people who are very good. When interviewing we mark all candidates out of 10 – we don't bother much about their CVs, qualifications are of little consequence, we want people with personality. We look for characters who could be called by names like Mr Keen, Miss Ambitious, Mrs Can be Done, Mr Punctual, and Miss Happy. We now aim to only take on people who score at least 9 out of 10.

Today, with lots of applicants for every job, it is possible to have the pick of the bunch and over the last two years I have noticed the difference that has made to our business. We are now getting many more recruits who are keen and quick to learn new skills. They have no problem completing our apprenticeship within the required sixteen weeks and have the right approach to customer service.

We are able to fill the business with people who 'get it', which makes life a whole lot easier for the colleagues who work with them. It is much more fun to spend the week alongside characters with the right attitude, who are keen to come to work and earn as much money as possible.

Customers also notice the difference when they are served by shop assistants who want to be helpful. With so many retailers happy to pay the minimum wage to people who simply turn up for work, shoppers are surprised and delighted when they visit a shop where the person behind the counter really cares.

We don't always get it right. Sometimes interviewees are able to hide their true personality and in the odd weak moment we let a 7/10 through the net. It is a continuing campaign with the ultimate goal that every colleague, present and future, will score at least 9/10.

A few years ago a job centre was taken to task for advertising a post that looked for 'hard working applicants'. They were criticised for discriminating against people who are not keen on hard work!

Our success depends on the quality of the colleagues on our payroll and we will continue to discriminate in favour of the top performers.

Employee empowerment has ensured the successes of both John Lewis and Timpson; two British retail institutions established around 150 years ago! While John Spedan Lewis championed an 'employee-partnership', you introduced 'upside down management'. What do you consider to be the comparative advantages and disadvantages of the two business models?

I'm certainly not complaining about Timpson being quoted in the question alongside John Lewis. It's a privilege to be put in the same sentence as a prime candidate for Britain's best retailer but I am not sure they will be quite as flattered.

We are of a similar age. John Lewis was founded in 1864, a year before my great-grandfather opened his first shoe shop. But there is a big difference between The John Lewis Partnership's £10bn-plus turnover and Timpson at £200m. It is difficult to compare a cobbler and key cutter to department stores and supermarkets with award-winning advertising, when we don't even have a marketing department.

The Partnership has proved to be a marvellous business model but it might not suit my maverick management style. I also suspect John Lewis would be scared by the amount of freedom we give under Upside Down Management. We operate in different ways but the differences are not nearly as significant as the similarities.

John Lewis have partners and we call them colleagues, but we both recognise the importance of our people, especially those that serve our customers. Partners get a dividend and our colleagues are all on a bonus – both businesses realise that the way to make most money is to provide a great service.

Each company has a strong culture that has been created by decades of consistent management. In total, Sir Charlie Mayfield, Andy Street and Mark Price have worked at John Lewis for over 75 years, and James and I have a combined 75 years on the Timpson payroll. We are able to take a long-term view – keen to keep the culture but determined to stay up to date. John Lewis has seen a lot of growth online and Timpson is growing quickly in supermarket car parks. Both businesses have benefited from innovation. Waitrose now takes over 50% of The Partnership turnover and the biggest contributor to Timpson turnover is photo processing.

There has been a lot of talk of copying The Partnership

model and perhaps some people think that Upside Down Management is an assured secret of success. But it isn't just a process – it depends on having the right people. Success comes from the way we do business.

Duplicating a system doesn't come with a guarantee. It's no good just changing the way you pay your people: the important bit is to capture the culture.

As you go about your day-to-day routine do you still learn new things about the business?

Two weeks ago I spent a day visiting some of our shops in Scotland, starting in Kilmarnock where I saw the newly appointed manager Jim Malcolm. I first met Jim in 1988 at a shop we had just bought in Corby. Jim was on good form. 'I've just set a new shop record. I hate the thought of being beaten by someone else', he said.

Later that day I was in Braehead Shopping Centre near Glasgow where manager John Kelly was in his first week, having spent five years running our shop in East Kilbride. John was on a mission. 'This is like a breath of fresh air, just watch the turnover over the next few weeks. Prepare for a surprise.' Sales in Braehead have been fantastic since he took over.

I was reminded of a lesson I learnt from Dean Butler, the guy who brought the one-hour optical service to Britain under the name Vision Express. 'I had a shop in every major Canadian centre so I decided to stop investing in new shops and spend a year simply concentrating on having a great manager in every branch. It was the most profitable year I ever had', he told me.

Scotland has reminded me of three important lessons:

1. Always aim to have a great manager in every branch.
2. Every so often, move managers round to run a different shop.
3. Most of our best business ideas appear when we are out of the office visiting shops.

After many years of doing, I'm being promoted into a managing position for the first time. I've observed how my bosses have operated in the past but there doesn't seem to be any science or set way to encourage other people to achieve the targets against which I'll be measured. I am wondering what you look for in a manager so I can use it as a guide?

There isn't a magic formula. Good bosses come in all shapes and sizes, but there are a few signs of success.

You must have the courage to delegate authority but retain responsibility. Forget stereotypes of the boss behind a desk issuing orders. Good management is about helping colleagues to do their job rather than telling them what to do.

Don't spend your life stuck in meetings. Some managers take up too much time talking to other executives. You can't manage your people if you don't see them face to face.

Your job is to clear away the obstacles that get in the way of your team. Use plenty of praise and be careful with your criticism but don't be a soft touch. Set high standards by never walking past a problem.

Trust your team with the freedom to make their own

decisions. Earn their respect by getting your coat off and doing some of the dirty jobs and fighting causes on their behalf. In particular always fulfil every promise you make. Typical critical comments are, 'My boss is always too busy', and 'He said he would – but I am still waiting'.

We carry out a six-monthly survey of all our colleagues to produce a 'Happy Index' for each team. We find this is the best way to measure our managers. If you are a natural people person you should have no problem passing the test.

I'm a freelance training provider delivering specialist face-to-face 28-week courses which lead to a professional insurance qualification. I find it increasingly difficult to have the courage to put up my fees. In fifteen years my charges have hardly risen at all. I'm scared that an increase will push my hirers into the hands of alternative providers. Have you got any advice?

By waiting so long you have made matters much worse. To keep up with inflation, it is always best to change prices little and often.

What are you frightened of? Do your competitors charge less? Are you giving your customers a poor service? If you put your fee up by 5% would any of your business disappear? I am pretty sure you have been guilty of some expensive pessimism. Do yourself a favour and, from now on, be bold.

Some businesses can cut costs and use cheaper imports to keep prices at the same level. You can't. If you give face-to-face training courses there are few economies of scale to be made. But, if it makes you feel better, try tweaking your product.

When I raided our biscuit tin last week I found an 'original' Penguin. It isn't like the original Penguins I enjoyed as a child – it might taste the same but it's half the size. I am not suggesting that you cut your course to fourteen weeks for the same fee, but you could justify a price increase by designing an updated package – new visuals, more handouts, unlimited free coffee, perhaps with a Penguin biscuit.

Even if you keep your course exactly the same, it is time to forget your fears and simply put up the price. I am sure you are worth the extra money.

I am a final year student currently writing a dissertation focusing upon motivation. I have found many of your articles very useful. I am studying Business Management with Hospitality and Events. My dissertation focuses upon racecourse management where much of the work is outsourced to other companies. Do you have any thoughts regarding how the racecourse manager can motivate employees who are working at the venue for only a short period of time?

A racecourse that only opens for business on twenty or so race days a year is faced with a major challenge. How can they provide their punters with a proper service when the bookmakers, barmen, burger bars and those behind the buffet table only turn up for the day?

I see a lot of racecourses in my role as financial supporter and husband of a racehorse owner and experience a big difference in atmosphere as I move from course to course. I can still remember a grumpy car park attendant at Hereford and the tepid tea at Towcester. A freezing day at Leicester is far less fun than the Cheltenham Festival, but each venue has its own character. I enjoy the country charm of Bangor-on-Dee, and the special care given to owners and trainers at Haydock. Uttoxeter has a different theme for nearly every meeting to attract new racegoers but there is no spectacle more entertaining than Ladies' Day at Aintree, on the day before the Grand National.

Each course has its own culture, which is strongly influenced by the management team. Every course manager should visit lots of competitors to sample different racedays and pinch some ideas that work and weave them into their home racecourse package.

Whether the aim is to be universally popular, exclusively posh, attract serious racegoers or cater for families looking for a fun day out, every racecourse needs to be good at looking after customers, and they rely on a range of franchised service providers. The temptation is to tie everyone down with a list of rules – DON'T!

The course manager should pick franchisees with care, then give them the freedom to look after customers the way they know best. No one can create great service by issuing a set of rules. Great service champions have a strong culture and trust their colleagues to play a full part.

It won't always go well. The racecourse manager must give everyone freedom but watch them all carefully. On raceday he must be permanently around and about, praising anything good, but never walking past a problem.

The racecourse is an extension of the manager's personality. By meeting lots of colleagues and customers face to face he will establish his individual mark and make a difference.

I live in Wilmslow and I am sure you are aware that there is another good cobbler in Wilmslow besides Timpson's. I wondered if and how you benchmark your stores against the competition?

We don't do formal benchmarking, have steered clear of focus groups and never used market research to categorise our customers by socio-economic group. We simply spend time walking the high street, to visit our shops and sometimes pop in for a chat with our competitors, most of whom are independent traders like Mark Rogers in Wilmslow.

I know Grove Street in Wilmslow as well as anywhere, having lived near there for nineteen years after Alex and I got married. I first met Mark when he managed our shop in Macclesfield, before he decided to go it alone down the road in Handforth and then opened a second shop near ours in Wilmslow. I never feel bitter about someone who leaves us to start their own business.

We are always looking for new ideas that work. A lot of other cobblers copy the way we have developed key cutting and watch repairs, but some like Mark also have a mind of their own and give us plenty of food for thought.

If we did use outsiders to do a bit of benchmarking I am pretty sure they would tell us that customers want an expert job with memorable personal service. I know we don't always get it right, but that is exactly what we aim to do.

Many of your shops have only one or two staff. How do you deal with holidays and sick leave? Do you have a pool of people that you 'parachute in', and are you able to do this at short notice, if someone phones in sick at say 8.00am?

You've put your finger on one of the trickiest bits of running our business.

With so many shops staffed by only one person, it isn't easy to ensure we are always open for business, but most of the time we do. In the last twelve months, I have been at nearly 100 branches before 9.00am and only found two that weren't open – one because the manager's car had a puncture and at the other a colleague was waiting outside for the person who had the key.

We have 27 areas, each supporting about 40 shops. The Area Manager has three assistants and at least three mobile managers who cover for sickness, holidays and days off. As a lot of our shops are open for seven days a week, the mobiles play a vital part. Up to fifteen years ago this roving role was given to junior colleagues, as part of their management training, but today we pick our best managers so they can check our standards as they move from shop to shop.

The area team doesn't have an office. Everyone does their management job out in the shops, often giving skills training while also serving customers. Every member of the area team is promoted from within, having started as an apprentice.

One person in each area is responsible for all the staff movements. They sort out the holiday rota, plan the programme for each mobile manager and deal with sickness and emergency absence on a daily basis.

Recently I got to our pod in the car park of Tesco Burgess Hill at 8.40am to find Assistant Area Manager Lindsay on the phone. Lindsay is responsible for movements and she was sorting out a couple of sickness issues while, at the same time, running the branch. 'It helps if people are ill before 7.00am', she told me. 'It gives enough time to sort it out.'

We don't have a company-wide process – every area has their own system. Lindsay showed me her notebook and iPad, listing everyone in the area with holidays, birthdays (it's an extra paid day off) and future medical appointments or family celebrations that require time off. 'The important bits are already in my head', said Lindsay. 'You need to know who won't work Sundays, who wants some longer hours for extra cash, where they all live, and who has a car.'

Lindsay always has an interesting but difficult week; every day is different. She does a great job but is quick to point out: 'My job is made a lot easier by working with a crowd of colleagues who are keen to get to work and earn a big bonus.'

One of my long-standing suppliers is letting me down. It is not just a one-off and I fear they may be struggling. They're based just down the road and the last thing I want is to see them close down. So what should I do?

There is no harm in having a social conscience and being a nice neighbour but sometimes you can be too kind for your own good. This is not the time to be sentimental – your business must come first.

You have already given this supplier enough chances to provide the service you need. Ask around the trade and you will almost certainly find that other customers are having similar problems, whether they are to do with late delivery, poor quality or uncompetitive prices.

If you want to be helpful, tell him the truth. Put forward your findings in a face-to-face chat. He has been finding life difficult for a long time, so the more you dig into the detail, don't be surprised to discover that the business is in an even worse state than you imagine.

Although you describe this as a long-standing relationship and he is probably a friend as well as a supplier, don't allow loyalty to go too far. Your priority is to find a replacement who can come up with the goods and still be around in five years' time – long after your local man has gone out of business.

Have you ever received competitor information by mistake or via a rogue supplier or employee? If you have, did you act on it?

It is impossible to stop bits of information coming from competitors but most of it is useless.

Confidentiality is overrated. Most secrets are of little interest to the rest of the world, so feel free to keep your colleagues fully up to date with company progress without any fear of losing a competitive advantage.

In 35 years I can only remember one occasion when indiscretion gave me the upper hand. We were in the early stages of a deal but despite us signing a confidentiality agreement the prospective vendor was only providing sparse information – top-level figures flattered by using earnings figures before interest, tax, depreciation and amortisation were taken into account. We needed branch-by-branch detail.

Suddenly everything we asked for, and more, arrived in one email. The next day we found out why the other side had been so forthcoming when we received another message. 'We wish to retract yesterday's email which was sent in error. Please confirm that you have deleted the message, destroyed all hard copies and will not use any of the information you have received.' I would never indulge in industrial espionage, but if intelligence is handed to you on a plate you might as well use it.

What do you make of these 'discounts' companies ask for from suppliers for 'early payment'? It seems to me they're being used as an excuse by some to squeeze the supply chain – one retailer has scrapped normal payment entirely, insisting suppliers take at least a small hit to be paid in 60 days, or a bigger one to be paid faster. Not cricket in my view, what do you think?

The way a man does business says a lot about his character. What might be seen as fair play by one could be called unethical trading by another.

A circular to all suppliers demanding another 30 days' credit may seem a simple way to beat the board's cash flow target. But good business is not as easy as that. A short-term ploy could be to your long-term disadvantage.

The best trading relationships are based on trust. Business

should be a partnership, not a battle. Normally a supplier is expected to support their customer but it works just as well the other way round. Good buyers act in the interest of their suppliers – especially if they want a lasting relationship.

Much depends on what it says in the contract. A deal is a deal and for a big customer to demand a one-sided change to the trading terms, as well as being a breach of contract, is the deed of a big bully. On the few occasions we have been on the receiving end of such a selfish demand we have flatly refused and the culprit has climbed down. Many don't find it as easy to say 'No!', but if they give in it won't be long before the supplier comes back for more.

It is not just customers who can play to a thin moral code. Suppliers can be economical with the truth about passing on discounts, pocketing commission or secretly switching production to a much cheaper foreign source. There have been times when we thought we were working to an open book but the supplier didn't tell us the full story.

Anyone who is prone to take advantage of tough tactics should bear in mind that business people have long memories and may well have the opportunity to get their own back. Revenge is sweet, especially when you expose the weakness of a big business bully.

An important part of an executive's job is to judge the other person's personality. As I hinted at the beginning, a man's character will give a good hint of the way he will do business. Everyone has a choice. As I was told many years ago: 'If you want to sup with the devil, make sure you use a long spoon.'

How hard have you pushed suppliers recently? I know we all have to get along but our business still needs to cut costs and making our suppliers feel some pain seems like a good way to do it.

Business might be bad but this is no reason to turn your chief buyer into a Rottweiler. Even in difficult times keep thinking a few years ahead, and look after your key suppliers – you will need their support when the recovery comes.

Obviously you don't want to be a soft touch. Drive a hard bargain to ensure you are not paying more than your competitors, but once a deal is struck, stick to it. I strongly disapprove of companies who bully their suppliers by changing terms halfway through a contract by demanding an extra discount or extended credit.

Real business is not based on the macho techniques made popular by programmes like *The Apprentice*. Good business is more likely to come from friendship and politeness than blunt talking or mind games.

Your suppliers are probably already suffering enough pain without having to share some of yours. If you turn the screw any tighter you may drive them out of business and lose a good source of supply, and if they survive they will be out for revenge by charging you their highest prices or cutting you off their customer list altogether.

Buyers don't need to be aggressive to get a good deal. When I was a buyer we built up buyer/supplier relationships based on good manners and mutual trust. We consistently worked closely together with a number of key providers over a long period.

By all means make sure your trading terms are keen and competitive, but never lose sight of the value that comes from long-term relationships.

We are switching away from a key long-standing supplier because we can get a better price and hopefully service elsewhere. How do you handle it?

Sadly, from time to time the bond between buyer and seller breaks down. Often the supplier simply fails to keep up with the market, or sometimes they get too greedy (if they park a Ferrari in your office car park you start to wonder whether they are taking advantage of your generosity).

It's often a mistake to drop a supplier on a whim. It isn't just a question of price – think about service and after-sales support. Before making the decision don't just work out how much money they are making out of you; think about how much you make from the business you do together. The rival salesman who has offered an amazing price that you feel you can't refuse may not have the infrastructure to deliver his promise.

It is a big decision – you are ending a long-term partnership – but if you have lost faith in your partner, it is time to act.

Check the contract to make sure you are not about to trigger off a penalty clause and look at the purchase ledger – is there a credit balance to cover compensation for the future return of faulty goods?

Tell them face-to-face, be blunt but be friendly, and tell them the real reasons why they have lost the contract. The news will almost certainly come as no surprise, especially if they have been getting greedy margins at your expense.

Listen carefully to their side of the story but be firm – it is unlikely that they are going to tell you something new. You have taken a lot of time making your decision, so stick to your guns – but nicely. You never know when you may want to do business with them again, so try to part as friends.

The business that I started on my own is thriving and more money is coming in than ever before. When is the right time to appoint a Finance Director?

You will always need someone who you can totally trust to look after the company's cash but he or she does not need to be a director. As long as you see your bank balance every day, management accounts monthly, and get regular annual profit forecasts that you can rely on, you will sleep at night without any worry.

As you grow and the finance function becomes a bigger executive role, you will need someone who can negotiate insurance premiums, control electricity charges, meet the bank manager and talk about tax to your accountants. That means a finance controller who will probably be on your board, but be careful: this recruitment is almost as critical as choosing a wife.

The CEO/Finance Director relationship must be based on trust and respect. If you fall out, the whole company will suffer. Beware the accountant on a crusade to bring systems up to date – he will upset lots of long-service employees and may not be satisfied until he has your job. A good Finance

Director, like a football defence, is good at preventing mistakes and avoiding own goals, but don't employ an accountant who wants to become a striker and take over the captaincy.

Some supermarkets are interested in my food brand, which is already selling well in independent retailers. I'd love to grow my business but handling a much bigger production operation is a big leap and I also don't like the idea of waiting months to get paid (I've heard some horror stories). What do you think I should weigh up when deciding whether to take the plunge?

Why do you want to expand into supermarkets? Do you want to get bigger, become better known, or do you see it as a way to make a lot more money? Think carefully – you may do a lot more business and fail to achieve any of these objectives.

There is probably some truth in the stories you have heard. Most supermarkets expect to pay a lower price than you charge the independents. In addition they may want you to hold reserve stock at your own expense and make a contribution to the cost of marketing. They could also carry out a range review, discontinue your current lines and require the replacement stock to be supplied for free. When times are tough, some have been known to demand extended credit and an extra bit of discount.

Dealing with supermarket buyers takes time – so much time that your existing customers may wonder whether you love them any more.

If I haven't put you off, I suggest you start by simply supplying a supermarket in your local area and don't drop your price. Given the chance, the buyers will keep chipping the deal until you are selling below cost. Have the courage to say 'No'. If you deal with more than one supermarket, charge the same price otherwise you will finish up getting the lowest price from them all.

Before making a move, carry out a risk assessment. Answer the simple question: 'What happens to my business if my brand is taken off every shelf without notice?'

Always make sure that they need you more than you need them.

If you could be a fly on the wall in another business, where would you find yourself?

The obvious place to pry is their Finance department but I'm not sure a glimpse of someone's management accounts tells you what is really going on. It would be better to eavesdrop on a board meeting to hear the argument when the FD is accused of producing pessimistic figures and being a prophet of doom.

I discover most about my own business by visiting our shops where I can meet customers and talk to the colleagues who put money in our tills. You can learn a lot on the shop floor but if you want to discover the inside track in the office, hang around the canteen – or even better, stand near the smoking shelter.

When we had our own transport fleet, the best source of information was our delivery drivers who flitted from shop to shop spreading gossip wherever they went.

Some years ago one of our competitors got their field team to dial in to hear a recorded weekly strategy briefing.

We somehow obtained their magic number so we too could ring in for a regular update.

Today the most interesting titbits are spread through the internet, so why not tap into the company grapevine by adding their top gossips to your list of Facebook friends?

It may or may not be useful to know your competitor's hidden agenda but it is always helpful to have the fly on the wall's view of your own business.

We never announce our shop visits, so when James and I visited our shop at Parkstone at 8.30 one morning before Christmas it was a bit of a shock for the guy in charge. At Poole a few minutes later, our shop was busy so when the phone rang James picked it up. 'Just ringing to say that John and James are on their way', said the voice at the other end. 'I know', replied James, 'we have just arrived.'

It is not easy being an undercover boss.

I've been invited on an employee's stag do. I accidentally said that I would go when he first mentioned it. How can I come out of this unscathed?

You don't say where the stag party is taking place, what you are doing, or how long it goes on.

If the plan is to have a few pints at The Pig and Whistle prior to a night on the town, you could turn up early, get in the first round and, as soon as you get the chance, make an early exit.

If you're talking of a two-night cultural trip to Amsterdam I can't help wondering what possessed you to sign up. All I can recommend is that you put enough money in the pot to buy the team T-shirts and then make sure you are struck down with a desperate illness twelve hours before departure.

You can be pretty sure they will have a much better time without you.

What is the best corporate hospitality to offer important clients, in your view? I'm a little bored of taking them to football matches.

A lot of corporate hospitality is a waste of time and money. You feel you have to invite them, they feel they have to come, and everyone is glad when the event is over.

If you want to impress, do some research. Find out what your client really likes and offer the invitation they can't refuse – make it relevant and make it different. Centre Court seats may be just the ticket for tennis players, but Take That fans are unlikely to fancy the opera.

Avoid weekends and include your client's partner. Motor sport activity days are pretty popular (how else will they drive a Jaguar round a race track at 160mph?), and most will enjoy a private box at Aintree (Ladies' Day has to be seen to be believed). But to make it particularly personal, invite them to your home or your local pub and really get to know your client without allowing a mediocre game of football to get in the way of good conversation.

I'm passionate about my business yet hate the sales aspect of my role. Any tips on how I can get over this fear?

You are probably shy and hate the idea of failure, but you

possess the most important characteristic a salesman can have – you are passionate about your business. Make yourself have a go and make it fun at the same time. Set yourself targets: aim to meet all your major customers every four months, see how many calls you can make in a day and how many business cards you can collect in a month.

A friend of mine has turned his whole selling operation into a company-wide challenge. Recently he acquired a company with 5,000 customers and wanted to welcome them as soon as possible with a personal call. For a week all his 100 employees – including the managing director, maintenance manager and the girls in purchase ledger – became part of the sales team. They each made ten calls a day. By Friday all 5,000 customers had been contacted and Peter in the postroom was sales champion, winning more new business than the top sales rep of that year.

Once you have overcome your inhibitions you will enjoy the sales role and start to learn a lot more about your business. Don't be the type of pen-pusher that gets stuck behind a desk. Never rely on the sales reps to tell you what's happening – meet some customers every month and find out for yourself.

I keep hearing about the four-hour week phenomenon. Some bright spark thinks it's possible to get rich with almost no effort. Is this actually possible? Is it damaging to preach theories like this?

The term 'four-hour week' comes from the cover of a bestselling business book in which author Timothy Ferriss tells the story of how he increased his income twelve times by cutting his working week from 80 hours to four. He discovered how to make money by hardly lifting a finger through outsourcing to 'virtual assistants' and checking emails only once a day. He turned Parkinson's Law ('Work expands to fill the time available for its completion') on its head by completing all his work in the minimum possible time. *The 4-Hour Work Week* is such a great title it sold over 1.3 million copies.

At first glance the concept sounds appealing but I can't help being a little bit peeved by perfect people. This four-hour week man is now another on my list of executives who appear too good to be true. From time to time I come across a seriously successful superman who seems to run a great business while living life to the full. But I wonder how anyone can socialise with A-list celebrities by night but be back in the office immaculately dressed at 7.30am after a session with their personal trainer to keep fit for the fortnightly triathlons. These role models have a perfect holiday home by the sea, four well-behaved children and a golf handicap of three, and I find the whole package pretty irritating.

I prefer people with the ability to make a few mistakes, like me, mixing making money with a few day-to-day disasters – leaving a diary on the train, putting petrol in a diesel car and spilling coffee down my shirt.

I don't envy Timothy Ferriss. With only four hours a week devoted to work, what would I do with the rest of my life? There is a limit to how much time I want to spend on the golf course or tennis court, and if I was on holiday for most of the year, it wouldn't feel like a holiday.

Our business is my number one hobby. I really like work, so a four-hour week doesn't sound much fun.

When I was skiing in Austria recently nearly half the guys on the chairlift were tapping away at their BlackBerrys. Do you think it is right to mix business and pleasure in this way?

Posers using BlackBerrys on the button lift can be pretty irritating, but I bet it gives a lot of pleasure whenever an unfortunate captain of industry drops his vital little device in the snow. I suppose some may simply be arranging to meet with the rest of their party for lunch, but most will be addicted to opening every email within seconds of seeing the flash of a red light.

I feel sorry for the poor PA who was hoping for a week of peace but instead is pestered by a paranoid boss who delves too deep into the detail.

The chairlift communicator may impress some fellow skiers, but in reality he is showing a sign of weakness. He clearly hasn't created a team he can trust in his absence. He would be much better keeping the BlackBerry in his pocket, taking in the Alpine air, and showing he hasn't a care in the world by looking cool and totally relaxed.

It is good to let go, feel far away from the office and stop constantly turning business problems over in your mind – that is what holidays are for, to give you a break.

But I also think it is good to keep in touch once a day. It reduces anxiety and avoids the trauma of coming home to a mailbox full of surprises.

Some skiers will never be able to resist checking their emails every time they board a cable car but the smart executive waits until he is back at the chalet so he can read his BlackBerry in the bath.

A colleague who runs an events company asked me to be a keynote speaker at an upcoming business conference on mobile working. I'd love to, it's my pet subject, but he hasn't offered to pay me. I'm a conference novice – what's the etiquette and how much should I expect?

Don't ask for money until you have a better idea of what you are worth. You obviously enjoy speaking and think you are well worth listening to, but the only people who really know are the audience.

If you have a talent for talking (a lot of conference performers don't!) you will soon get more invitations. That is the time to start asking for a fee. I suggest you donate the money to charity – it feels good, takes the embarrassment away when asking for a fee, and avoids the chore of putting it on your tax return. Set a minimum price (is it really worth preparing a talk and travelling 200 miles for less than £1,000?) and ask for more than you dare. Many speakers on the circuit get over £2,000. Perhaps you can get more – it all depends on who is running the conference and the size of your reputation.

Once you get in the swing of it, speaking is good fun, but don't accept too many engagements (six a year is enough). Keep your novelty appeal and never forget your main job is to run the business.

We're running well under capacity and are trying to think of ways of managing this. While we've cut out unnecessary costs there must be something more

positive that we can do than just waiting for demand to pick up? The problem is that being busy in this trading environment doesn't actually mean making money.

You have done all you can to deal with the downturn – cut costs, controlled your cash, and kept the bank manager happy. Now it is time to prepare for the future.

What will your business be doing in five years' time? Where are the opportunities and what are your big ideas? There is no need to pay a consultant or employ a strategic planner – you can use your own crystal ball. All you need is a biro, an A4 pad and time to think.

Clear the clutter of day-to-day problems from your mind and let your imagination take over. Record the results of a free-range romp through all the possible ways to grow, then decide where your ambitions lie. Within a matter of hours you will have started to create a new business plan.

It may be too early to put your plan into action, and the bank will probably not be ready to authorise any capital expenditure, but at least you can look after your people. Your future success will depend on the loyalty and contribution of key team members.

Talk to them about your plans and listen to their views. Outline the important part they have to play and tell them how good they are. Even if you are strapped for cash, show your confidence by giving the superstars a special bonus.

A Chief Executive always has plenty to do. As a friend once told me: 'If you sit around waiting for something to happen, the only thing to turn up will be trouble.'

Cheating in our society is rife, to the detriment of family life, business, sport and politics. Cheating on family, friends and colleagues is unacceptable but are there forms of cheating which are acceptable? I have won orders by enhancing, in a non-monetary way, the lifestyle of buyers employed by my customers. Once I obtained a very large contract by nullifying a competitor's plans received from a disgruntled employee of his. Recently, I won a round of golf in my club's knockout tournament by refraining to tell my opponent, who is an unpleasant fellow, where his ball was when he lost it at a crucial moment. Are there some forms of acceptable cheating or is it a slippery slope?

No one is a paragon of virtue, but when does a sharp dealer become a cheat? As a simple guide, if it worries you, don't do it. Don't get involved in anything that you think might embarrass yourself or anyone else. It's a question of personal pride – not rules. You are much better aiming to satisfy your conscience than trying to comply with a set of guidelines.

Business entertaining becomes bribery when you put a buyer in a difficult spot. Paying cash or funding a holiday is clearly out of the question, and expensive tickets to Cheltenham races could be a step too far. Dodgy dealing may be used to gain a short-term advantage (and sometimes gaining the satisfaction of scoring points against an irritating competitor) but don't be surprised if your victim gets his own back some years later.

It is possible to make lots of money and be nice, decent and honest at the same time. You don't have to lower your standards to the level of your most aggressive competitor or play games with unpleasant opponents.

If you get drawn against the same guy in the golf knockout next year, I'd give him a walkover.

I am the Managing Director of a large construction company. We have a number of buyers who are responsible for all our purchases. The second most senior, who has been with us for over twenty years and is extremely popular, has been accused by the Managing Director of one of our suppliers of suggesting he is open to bribes. The supplier has asked me for a meeting to discuss what I am going to do.

I have faith in all our colleagues, particularly those I've known for a long time, but there have been times when that trust has been abused by a star performer. When it comes to people it is wise to expect the unexpected – you should never be too surprised.

If your buyer really is looking for backhanders you have a serious problem. I watched one big business implode due to bribery and greed. The buyers had created much of the company's success but bribery was endemic. I'm not just talking about a couple of cases of wine – these buyers expected free foreign holidays and money in Swiss bank accounts. When a new management team took over and fired the culprits, their merchandise lost its flair and the business was never the same again.

Don't jump to conclusions too quickly. So far you only have one person's story. You need to find out more. After employing your buyer for twenty years you can afford to take a few weeks to find out the facts.

First go and meet the supplier, ask him exactly what happened and check whether he knows of others who have received a similar approach. If your buyer has asked one customer for a bribe he has probably approached many more – it could be common knowledge in the trade. Dig as deep as you can, but you might not be the best person to do the digging. It may sound dramatic, but consider hiring a private detective.

Did you fail to see some obvious warning signs? Perhaps you have been funding some bribes through higher cost prices. Or maybe your buyer has been reluctant to change to new suppliers.

If your supplier's suspicions are confirmed you will, no doubt, be more vigilant in future. But first you must dismiss your star buyer for gross misconduct.

I am in the process of going through a rather nasty divorce. My soon to be ex-wife used to be my confidante and sounding board about my business. She knows all my fears – and the mistakes I've made over the years. She is now using this inside knowledge against me, threatening to reveal secrets to colleagues, employees and clients unless I give her what she wants in the settlement. What shall I do?

There are two sides to every argument but after seeking some feminine intuition from my resident expert, I'm on your side! Alex got straight to the point: 'The wife doesn't sound a paragon of virtue – if she's that vindictive she'll blow the whistle even if he gives in to her blackmail. I'd tough it out, fight for every penny and let her dish out the dirt.'

We all love a bit of gossip but have you really messed up so badly you need to cover up your past? Everyone makes mistakes, they show you are human. Perhaps you are particularly accident-prone, but most people worry about minor personal faults that don't bother the rest of the world. It's like golf: the saddest thing about playing really badly is that no one else cares.

Companies get paranoid about confidentiality but most competitors wouldn't believe your figures and, if they did, probably wouldn't know what to do with them.

It's tempting to pay up and move on but your ex will still want to spill the beans. However, if she sets out on a spiteful whistle-blowing campaign, others will see her for what she is – bad news!

I hope your story doesn't deter others from seeing their wife as a mentor – from my experience a wife makes the best possible type of executive coach.

Unless you're keeping a mammoth problem under wraps I reckon your only major mistake was to marry the wrong woman.

I hope you have a good lawyer!

I've been approached to take part in one of those fly-on-the-wall documentaries. A film crew wants to follow me about as I start up my new business. I know it will be great exposure but I'm not a very politically correct guy

**and worry that it's an attempt to make an idiot out of me
and my venture. Is it worth going ahead anyway?**

Notwithstanding any attempt by the production team to por-
tray you differently, the camera doesn't lie. Be yourself, and, if
you're a nice guy, viewers will recognise your true personality.
Don't be tempted to act the part. If you put on a false face
for the television crew you will come across as a fake in the
finished film.

You will have plenty of time to decide. Most TV production teams have to go through a long process before the big
bosses can sign off a proposed new programme. They will
want to meet you, thus giving a golden opportunity to size up
their motive. Do some research – previous programmes the
producer has made give a flavour of the way he or she thinks.
Be guided by the way you respond to their personality. It is
easier to make a good programme with people you like. The
working title should also give you a clue. It's OK to take part
in a series called *Business Superstars* or *How to be a Great
Boss* but go carefully if the current title is *Rogue Traders* or
Management Cock-Ups.

Don't get too excited; most proposals fail to get financial
backing. I've talked to several programme makers about the
Timpson way of employing people from prison. They all seemed
desperately keen to make a major programme (or in two cases a
series) but so far none of the proposals has gone ahead.

It pays to be patient and, if you eventually receive the go-
ahead, get on as well as you can with the crew – they have
editorial control and you don't want the best bits left on the
cutting room floor.

They won't give you a preview before it goes on air, so you're bound to be nervous when you watch yourself on TV for the first time – will you be hailed as a prat or a hero the next time you meet up with your mates?

As a new business this is a golden opportunity to gain a good reputation, and, apart from personal pride, you have little to lose. This is a chance worth taking. Go for it!

Shops and Salesmanship

I expected a lot of questions about the high street but was surprised to discover how many Timpson customers use the 'Ask John' email address to send compliments and complaints (in equal measure) about their Timpson shopping experience. It's great when people take the trouble to tell me about amazing service but the complaints provide a constant reality check. I still remember the Sunday when a customer demanded an immediate response to his 2,000-word rant about a shop manager who called him 'mate'. I find the best way to deal with an angry complainer is to ring up and talk it through – especially on a Sunday evening.

Apart from telling me their Timpson shopping stories, the retail questions covered car parking, click and collect, landlords and business rates. Everyone seems to be a bit of a retail expert but I don't think anyone really knows what will happen to shopping. For over 50 years I've been trading on a changing high street that has never been short of surprises. Out-of-town shopping, Green Shield stamps, Sunday trading, home delivery and internet shopping are just a few of the innovations that have been good news for some shops and very bad news for others.

The first time I appeared in print was while I was at Nottingham University in 1963, when the *Financial Times* published a letter I wrote under the heading 'RPM and shops' location'. My letter suggested: 'The proposed abolition of Resale Price Maintenance will hand a big advantage to the new supermarkets being opened out of town to the detriment of the high street trader and corner shop. Are we about to see a big geographical shift in our shopping habits?' I had certainly spotted a trend but didn't anticipate how much the high street would change in the next 50 years. Likewise, today, we don't know how much difference the internet will make and we haven't got a clue what development will make the next massive shift in the way we shop.

Empty shops have become headline news, with the media mixing doom and gloom with a range of reasons for each retail failure. But in most cases it is easy to see why a retailer has gone into administration. They went bust because they failed to keep up to date with the market – consumer demand and shopping habits are always on the move, and retailers must constantly change to keep up with their customers. Fortunately, I don't like the status quo. The fun in business comes from finding new ways to make money – being a bit hyperactive does no harm if you are a retailer.

Having to answer these questions has made me think, especially at a time when our business is making a big investment in new branches that are linked to some of the major supermarket chains. We are hedging our bets and splitting the trade between the traditional high street and out-of-town shopping.

Through all this change one thing has been consistent. Customers want good service. Whatever happens, consumers are looking for an easy life with friendly help whenever it's needed. Simply changing the branch manager can make a 50% difference to sales. The best people make the most money.

I am not going to pretend that I can see the future of retailing any better than Bill Grimsey, Philip Green or Mary Portas. In 1960, few gurus would have guessed that Woolworths would disappear or that you could happily go out shopping without carrying any cash. Thirty years ago, no one would have heard of Carphone Warehouse, Primark or Pret a Manger. It's safe to predict that at least half of the most popular shops in 25 years' time have not yet been invented.

In a world full of so much uncertainty we can at least be sure, despite clever computers, that people will always be the most important ingredient that makes one business better than another.

*

Cobblers repair shoes. Why do they also cut keys? Locksmiths cut keys. Even my local cobbler can't explain what mutual skills or machinery are common to both trades, or explain why locksmiths don't repair shoes.

Good question! Fifty years ago shoe repairers stuck to cobbling. With most people wearing all-leather shoes, made in the UK, cobblers were easily able to satisfy the economic law of shoe repairing – as long as your repair costs no more than a third of the cost of a new pair, you are in business.

In the 1960s shoe shops started to sell synthetic imports at half the leather prices and shoe repair demand dropped by 15% for three years running.

Cobblers tried all sorts of things to make up the loss: knife sharpening, hosiery, leather goods, rubber stamps, and straw shopping baskets – but the one that really worked was key cutting. The new service was introduced at a time when more people were moving house and ironmongers (who all used to cut keys) were disappearing from the high street.

Key cutting is now 35% of our total turnover (even more than shoe repairs) – that's why cobblers cut keys.

With reference to Mary Portas' recent report, my question is to query whether the high street is worth saving? Customers are moving to the internet and to retail parks through preferred choice so no amount of subsidies or papering over of cracks will stop this trend. Would it not be better to develop 'dead and dying' high streets into lively communities with affordable housing and recreational areas and in other sustainable directions?

I can't conceal my concern when I see a high street or shopping mall blighted by a clutch of closed shops. Some streets have had an unfair proportion of the number of names that have gone into administration. If a centre has been host to Clinton Cards, Game, Peacocks, Hawkin's Bazaar, La Senza and Barratts it is bound to look less prosperous.

But well-known names have always been disappearing from our high street. When I started work as a shoe shop assistant in 1960 we were trading alongside Home and Colonial, MacFisheries, Timothy Whites, Freeman Hardy and Willis, John Collier, Dewhurst, Dunns and a nationwide chain selling Singer sewing machines. All these names and hundreds more have gone during the last 50 years.

We can already confidently forecast that the high street

will continue to change, but it would help to know what people will want to buy from shops twenty years from now.

The internet will have a big influence. Bookshops, music stores, and almost anyone else selling merchandise available online will face a major challenge. But there are some things you can't buy from a website. Service retailers will continue to flourish – hairdressers, coffee bars, opticians, nail bars and, of course, key cutters will still be in demand in 2032.

In addition to service shops, people will always spend money in stores that give great service. Even the best website can't provide the chance to touch the goods and get face-to-face advice from an expert. The internet might offer the best price but a shop with amazingly helpful assistants will still give the best value.

There is one obvious magic wand that will bring customers back to the high street from the supermarkets and out-of-town shopping. Shopping centres need easy-to-find free parking.

Most shopping areas have too many shops, and some local authorities make matters worse by approving plans to knock a few down and build even more in their place. Next time they should replace the old stores with an enormous free car park, then shopping on the high street will be just as convenient as going out of town.

One of my shops is in a small town, which is becoming more run down each week. I am sure you will be familiar with the scene. Shops are closing and customers are disappearing. I have three other shops, which can

support this loss-maker but not for ever. Have you any advice as to when I should cut my losses and close the shop?

Cut out the loss-maker as quickly as possible but before deciding to close, check that it really should be losing money.

Textbooks say that retailing is all about location – if you have a pitch in the perfect spot you are bound to do well. I disagree. In my experience the critical factor is people – multiple retailers should aim to have a first-class manager in every branch.

There is no shortage of excuses when turnover is down. For years I've listened to the same reasons for poor performance: 'Car park charges have doubled'; 'We've had road works for five months'; 'A lot of local factories are laying workers off'. I often encounter the problem you appear to be facing – 'The town is very quiet ... everyone's complaining' – but often a change of personnel can prove that there is a lot more business available.

Before you throw in the towel, organise what we call a busman's holiday. Move the existing manager to another shop for a month and replace him or her with a proven superstar. If your top salesman takes no more money, you know there is a fundamental problem with the property.

Don't start a closing down sale until you have checked the lease. Even if you stop trading, the landlord will still want the rent and may bill you for some dilapidations – you could lose even more money by shutting the shop. It's worth seeing if the landlord will do a deal.

It is tough taking the decision to close part of your

company, especially having invested so much time and money in the venture. But if you are making a loss in a declining market, get out as soon as you can and concentrate on places where you really can make money.

Tailors of London's Savile Row are up in arms about the arrival of Abercrombie & Fitch's planned kids' store, saying it will make the street a less desirable destination for their affluent customers. Have any of your stores ever been affected by an unwanted neighbour? And have you ever experienced being on Abercrombie & Fitch's side of the fence?

On today's high street having any neighbour is better than trading next to an empty shop. But I prefer being alongside Greggs or Pret a Manger rather than a Cash Converters, bookmaker or sex shop. I was located next to the latter when I made the mistake of opening a shop in Wardour Street, Soho. There was plenty of passing traffic but we were providing the wrong sort of service for that part of town.

Shoe repairers used to be regarded as the C2s and Ds of the retail world – noisy, smelly, dirty and fit only to be hidden in a back street. That impression still lingered on eight years ago when I was summoned to Ely's department store in Wimbledon to be told that our prominent ground-floor concession was being re-sited to an upper floor. We turned down the new site and fortunately found an empty unit on a busy part of the main street where we now do more than three times as much business.

Cobblers are an asset to any shopping area, but I thought

we might be stepping out of our class when we opened our shop on the King's Road in Chelsea. Thanks to the loyal following built up by Andy and his team, we now feel very much part of that community.

We have proved that there are no social barriers for a shoe repairer but top tailors have no need to worry. I have no plans to open in Savile Row.

Labour wants us to have a 'Small Business Saturday' to encourage people to shop with independent traders. What do you think of that idea?

A few of today's independents will grow into the biggest retailers 25 years from now. Any measure that encourages budding entrepreneurs to bring new ideas to the high street is to be applauded.

I see absolutely no reason why we shouldn't have a special day for Small Business – after all, there is a national awareness day for just about everything else.

We've got Apple Day and British Egg Week to promote healthy eating, which we can abandon during British Pie Week and National Doughnut Week, which are understandably followed by Walk to School Week. Most of us have heard of No Smoking Day but there is also a Stop Snoring Week and International Kissing Day.

Most are worthy causes. I certainly approve of Plain English Week and Foster Care Fortnight and have no problem with adding a Small Business Saturday – but beware, in America, where the idea started, it is now preceded by No Shopping Day.

People as old as me wax lyrical about the wonderful shops we had in our youth and the magical names that have disappeared from the high street, like Hepworths, MacFisheries and Timothy Whites. But shopping was bound to change and the shift from independents to big shops and supermarkets was accelerated by two bits of legislation: the abolition of resale price maintenance through the Resale Prices Act in 1964, and the Sunday Trading Act in 1994.

These laws have made life more difficult for the small trader but not impossible. Compared with the big boys, independents have more flexibility, are well placed to innovate and should always be able to give great personal service.

A Small Business Saturday may bring a mini boost to the local shop but their long-term prosperity will depend on delivering goods and service that customers really want on every shopping day of every week.

It can be done. The nearest shop to my home, The Hollies, an independent and innovative farm shop, keeps finding new ways to attract more customers and as a result gets bigger and better every year.

There's a lot of talk about the high street and e-commerce coming together through things like 'click and collect' where you order online and then pick up when you do your shopping. What do you make of this? I assume this doesn't apply to your shops?

I can still remember the coffee aroma in Cadman's, the independent grocer in Hale, Cheshire when my mother called to place her weekly order, which was delivered to our house the following day. The modern concept of 'click and collect' works the other way round – you order from home (or on your smartphone) and pick up from the store.

It doesn't work for watch repairs or cobbling and there are plenty of other trades that still need a personal service – you can't get your haircut on the internet.

Click and collect could attract more shoppers into town but only where there is plenty of easy parking. We are always keen to have busy neighbours but I guess the popular collection points will be at supermarkets or out of town. It is unlikely to bring people back to the high street.

Shopping habits keep changing and shopping centres must keep up to date, but it is nonsense to suggest that buying online will kill the high street. People still need to leave home to go to nail bars and coffee shops. Good cooks will prefer to pick their pork chops in a butcher's rather than on the internet. Retailers can offer much more personal service than a website, and shopping will remain a leisure activity – for a lot of people it is more fun to try on clothes in a lively fashion store than select styles on an iPad and hope the parcel contains something that fits.

The perfect high street twenty years from now will have free parking (knock down some of the empty shops to create the space), plenty of shops offering personal service, including a bank manager you can meet face-to-face, a bus station, wheelchair access, a range of pubs, restaurants and coffee shops, public loos and policemen on the beat.

Even the most dedicated techie will go to town for exciting shops that give a proper personal service – so it isn't surprising that one of today's most successful outlets, the Apple Store, sells all the kit you need to go online.

The high street is going through a lot of changes but I don't expect customers to click and collect from a key cutter.

In these days of permanent 'sales', how can a business make a powerful impact on customers in the new year, encouraging them through your doors?

For many shopkeepers mid-January to the end of February can be pretty desperate. Add a decent dose of snow and the retail trade becomes a nightmare.

It is tempting to try to pick up extra business with amazing special offers but you can't stimulate a demand that doesn't exist.

There are some shops that totally rely on price reductions to stimulate demand, as I discovered many years ago when I ran a business that specialised in fur coats. But even with products like carpets and furniture, where customers consistently look for savings, continual price cutting can become a drug that quickly erodes margin.

Great retailers are good at what they do, not just good at offering low prices. The product range, window displays, shop layout, location and attention to detail all play a part in success. But despite the woe of winter, customers like to be greeted by smiling, knowledgeable sales assistants – they're the biggest influence on performance.

My landlord has offered me a terrible new lease. Have you had many problems with rent increases, surcharges etc.?

We have all been on the wrong end of a tough negotiation with landlords, but since 2008 the tables have turned. Tough trading and a lot of empty shops have brought rent levels down and in most of the country you should be able to get a better deal.

However, despite these changes some landlords (usually individuals rather than institutions) think they still have the upper hand and hold out for some unreasonable terms.

As this is the renewal of an existing lease you always have three options:

1) Give in to his unreasonable demands.

2) For some leases you can take the matter to court (but this can be expensive and you will need advice from specialist lawyers and surveyors).

3) Threaten to leave (a realistic option if there are empty shops nearby).

It all depends on whether there is someone else in the wings who is willing to pay what the landlord wants. My guess is that he is in cloud cuckoo land and if you dig your heels in you will win.

A retail surveyor with experience of your particular town should be able to tell you the going rent levels and advise you how best to tactically manage your lease renewal. If you are trading near a Timpson, Max Spielmann or Snappy Snaps I would be happy to share our property information with you.

We're a retailer and need to shift some stock as we've over-ordered. What works best?

The best stock clearance sale I ever had was in 1975. At that time the Timpson shoe shops were part of the UDS Group (along with other retailers like John Collier, Richard Shops, and Allders). I had just been put in charge and like many new MDs was keen to clear the decks by attacking a lingering legacy of slow-moving stock.

It was a bold move. I closed all 250 shops for two days, completely covered the windows with posters and advertised on television: 'Our shops are shut to prepare for our biggest sale in 110 years – it starts at 10.00am on Thursday.'

On the Wednesday afternoon I received a pretty tricky phone call from UDS Chairman Bernard Lyons, who thought I must have lost the plot: 'How can you make money if all the shops are shut?' I was wondering whether he was right when I was in the centre of Sheffield at 9.30am on Thursday. Our five city shops were still shut and shoppers were walking past the poster-covered windows without, seemingly, taking the slightest notice.

At 9.45am queues started to form and within twenty minutes I knew my gamble would pay off. In the next three days we set an all-time sales record, beating figures set over a full week the previous Christmas.

So the secret is simple: set some sensational price reductions and surround them in drama. But be careful – you can become a victim of your own success. My 'super sale' cleared so much stock that for the following six weeks I didn't have enough shoes to serve our regular customers.

Gerald Ratner took a lot of trade from his jewellery competitors with his cut-price tactics. One year he decided to start his January sale at the beginning of December. His turnover was phenomenal. It had to be – he was taking a big chance slashing margins during the peak pre-Christmas period. It worked so well that the following year Ratners ran another pre-Christmas sale, this time with even bigger posters and deeper discounts. It worked twice but didn't do the trick the third time. Price cutting probably caused as big a problem for Ratners as the famous 'crap' comment to the Institute of Directors.

If you have stock that isn't shifting, slash the price but don't get addicted. For many retailers price cutting has become a drug, and as a consequence today's high street has too many special offers. Early in June some shops, like Clarks, have already started their summer sale. It's fun to look at the high sales figures that accompany the cut-price promotions but it's much more satisfying to sell stuff at full margin and make loads of money.

I enjoyed the dramatic price offers in my past but I am happy that these days Timpson is totally involved in the selling of services – no fashion, very little merchandise to worry about, and never enough mark-downs to run a sale.

Do you sponsor personalities to promote your company? I would travel to see Jessica Ennis open a new Timpson shop in my locality and to look at her gold medal. My

question is whether the local publicity would generate sufficient interest and future sales?

The last people to open a Timpson shop were Peter West and David Nixon, both television personalities in the 1950s well before *Hello!* magazine started to talk about celebrities.

Plenty of people came to watch them declare the branch open and a gang from head office turned up to rub shoulders with someone famous, but the shops they opened (in Norwich and Coventry) didn't take much money in the first month.

One set of celebrity openings that did make an impact was in the 1980s when a number of Burton branches were turned into Top Man. They hired topless model Fiona Richmond (fairly fully clothed) to cut the tape. Her presence certainly emphasised the change from a stodgy retail format to something with a lot of attitude, and an even bigger gang than usual came from head office.

I can think of a number of people I would like to meet – including Jessica Ennis, Mo Farah and Usain Bolt – but I don't think a connection to Timpson would persuade customers to get more keys cut.

We are currently opening one or two shops every week, mainly with Tesco and Sainsbury's. There is nothing official – we simply open the doors and start trading. Each shop's success depends on our quality of service.

As far as I am concerned a talented branch colleague is the only sort of personality who can make a difference.

How often would you recommend a shop revamp? It can be expensive but I think customers and employees need to see changes from time to time.

Take a look at a photo of the high street in 1960 (when I started in business) and you realise how much shops have altered. It is vital to keep your shops up to date, but don't change the look for the sake of it – there is no need to spend a fortune to get the image right.

The last time we had a major revamp to the look of Timpson was sixteen years ago (perhaps that is why Mary Portas says we look old-fashioned; I, however, like to be traditional – it fits in with being a cobbler), but each shop gets a minor change about every five years.

There are three reasons why retailers have a refit: 1) Brighten the store; 2) Change of image; 3) Increase turnover. Whenever we spend money I expect an increase in sales to justify the expense.

Don't confuse refits with housekeeping. You shouldn't have to refit a store simply to keep it looking smart, but day-to-day cleaning doesn't always come naturally to a craftsman cobbler. We ensure every shop has its spring clean by running a 'Perfect Day' competition every year (an idea we borrowed from Asda). Every shop is checked out on the designated day and it is well worthwhile winning the Perfect Day prize.

Most of our refits coincide with the introduction or extension of a new service. In the 1970s key cutting made a massive difference and more recently watch repairs have become a major part of our turnover. The refit gives our colleagues the chance to take more money and increase their bonus. It gives everyone an excuse for performing better.

We never have a rigid plan and don't use design consultants. We want functional shops created by practical people from our own team. A lot of the new features have been developed by in-branch colleagues who have the freedom to try any idea they believe will make us more money.

We like shops that look good but the image is not created by a logo. Our reputation totally depends on the service given by the colleagues who meet our customers.

Our biggest client loves a big night out on the town; frankly, he'd like regular lap dancing trips. I'm his main contact and responsible for keeping the contract, but all that is not my scene. What's your advice on balancing client service and betraying your principles?

You could be a wimp and pretend to be unwell or delegate the job to a colleague but it is better to stick by your principles and refuse to go clubbing!

If you give in now, next time they may want to take the lap dancers home. Surely these customers enjoy something else other than sex? If they really need to be pampered, why not offer to take them to a top theatre or book a table at a Michelin-starred restaurant? If they want to go on somewhere else, make your excuses and leave, clearly stating that the rest of the night is at their expense. (Would they expect a female sales executive to take them to the fleshpots?)

It's not just a question of your principles, it also affects your company's reputation. If your product is good enough you don't need this type of incentive. If they insist on this barely concealed bribe, let them buy from someone else.

Would you ever dream of changing your brand, logo, corporate image? It's easy to scoff at branding experts, but I have a feeling that our corporate image needs a modern makeover. The world is changing fast and we run the risk of looking dated and losing potential young customers.

The Timpson name has been on the high street for nearly 150 years and we are not going to change it now. We don't advertise and don't have a marketing department; our brand is created by the people who work in our shops and the service they give our customers.

Twenty years ago consultants advised me on our shop design. After six weeks and £10,000 they told me to promote each of our services with a different colour – that was it, that was their big idea. The week after paying them off I went to Bath and took a photo of every fascia I liked (all old-fashioned and traditional). We stuck the pictures on a wall and picked the one we liked best – that is what our shops still look like today.

Rebranding is expensive – consultants don't stop at fascias, they stipulate your signs in reception and the look of your stationery.

Some rebranding exercises have been spectacularly successful, like the change of Chelsea Girl to River Island and a conversion of Kendalls Rainwear to become the first Next shops. But rebranding can be a spectacular waste of money.

What good has been done by changing the DTI to BERR and then to BIS (other than to the profits of their printers and sign suppliers)?

Is design your top priority or do you have more pressing problems? Think twice before betting your future on a corporate image – it might not be the magic wand you are hoping for.

September is always a frantic month for us after the summer lull. What are the best and worst business ideas that you've dreamed up while on holiday and put in place when you got back?

Alex won't let me work on holiday but she can't stop me thinking about it. Sitting on the beach with a clear mind, the business seems so simple and the ideas start to flow – each one an obvious winner, but I can only remember one holiday brainwave that turned into a real success.

Fortunately, all my other fancy suggestions never got much further than Manchester airport. As soon as I was back in the real world my great ideas didn't seem so great. When I put each scheme forward to my colleagues they were unconvinced. They refused to back my enthusiasm for a range of projects that included 'Sew Easy', a chain of garment repair and alteration shops, and a mobile shoe repair service I wanted to call 'Heels on Wheels'.

These holiday dreams didn't get off the ground so I will never know whether they would have worked. But the board foolishly let me go ahead with a retail idea called 'Security Now', which combined key cutting with an off-site locksmith and burglar alarm service. It was a good name but didn't turn out to be a good business. We opened three shops and lost £75,000 before admitting defeat.

At least I can claim one success. In 1987 while taking a camper van from Seattle to Los Angeles I spotted a chain of shops called 'Things Remembered' which did personalised engraving. It helped me see the potential of a new service. Today our while-you-wait engraving of tankards, jewellery and other personal gifts brings in sales of over £7m a year, but one brilliant brainwave in 25 years can hardly be called a recommendation for strategic planning on the beach.

Why do you consider it worthwhile to put 'Est 1903' on your fascia boards?

When we changed the look of our shops in 1995 we wanted to keep up to date but still retain a sense of tradition. We decided to display the date we started trading on the shop fascia but there was a problem – we didn't know what date to put.

My grandfather started selling shoes in 1865 but the shoe repair service came much later. The old pictures of our original shoe repair factory and the horse and cart delivery service were taken in the 1900s but we had to guess the exact year. 1903 provided the perfect answer because it meant we could celebrate our centenary in 2003, when we had a big party, presented lots of awards and gave everyone their birthday off to celebrate (a perk that was so popular it now happens every year).

The 'Est 1903' on our fascia not only underlines the long tradition of experience we have in the trade, it also shows that we are members of an exclusive club – a multiple business with hundreds of shops that has been on the high street for over a hundred years.

With so much current talk of retailers going into administration it is perhaps surprising that a number of other well-known names like Boots and W.H. Smith are well into their second century of shopkeeping – something well worth shouting about on the front of the shop.

We've seen various places try alternative currencies to boost local trade, like the Bristol Pound. What do you make of these initiatives? Would you accept such a currency if it helped local high streets?

You have to admire the determination of Bristol and other locations like Brixton, Lewes, Totnes and Stroud who have developed their own currency to protect local business. But I am not sure the local pound will do any long-term good.

To be honest I am struggling to work out whether the scheme will make much difference. It is similar to the system we have at our golf club where I put credit on a card that can be used at the bar – visitors use cash and pay a higher price. I can't say the card causes me to call in to the club for an extra pint but it is satisfying to know that, if I did, my drink would be subsidised by the visiting parties.

I wonder what will happen if most parts of the country copy Bristol? It may start in pockets of independence with the Plymouth Pound, Peterborough Pound and the Tarporley Pound. Before you know it, new currencies will be cropping up from Land's End to John O' Groats.

For a moment it occurred to me that we could be seeing a community form of quantitative easing, but although they are producing banknotes they haven't got a licence to print money – we will have to leave that to the Bank of England.

One benefit of the Euro (perhaps the only one) is the way it allows you to move through Germany, France and Italy without having to change your money. I am not keen on having to handle different kinds of UK cash from county to county.

You ask whether these new pounds will be welcome at Timpson. The simple answer is yes (if the locals let us). We don't make our customers stick to any rules – as long as the payment is legal, we will accept whatever we are offered.

The Bristol Pound has already created a fair bit of publicity and should do some short-term good, but I am sure the traders know that the only way to ensure long-term success is to provide the public with value for money in the goods and services that customers really want.

Do you ever recall the mistakes made by your past high street competitors to inform your current management decisions? I was wondering the other day what happened to Sketchley?

Let's start with Sketchley.

In 1985 Sketchley was the UK market leader with over 600 dry cleaning shops. They got close to dominating the market when they bid for Johnsons the Cleaners. After losing the bid battle they bought several service companies including SupaSnaps, a photo processor previously owned by Dixons.

Sketchley struggled throughout the 1990s. Demand for dry cleaning declined and the tiny SupaSnaps outlets couldn't compete with other photo shops that installed in-store mini-labs offering a one-hour service.

To reduce property costs some SupaSnaps shops were merged with their local Sketchley. This move blew the business off course. Unprofitable shops were closed but to camouflage the closure programme and stay in favour with City investors Sketchley announced a major out-of-town expansion with Sainsbury's.

Eventually Sketchley was bought by our shoe repair competitor Mr Minit UK (owned by Swiss bank UBS), who used the acquisition to create a multi-service concept branded Minit Solutions. This new venture was a spectacular failure, losing £120m in four years.

In 2003 we (Timpson) bought Mr Minit in a deal that included Sketchley, which by then had withered to 120 high street branches. After a year we sold Sketchley to Johnsons.

Sketchley is one of dozens of household names that have disappeared from the high street, along with Freeman Hardy and Willis, John Collier, Richard Shops, Littlewoods, C & A, MacFisheries, Cyril Lord, Radio Rentals, and of course Woolworths.

Every retail failure reminds me how difficult it is to survive on the high street. To retain customer loyalty you must provide good service year in and year out.

It is unwise to be complacent.

A customer (who has spent a lot of money with us over the years) is giving one of my shop assistants a hard time. He makes rather personal comments about her weight. I know 'the customer is always right' but should I step in?

Your priority is clear: colleagues come first, not customers. This man is making your sales assistant's life such a misery that she could, if she wished, sue you for harassment. And, if you don't support her against this ignorant man, she deserves to be awarded substantial damages.

Although we have built a reputation based on customer care, I do not believe 'the customer is always right' – indeed, you should always be strong enough to refuse customers who cause more trouble than they are worth.

Meet this cruel customer face-to-face and tell him why he is out of order. If you want to keep his custom, ask him to ring before he comes to the shop so you can be there to serve him yourself.

If you want to take a stronger line, that's fine – ban him from your shop. You are totally entitled to just serve the customers you want.

Strategy and Culture

I'm sure many readers will disagree with some of my answers, but that doesn't mean any of us are wrong. Each business has its own character, a combination of strategy and culture. My replies reflect our Upside Down Management style, but I can understand why others wonder whether it can work for them.

It took me five years to make this novel way of management an established part of the Timpson culture and the main problem was middle management. There were two concerns. First, they were reluctant to delegate: 'How can I be held responsible for results if I can't tell my people what to do?' Secondly, they worried about their jobs: 'If I let my team do all the work, what will be left for me to do?' It took time for them to realise they had a different but more interesting role planning the future, picking the team and giving them their support.

The same applies to senior management, whose job is to create the culture and set the strategy. Upside Down Management doesn't mean that you delegate future planning – that's your job.

I give our colleagues a lot of trust and respect but we are not a democracy when it comes to the big decisions. I've no time for policy committees or strategy retreats in the south of France. Leaders create culture, not committees – and I certainly wouldn't want a consultancy to do my job. If you need to call in a consultant to tell you which direction to go, it is time to work for someone else.

Seek as much advice as you like, but I find the final thoughts only begin to flow when I am sitting down quietly scribbling away on an A4 pad. That is when the experience of visiting our shops two days a week comes in particularly handy.

The culture should be consistent but strategy must always be on the move. Every business needs a lot of luck but you still have to spot the opportunities and take advantage.

We have developed a strong culture at Timpson but it would not take much to lose it. Most new recruits come from the world of command and control. They soon know we are different but it takes two years before our way becomes their way of life. As we grow it will get even more difficult to keep our culture, but that's our big challenge – to get bigger and still feel like a small business.

*

Does your business ever make use of business plans and if so, what do you put in them?

Recently I was clearing out some files when I unearthed our shoe shop corporate plan for 1985. The management team had compiled the document during a two-day retreat in Stratford-upon-Avon. It was an early example of joined-up thinking with detailed projections for each of the next five years. We believed that if we all aimed for a common purpose, success was assured – but it didn't work. Within eighteen months the business was performing so badly I sold it.

I believe in planning but I don't believe in planning committees or planning departments – strategy is my job.

Businesses evolve but they don't evolve on their own. If life was logical, planning would be easy and you could leave it to the number crunchers. But experience has taught me to expect the unexpected so I prefer to doodle on a pad and produce rough figures on the back of an envelope.

Firm financial figures forecasting for five years can be dangerous if they are taken too seriously. No one can accurately predict that far ahead. My plan is a dream scenario with plenty of provisos and I quite often change my mind, but it indicates the direction we should travel and it helps to set our priorities for the next two years.

Strategy should not include firm targets – it should simply get the thinking straight. Common sense only takes you so far.

What is the best way to work out your priorities? I can see promising projects and problems at every turn but end up doing too many things at once.

Join the club! If you are one of life's 'doers' you will always have too much going on and too little time to do it all. Every true entrepreneur faces the same problem.

Follow your instinct. Pick the things you want to do (not what you feel you ought to do). You are more likely to produce profits from your pet project than a scheme suggested by someone else.

Back your judgement. Give priority to the 'no brainers' – the ideas you believe are sure of success. But never be surprised. Racing certainties can let you down and some outsiders win at 33/1.

One thing, however, is certain: you must make yourself and your family the top priority. With so much going on in the business you could be in danger of having no time left for your personal life.

I've been running my jewellery business for fifteen years but I'm spending too much time stuck in the office working on strategy. How should I divide my time between visiting stores and dealing with the 'bigger picture'?

How much strategy do you need? You are making life too complicated. I understand you have 60 shops and that you haven't visited some for over a year – that is not good enough. You make your money out of selling the right product and providing a good service, so it's the staff in the branches that create your profit – go out and talk to them. Aim to visit each shop at least three times a year so your people know you and trust you. They will give you more hints about strategy than you will ever find in the office.

Get a driver and a BlackBerry to help you keep working while you are on the move. Plan your diary so that you are out at least two days a week. After a time, you will find you know so much about the business that you won't need a lot of the details currently supplied by your FD, and the strategy will become so obvious you'll be able to work it out in the bath.

I have used a number of your shops and almost without exception have been impressed by the helpful attitude

of your staff – most give service with a smile. How do you find so many good people – is it luck or is there a secret?

About eighteen years ago we suddenly realised what is now obvious. The only way to give great personal service is to trust customer-facing colleagues with total freedom to look after each customer the best way they can. You can't create legendary service by issuing a set of rules.

We soon discovered that this 'Upside Down Management' only works if you employ the right personalities. For years we had been recruiting shoe repairers and key cutters when we should simply have looked for people with the right personality. You can teach key cutting to a positive personality but you can't put personality into a grumpy cobbler.

We had to persuade the managers, who do our recruitment, to stop just looking for craftsmanship and help them to spot people with personality. The answer was our novel Mr Men interview form that we have been using ever since. We simply ask the interviewer to tick the boxes under those cartoons that are most like the applicant.

For the last fifteen years we have taken little notice of qualifications, we haven't bothered much about what is said on the application form, and have certainly never used psychometric testing. Our main aim has been to recruit for personality and the Mr Men form has played an important part in picking the right people.

My pest control business has just bought a competitor which provides a complementary service. The process

was pretty straightforward and I'm happy with the deal, but I worry about integrating the new staff members. The company I bought seems to have had a very different culture – how do I go about combining two very different teams?

There isn't a foolproof formula to follow after a takeover – every acquisition is different – but I don't believe you can have two cultures in the same company. It is, therefore, either their way of working or yours and, assuming your way works well, you will ultimately have to establish your culture in the new acquisition.

Start by telling everyone, from senior management to shop floor, all about your existing business – what it does and how it does it – but don't expect anyone to change overnight. Go and meet as many people as possible and try to understand what makes them tick. In the process you will learn a lot about your new business, and will almost certainly identify some real superstars (but they may not be the senior managers!).

Whatever you do, you will be viewed with suspicion. The newly acquired colleagues won't trust you until they see that you understand their business. Find some ways to make a mark – improve their employment package, get rid of some silly rules or, better still, find a way to increase sales and improve their bonus.

While all this is going on there will be plenty of ways to improve profitability. It will take years to change their culture but within the first few weeks, by saving on overheads, you are bound to find a few ways to improve the bottom line.

Have you ever found yourself in what's now called a 'turnaround' type situation? If so, is there a template you can follow to salvage a struggling business – what's the first thing that should be addressed?

You can't manage a business for nearly 40 years without having some wobbles along the way, and I have had my fair share. It would be neat to come up with a universal rescue remedy to save any business in trouble, but every problem is different and sometimes you can't find the solution. I still regret failing to find the right formula for our shoe shop chain in the 1980s – my only answer was to sell it.

But we have had some successes, and one of the most spectacular has happened in the last few years.

In December 2008 we bought just under 200 photo shops called Max Spielmann out of administration. They were losing money, the photo market was being hit by digital cameras, pictures on mobile phones and competition from online photo processors. Sales were falling by more than 20%. Four years later the shops are making a healthy profit.

If you buy shops from an administrator they come without a lease. 2009 was a great year to bargain with landlords. We were able to reduce rental terms by around 20% and in many cases negotiated a rent-free period or a capital contribution to refurbish the shop. This property windfall gave us a good start, but the biggest savings came from closing their Glasgow-based head office. We kept a warehouse in Chester but all administration was absorbed by the Timpson team at Wythenshawe, saving over £2m a year. Most successful turnarounds include a substantial slice of cost cutting, especially at head office.

Lower rent and fewer overheads put Max Spielmann into profit but didn't solve a more fundamental difficulty – turnover was still sinking fast and the market seemed likely to get even worse. Margins were poor; competition in digital cameras had cut prices so low that if a camera was stolen we needed to sell six more to recover the lost profit. We desperately needed to find a new source of sales.

Then we had a bit of luck. As we were already providing a growing passport photo service, it was a short step to introduce instant portraits (mainly pictures of young children). The new service proved popular and started a major change at Max Spielmann from photo processor to picture maker. Photo restoration and while-you-wait photo gifts on canvas, posters and even mugs have brought more sales at better margins.

Today, Max Spielmann branches look very different, but shop design would have done little to rescue the company without having people who were happy to provide a personal service. Without building a team of enthusiastic colleagues our strategy would never have worked.

You ask for a template to help a struggling business, but I must disappoint you – there are no golden rules. You should almost certainly try to cut overheads, increase margin, and get a tight grip on the cash, but whatever happens you will need the support of some exceptional colleagues, a generous slice of luck and a lot of patience.

Common sense only takes you so far. Timpson must have some rules. What are they and how do you justify them?

Rules often do more harm than good! If you run a business by the book you could be creating a compliant workplace by stamping out initiative and profit-making flair.

I believe in giving colleagues the freedom to get on with the job, unfettered by the structured process used by most professional managers.

The fear of falling foul of legislation in areas such as employment, health and safety and governance causes most companies to create a code to keep everyone within the law. We, too, must follow the legislation and have guidelines to keep us legal. But I believe in making everything simple. A long list of rules makes life complicated. It is very expensive to control the detail from head office. I don't like telling colleagues what to do.

However, even I recognise the need for a few rules. We have three:

Two for our shop colleagues:

Rule 1. 'Look the part.'
Rule 2. 'Put the money in the till.'

One for everyone else:

Rule 3. 'Do all you can to help the colleagues who serve our customers.'

Ask John

We also have two unwritten rules for management:

Rule 1. 'Don't issue orders.'

And:

Rule 2. 'Don't make any more rules.'

Have you considered running your business by the 80:20 rule? If you shut 80% of your shops, would you retain 80% of the profits from the remaining 20% high flyers? If you did this, I'm sure life for you would be a lot simpler.

The 80:20 rule is a statement of the obvious that offers very little help to the experienced entrepreneur. In a nationwide chain some shops are bound to perform better than others. It is much easier to take money in Windsor, Winchester and Witney than tougher trading towns like Bootle and Billingham.

Accountants and statisticians who stick in the office running a business by numbers think that if one shop can take £12,000 a week all the others can do the same. But it doesn't work like that; there is bound to be a variation in performance.

I have never closed a shop that is making a profit – it only takes a day to shut a shop but it takes years to establish a new business. As long as the branch is making a contribution to overheads I would always keep it open.

If we were to cut out all the plodders and concentrate on the superstars we would have to reduce our chain from

152

900 shops to about 250 and cease to be a national brand. We like having shops everywhere and employing people all over the country.

Of course you should close any loss-makers but closing the poor-performing 80% is a recipe for disaster. And guess what – if you did cut back to the top 20% the 80:20 rule would still apply to the shops that remain!

I have read that you have a number of non-core businesses in your group of companies, such as two pubs, a manufacturer of house signs and an events business. Don't these activities take up a greater proportion of management time and deflect attention away from the main business?

Yes, you are spot on! Non-core businesses are bound to soak up a disproportionate amount of time, and there are plenty of times when I wonder why we bother to venture outside our comfort zone.

But every so often a new activity blossoms into a big business – like our adventure into watch repairs. We first offered a modest watch strap and battery service in 1996. James was convinced it would work but I was doubtful whether customers would come to a shoe repair shop with their watches or whether cobblers would be willing to tackle a watch.

During the first two years we were spending over 25% of our time on less than 2% of our turnover, and watch repairing was making a loss. But before long James had proved me wrong and our watch repair service started to grow. Sixteen years later we have a comprehensive watch repair service that is the biggest in Britain.

It is tempting to think that, just because we are pretty good at running a shoe repair and key cutting company, we can create success in another sector. But it is seldom that easy. Most attempts at diversification end in tears, but even if we make a loss, hopefully we gain something from the experience.

It is in our nature to keep trying new ideas, but we will never forget that most of our money is made from cutting keys and repairing shoes.

Very few 'serial entrepreneurs' fully repeat the success of their first big enterprise.

How do you approach launching new business projects? Is there a formula that you follow to ensure success?

Developing a major new idea is the most enjoyable part of running a business but you need a lot of luck and plenty of patience.

There is no guaranteed formula for success, but bitter and sweet experiences have taught me what seems to work and what to avoid.

I am not a fan of business plans that extrapolate dreams into a five-year spreadsheet before the idea has been given a proper trial. New projects often emerge by chance, and management's job is to spot them when they appear. It is dangerous to conjure up something new simply because the think-tank at your executive retreat decides the company needs more innovation.

Don't rush – it often takes years to develop a new idea. In 1996 we put watch repairs into four shops and were delighted with sales of £500 a week. Eighteen years later this side of our business has reached over £20m a year and is still our fastest growing service.

Start in a small way and if necessary get outside help from an expert. For the first year you probably need someone to teach you the technical tricks of the trade, but pick a project leader who understands your company culture. That means an internal appointment.

Don't be seduced by the thought, 'If it can work there it will work anywhere.' Test the project with the person and in the place where it is most likely to succeed – if they can't make it work you can forget the whole idea.

Your first attempts will need changing several times before you have something that will stand the test of time. When one of our competitors introduced watch repairs they spread it to 300 shops within six months and provided such a poor service that customers and shop staff lost confidence.

You might think you have a great idea but it won't work unless you can convince your colleagues – particularly those who are putting the project into practice – that they have a winner.

We have found quite a few failures among the gems (I still don't know why we couldn't make jewellery repairs work in our shops) but don't be deterred by the odd disappointment.

I still get the same sort of thrill out of our latest locksmith and portrait photography developments as I had when we introduced key cutting over 40 years ago.

If you lose the desire to develop new ideas it is time to retire to the golf course.

Everyone's always banging on about the emerging markets. But can just any business set up shop in Brazil or China? Can you see yourself opening a Timpson's in Beijing?

It's true, new markets are appearing all the time and every up to date business is expected to 'think global', but I make no apology for keeping all our business within easy distance of Wythenshawe.

I have just returned from New Zealand (Alex and I were completing another leg of what we call our geriatric gap year – over the next decade we intend to follow in the footsteps of our backpacking children at ten times the price). While away, I noted the enterprise of many founding fathers like Captain Cook, saw successful Kiwi branches of British chains including Lush and Body Shop, and even watched Stockport's local brewery Robinsons being featured on New Zealand TV.

In preparation for our home-bound stay at Singapore, I read a book about Sir Stamford Raffles, who emerged from being an East India Company clerk based in London to have a great influence far away from home.

Such an adventurous life was never for me, but I wouldn't want to deter those with the right personality and attitude to be a pioneer. However, recent history shows that a British-based business doesn't always travel too well. On top of character and determination you also must understand the local people and their culture. Trading overseas is bound to bring loads of extra administration but there is no point in mastering the red tape if you can't understand the people you are dealing with.

Knowing the personalities who run our shops is essential to our success. I don't believe our formula would be nearly as successful if we tried to trade too far from home.

That's why you won't be seeing a Timpson shop in Beijing, Bangkok or Brisbane, but we will shortly be opening in Orpington, North Shields and Glasgow.

My staff are clamouring for free gym memberships as a perk. I think it's an unnecessary expense as these places charge a fortune. Why can't my employees just run to work?

I'm tempted to ask what your last slave died of. Perhaps you think your employees are lucky to have a job and all you have to do to get their grateful thanks is to pay the minimum wage, but it simply doesn't work like that.

Good bosses don't cut down on colleagues' perks, they look for more ways to care for their star performers. Never take the goodwill of your colleagues for granted.

We don't do free gym membership (I agree most gyms are expensive and after a month many members lose interest in regular exercise) but we have a gym at the office with a fitness trainer twice a week and a thriving running club.

Our other treats include free football tickets, holiday homes, and everyone's birthday is an extra day's paid holiday.

You can't put a value on a benefits package. Many

managers might think we are far too generous and be tempted to reduce our perks to save money. In my view you can never do enough to look after your key colleagues. You won't be able to run your business without them.

I have read in one of your previous answers that you give all your employees the day off on their birthday. That may be admirable but can you really justify the cost and management time involved in finding cover in your one-person shops, and isn't it creating a headache for your management team?

It is certainly not something we have thought worthy of a financial appraisal, but if there is a significant cost it is money very well spent.

We introduced our birthday off with pay to help colleagues celebrate our Shoe Repair Centenary in 2003. The move was so popular we made the perk a permanent fixture. We like making our people feel appreciated, especially in a way that is noticed by their family and friends.

Sure, our area team has to rearrange the staffing rota but if that was such a big problem they would soon let us know. Our birthdays off get their full support – they think it helps to improve our attendance record. On average a Timpson colleague is off for four sick days a year (in the public sector the figure can be as much as three weeks!)

Our lack of sickies is helped by a bonus scheme that only pays out to colleagues who work a full week, and we make it easier for the area teams to open every branch by insisting that any colleague who is going to be sick must ring in before

7.30am (they are not encouraged to get mum to ring on their behalf).

I am pretty sure that by giving birthdays off we improve attendance for the rest of the year.

My son called in early at my home last Friday and, because he was wearing a jersey and jeans, I assumed he had taken the day off. He quickly pointed out it was Friday and therefore it was 'dress down day'. Do you encourage this in your company? What benefit does it serve and, if there are any benefits, then why not 'dress down' every day? Ironically, I was dressed in a jacket and tie because I was off to my golf club. Should I encourage a dress down day there?

Our office joined the 'dressed down Friday' club a few years ago. At first I didn't subscribe, showing my age every Friday by, rather pathetically, putting on a particularly smart shirt with a loud tie.

It took me a while to realise that I was the odd one out. Everyone else was at ease in casual clothes of their choosing, but my mind had been set by a strict uniform code in the sixties that required all men to come to the office in a suit (women were in skirts), and everyone wore an overall – grey for the bosses, white for middle management and blue for other ranks.

I now recognise that people who feel comfortable in what they wear will do a better job. My young colleagues might not have the same strict dress code but they are more talented and effective than any of their predecessors – so who am I to criticise their fashion sense on any day of the week? It's what they do that matters, not what they look like.

It is a different matter in our shops, where every customer-facing colleague has to look the part. That means wearing an apron and a tie – standards I introduced in 1979 to set us apart from our competitors.

Even golf has moved on. Most clubs, including Open Championship courses like Hoylake, have a spike bar where jacket and tie are seldom seen.

But I am all in favour of keeping a sartorial sanctuary for grumpy old members who can mutter about the good old days (even if it can no longer legally be called the men's bar!).

Senior golfers, sporting their club tie, may look from the clubhouse window where they can grumble about new members wearing shorts with the wrong length of socks or sneering at young men who haven't tucked in their shirt (envious that they hit the ball so far the committee have decided, at some expense, to lengthen the course).

It is right to maintain standards, but times change and it is also important to keep tradition up to date.

The media is suggesting that business' reputation is at an all-time low because of malpractices and scandals, yet business is leading the way in improving the UK's economy. What does business have to do to regain its standing with the public and the media?

It isn't a sin to make a profit but there are enough dodgy dealers and bad bosses to give business a bad name. Bad news makes good headlines and papers appeal to their readers by pandering to public prejudice so it isn't surprising that bankers are on the naughty step and every big bonus earner is labelled as a fat cat.

Our image is unlikely to change overnight, or even over a decade. Joe Public is pretty certain that business leaders use power to their own selfish advantage, while some commentators happily throw criticism from the safety of their glass offices.

The standard solution is to write a new code of conduct that includes a dollop of risk assessment and plenty of governance. But this is purely playing politics and will do nothing to change public opinion. Rather than wasting time on good practice, process and PR we should copy those companies that do a lot more than simply make money. They stick to their principles rather than process. They look after loyal employees, support suppliers and put something back into the community.

Like many other company chairmen I sleep soundly in the knowledge that Timpson does much more than cobbling and cutting keys. Helping colleagues with personal problems, employing people from prison, and supporting adoptive parents are some examples of why we can claim to do good by doing business.

We are not alone. UK companies can be proud of the wealth they create and the benefits they bring, which extend way beyond their own business. Perhaps one day the public will recognise how much good is produced by the private sector. In the meantime, despite the criticism, we will stick to our principles for the simple reason that we like doing things that way.

I work for a small privately-owned company. The owner is continually evading corporation tax in many ways and the auditors are failing to realise this. I feel strongly that if all companies did this, the country would be in greater difficulties, so I am leaving for another job. Should I blow the whistle or just walk away?

When I think of the huge percentage of our turnover that is paid in tax (not just company tax but also PAYE, VAT, dividend tax and rates on property), I, like you, get very irritated whenever I hear about companies that cheat. But before you blow the whistle check out the facts.

Are your company executives cooking the books or are they just shrewdly acting in a way that quite legally keeps their tax charge as low as possible?

We have a complicated tax system that has enough loopholes to create plenty of fees for clever accountants. If your company is simply trying to keep its tax down but keep within the rules, leave well alone.

But your letter suggests something more sinister. Perhaps there is a wholesale expenses scam or cash payments are taking place to avoid VAT or PAYE. If you have evidence of such improper practice there is no reason why you shouldn't contact the auditors anonymously in writing. (It is probably wise to wait until you are fully installed in your new job.) If the auditors appear to ignore your tip-off, it is time for you to contact HMRC.

A final thought: when you change jobs, don't be surprised to find some similar tactics going on at your new employers. With tax rates that are too high and a tax system that has become so complicated even the inspectors can't be sure of the law, businesses are bound to test the rules in an attempt to be as tax efficient as possible.

Blatant cheats shouldn't be allowed to get away tax-free. If you have clear evidence, go ahead and blow the whistle.

A business in which I have an interest is reluctant to allow members of staff to have access to important information for fear of them leaving and taking 'secrets' with them. In your business, you operate an 'upside down' structure in which you empower your staff in the shops with complete authority to make decisions relating to their retail outlet. How do you protect yourself against the threat of well-informed staff leaving and joining a competitor, thus causing damage to your business?

Some companies are too paranoid about confidentiality for their own good!

Employees like to know what is going on and value being trusted with the full facts.

Occasionally one of our leavers passes on a useful tip to a competitor but it happens so rarely I am happy to take that risk and continue to treat our colleagues with respect and tell them everything.

It would be different if we had a secret formula like Coca-Cola and Vimto, but there isn't any hidden magic in the way we repair shoes.

We go further – every year we invite our suppliers to a lunch to tell them what is going on in our business. The better they understand us, the more support they can give. This year we invited two of our biggest competitors!

If we have a secret formula it is the way we run the business (I have written several books to explain what we do). Part of that formula is to keep everyone fully informed.

I heard you talking about football and business at a conference last week. Surely there is nothing that a family-owned, stable, non-ego-driven business like yours can learn from a volatile, money-soaked industry like football – or am I wrong?

Lots of football lessons apply to business. Here are a few:

Football shows how a great manager can create success and demonstrates the damage done by selfish players who don't have 'pride in the shirt'. Many clubs can see the dangers of an interfering chairman and as a spectator you experience the importance of creating a club culture when the guy on the gate gives you a warm welcome. Football clearly shows the importance of winning and how it affects morale. Basic management principles apply to football, but a Premiership club is worlds apart from an ordinary business – we pay our star shoe repairers a lot less than Rooney or Suárez.

I wish my customers were as loyal as football fans, but I wouldn't want to run a company under the constant eye of the public with my performance published in the national press every week.

I am happy to learn lessons from football but not get involved. I'm a Manchester City season ticket-holder but my seats are as far away as possible from the directors' box.

The small sum I fritter away on sport is spent owning race-horses. I am not brave enough to buy into a football club.

Do you read management books? If so, which have influenced you the most, and how?

I always read a business book on holiday, sticking to stories about entrepreneurs and real companies – business experience rather than management theory. I have selected three that stay in my memory.

The Richer Way by Julian Richer is the first book that got me making notes in the margin. It is full of original ideas that work. We have put several into practice, including free holiday homes for colleagues, which became one of our most popular perks.

Boo Hoo, which charts the rise and fall of Boo.com, is a riveting read about the dot-com boom. It is an entertaining but cautionary tale, a reminder that disasters really do happen.

But my No. 1 choice is *The Nordstrom Way*. It changed the way we run our business. The book describes how US department store chain Nordstrom empowered their workforce who then performed incredible feats of amazing service. Their management chart was upside down – sales assistants at the top, Chairman at the bottom. I copied this chart and introduced 'Upside Down Management'. Our customer care immediately started improving and our business has been transformed.

A good read beats any conference or management training – but you need to pick the right book.

Do you think your key suppliers and partners have the same relationship with your son as they had with you? And does any difference matter for Timpson long-term?

Many years ago it became clear that my most important task was to train my successor. I am now more than twice the average age of our employees and am older than many of their grandparents. They need to work with someone who is nearer their age. Now it is James' turn.

Fathers aren't in the best position to give an objective view on their son's ability, but as James has been our Chief Executive for over ten years, everyone should have a clear idea of how he differs from Dad.

Of course our suppliers' view is important, but it is the respect of our own colleagues that matters most. Fortunately James and I have very similar values and follow the same list of principles:

1. The colleagues who serve customers have the most important job in our business.
2. We don't like rules, preferring to trust everyone with the authority to get on and do their job in the way they know best.
3. Go out of your way to praise success, but don't put up with poor performers.
4. Look after the colleagues who look after the business.
5. Only do business with people who 'get it'.
6. Keep down overheads and keep things simple.
7. Keep down the paperwork, avoid endless meetings and use the time to visit lots of our shops.

The management style we have developed at Timpson is much more likely to be nurtured by a family successor than a professional manager imported from elsewhere.

James is bound to have a slightly different approach from me, but I believe our company is fortunate to have someone with similar values and I am lucky that he still allows me to make a contribution.

Is there any other direction you regret not taking in your business career?

Your question made me wonder whether accountancy or the law would have shaped my personality in a different way, but I feel I've had much more fun from business. Being born into a family company is a big slice of luck – it is a privilege, not an obligation.

Any regrets were staring me in the face last weekend when I was tidying out my study. (Alex says we've reached the age when we shouldn't be leaving a mess for others to clear up when we have gone.)

I am a bit of a hoarder and wherever I looked I could see missed opportunities. The five-year plans we wrote in the 1980s (a futile practice that thankfully I haven't followed for the last 25 years) reminded me of the shoe retail chain I sold in 1987. I still have a nagging guilt that I couldn't continue the business my great-grandfather started.

I came across the draft ideas for a couple of books I have never written: 'Customer Service Champions – companies that really deliver', and 'Untitled', the novel I keep promising to write. I am ashamed to admit these books have been in my in-tray for over ten years.

Then I spent an embarrassing couple of hours sifting through old lists of things I intended to do, including: build a clothing repairs and alterations service; correct the misleading Timpson entry on Wikipedia; test a mobile cobblers' van under the name 'Heels on Wheels'; and many more.

The pile of business magazines was evidence of how little reading I do. I regret to confess that I never pick up a book between holidays.

As I put all these sharp reminders back in their place (hoping Alex won't notice I have thrown nothing away) I decided it is much better to enjoy what I did than to regret what I've missed.

Can business learn anything useful from the successful implementation of the London 2012 Olympic games?

I was lucky, I went to several Olympic events and saw at first hand the brilliant organisation and excellent customer care. It was a triumph, but it won't be easy for Business UK to follow in the footsteps of London 2012 or Team GB.

There were some special circumstances. It helps to have an enormous budget and building contractors working to a high profile and immovable deadline. It helps even more when 250,000 people apply for 70,000 jobs with long and unsocial hours, no pay and no perks other than a natty uniform.

Despite the unreal circumstances at Stratford there are some useful lessons. The Olympic organisers created a very strong team spirit – you felt they all had the same goal. From the guys at St Pancras in the morning to the girls who waved goodbye as spectators left Olympic Park, everyone wanted to make sure you 'had a nice day'.

The management set high standards, the clean-up every night was driven by the goal that every morning should look like the very first day. Problems were dealt with promptly. When a flower bed was trampled down by spectators trying to get a better view, the area was cleared and turned into a photo spot. Steps were taken to fill the seats left empty by absent members of the Olympic family.

It wouldn't have worked without the volunteers. It helps to have a workforce full of characters who love their job. They seemed to have the freedom to do whatever they thought would make us smile. You sensed the atmosphere as soon as you entered a venue and the volunteers kept up the buzz until the last customer went home.

It's contagious. We talked to people on the train and shared memories with strangers in the queue for hot sausages. Despite the security check and fairly uncompromising crowd control we didn't feel we were run by a set of rules. Employees were allowed to use their initiative.

For a magic month we experienced management at its best. It was so unusual I wondered whether it would last. Indeed, towards the end I cynically said to Alex, 'At least we only have to be nice to everyone for a couple more days.'

The Olympics showed that people who are inspired by the enterprise and enjoy their job are remarkably good at giving a great service.

They weren't paid but the volunteers enjoyed some fantastic work experience. 'I worked as a volunteer for 2012' will look great on a CV.

Doing Deals

We would never have created our current business without doing a few deals. I made a list of them when I was wondering what to write as an introduction to this section and was surprised to find how many we have done. Since 1983 I have been involved in 23 significant deals – nineteen acquisitions and four sales.

My first was a baptism of fire. The £42m management buyout from Hanson Trust is still easily our biggest deal and certainly the most complex. It was a big learning curve that took nine months out of my life and gave me my first experience of warranties, indemnities, lawyers' offices and a completion meeting. I was naive. I thought that when we agreed the heads of terms we had done the deal. I soon discovered it was only the beginning of months of draft contracts, sticking points, deal breakers and meetings where most of the time I sat waiting for a lawyer to tell me what to do.

I can't claim to have planned the management buyout. It was only made a possibility because my father had been ousted from our board in 1972 and Timpson ceased to be a family business. I had never heard about an MBO until I met Roger Lane-Smith, who proposed the idea and became my long-time corporate lawyer and non-executive director.

My next two big deals were planned for years before I got the chances I was looking for. I stalked Automagic, the 110-shop shoe repair chain, for eight years and the UK Mr Minit business was on our radar even longer. It was frustrating to have bids for our two biggest competitors rejected, but while we waited I spent the time getting to know their shops and studying the detail so closely that by the time we finally got to the negotiating table we knew their business much better than the people we were dealing with.

The research paid off particularly handsomely when we finally got the chance to buy Automagic. They went into administration so we had to think on our feet. The years of travelling the country and pacing the pavement to see their shops on the high street put us in a privileged position. We were so confident I was willing to mortgage my house for £1m to finance the deal. With all I knew about their business it wasn't a risk to me, but Alex was so unhappy she wouldn't speak to me. She thought I was taking an unnecessary punt on the rest of our lives.

Our ability to take quick decisions was a great help in our other purchases from an administrator. When Max Spielmann's holding company Bowie Castlebank went into administration we had no thoughts of getting involved in photo processing – but three weeks later we bought the business. We spent some of the time sitting in meetings and studying figures but James and I spent four days out of five travelling the country to find out about their shops. In very little time we needed to learn a lot about Max Spielmann and the photo market. That was one of many deals that have been based on intuition rather than financial forecasting.

Our quickest deal was the acquisition of Snappy Snaps, who were unhappy with a prospective purchaser, close to completion, and gave us six days to step in. We had looked at Snappy Snaps twelve months earlier so knew a lot about their business. None of our directors met before the day our board approved the deal; we were too busy looking at their shops. As requested, we completed the deal within six days.

Although we managed to make a lot of our money and grow the business through acquisitions, the small number of sales have been of equal importance. We have never sold parts of the company to make a capital gain: all our sales have been made for a strategic reason. Two disposals have been critical. Although, from a personal view, it was the most traumatic and unwelcome deal we have done, the sale of the Timpson retail shoe shops to Oliver Shoes in 1987 was the launching pad for our business today. In 2004 we had to sell Sketchley, which was losing up to £40,000 a week. After some tough talk we were finally beaten down to selling the business for £1 to Johnsons the Cleaners. I would have given them £4m to take it away. Sketchley was hurting our cash flow and the shops were too poorly located to make any money. The sale of Sketchley ended all my worries about cash and allowed us to concentrate on the bits of the business that made money.

It is easy to forget the deals you missed. We were close to buying InTime, the in-store watch repair chain that mainly trades in Debenhams. I also made a pass at Sketchley in 1998 but fortunately realised it wasn't for us. Both InTime and Sketchley were purchased by UBS on behalf of Mister Minit and Sketchley made a major contribution to Minit UK's losses of £120m during the next four years. A lucky escape.

Although it wasn't that big, my favourite deal was the purchase of fifteen shops in Scotland, trading as Uppermost, from an ex-Timpson employee, Brian McKeown. Brian and I agreed the deal over dinner at a hotel in St Andrews, including the stock valuation that was settled at the bar over a round of malt whiskies. The contract we signed three months later followed the exact terms we had agreed in the hotel. It is rare for lawyers to allow an agreement to get through to completion unscathed.

Plenty of commentators suggest that deals are often bad news, but I suggest the problems come when an ambitious CEO pays too much for a very profitable rival. We have done well by buying poor performers.

Financially our best deal has to be our original MBO. The shareholders paid £250,000 for equity that, four years later, Olivers bought for £15m. Max Spielmann was another stunning success. We created enough cash to pay back the £1.3m purchase price in nine weeks!

But don't just do deals to earn a quick return. Sales and acquisitions play an important part in developing the company strategy. Our deals have shaped Timpson today.

The MBO gave us the chance to break away from corporate conformity and create a different sort of company. In 1991, when I bought out all my management shareholders, I paid a massive £3.5m at a time when our profits had gone down to £400,000, but I have since discovered that control of 100% of the equity can be priceless.

The purchase of Automagic turned us into a serious national chain and introduced the Timpson name to central London. The big benefit of purchasing the Persil Services shops operating within Sainsbury's in 2008 was the wider experience they gave of trading in supermarkets, which, five years later, have become our biggest area for growth.

Our acquisition of Max Spielmann, which at first wasn't

much more than a speculative punt, has completely changed our business. The biggest Timpson service is now photo!

Doing deals has done us a lot of good but the hard work really starts when the lawyers disappear. The most difficult part of any acquisition is putting our culture into a different business.

*

I've just received an acquisition offer from a larger rival. The price is fair, but I do believe that in five years' time, my firm could be worth more. But who knows what might happen to the economy, or my competitor, by then. Should I hold out for a better offer down the line or take the money and run?

Only you really know whether and when to sell your business. To your professional advisors it's simply a question of money, but for you it is much more. You have to decide what you want to do for the rest of your life.

Beware of the bankers and lawyers who are just looking for another deal and talk in terms of EBITDA (earnings before interest, taxes, depreciation and amortisation) and P/E (price to earning) ratio. Once appointed they tend to take over the negotiations, but don't give your advisors too much freedom – the final decision must be yours.

There are plenty of things to consider.

Do you trust your competitor to deliver the deal on offer? The price agreed in the heads of terms can change dramatically by the time contracts are exchanged.

What will the deal do to your income? It might sound attractive to stick a big lump sum in your bank account (don't forget the tax) but will it provide enough income to match your current salary and dividends?

How's the cash? Does your company create cash or have you an overdraft that looks like getting bigger? If you owe money, will the bankers support you until your upturn comes?

What's the betting on the business getting better? If you know more about the bad news than your competitor, it is probably the perfect time to sell.

What would you do next? If you sell the business, what are you going to do with yourself? You may not be happy having endless holidays and just looking forward to pushing a trolley round Sainsbury's and pottering around the garden.

A lot to think about, but it is worth answering a final and critical question.

Is business fun? If you don't get any pleasure from your job it is probably time to sell. But if you still enjoy it, why give up such an important part of your life?

I've built a successful business with two partners from scratch. But I can see our nearest rival is making more progress than us. They have taken in some private equity and have outside non-executives on the board. Quietly they let on that the money is useful but the private equity boys are just as much of a pain as the banks, and just as risk-averse. Still, they've got something that we haven't and I'm wondering at what point should we bring in outside help?

Don't waste time wondering what is going on inside a competitor's boardroom, simply concentrate on your own company and take your own decisions.

You and your two partners are in a privileged position. As long as you are the sole shareholders of the business and keep within any bank covenants you are totally in charge. I can understand the temptation to borrow money to pursue an expensive pet project but I wonder how many Chief Executives, who are now calling in an administrator, regret getting too big too quickly.

Venture capitalists can be tough taskmasters. They require a very high return on investment and will expect the management team to deliver some minor miracles – the non-executive directors you mention will have been appointed by the VC to keep a close eye on performance.

It often pays to be prudent by only borrowing money you are sure can be paid back. Keeping within trading cash flow can prove an excellent discipline. With money in limited supply, investment is concentrated on the top priority. If someone offers unlimited credit it is only too easy to spend money you haven't really got.

Perhaps you have a lifetime ambition that can only be achieved with the help of venture capital, but if you are simply thinking of matching your nearest competitors at their own game, forget it! You will probably still be in business long after they are looking for a new job.

Your growth has been helped by acquisitions of competitors who were in a poor state and were bought

at a low price. BTR and Hanson used to do this and turn round these companies in the 1980s, helped by price inflation and asset stripping. What have been the successful ingredients with your purchases?

I have been involved in a few disappointing acquisitions but at least there have been enough successes for us to realise what really works. Here are some of the main lessons I have learnt:

1. It is much better to pay a low price for a business that is doing badly than to overpay for a profitable company. Some of our best deals have been done with an administrator.
2. Being good at running your own business doesn't make you an expert at running someone else's.
3. Acquire companies that are as close as possible to your core skills. A purchase that takes you into new territory can cause more trouble than you imagine. It is easier to simply do more of what you already do well.
4. If possible, buy assets with no central overheads. If you have to take on a head office, close it within the first few weeks.
5. Do your homework. The aim is to know more than the vendor about your target. If we are negotiating to buy a retail chain we would rather spend time visiting shops than poring over the prospectus.
6. Don't sign the deal until you know exactly what you are going to do with your new toy from day one.
7. You must have someone in charge you can trust. Put in your own people to run the day-to-day business.

8. Don't linger, put your plan into action as soon as possible.
9. Ignore price estimates based on P/E ratios and EBITDA (whether from your advisors or the vendor's). Be guided by your intuition and pay no more than you think it is worth.
10. If you have to borrow a worrying amount of money to complete the deal, forget the whole thing.

I've just acquired a struggling business because I wanted to add some of its customers to my existing company – I feel it will take us in a new direction. However, the state of the company is worse than I anticipated and I now realise I've got some serious turnaround work ahead. In times of difficulty, what's the first thing that companies should focus on: cash flow, management, or something else?

After most deals there is a disconcerting moment when you think you have made a mistake. Almost as soon as the contract is signed you wonder whether it could have been done at a lower price, or should never have been done at all.

If you acquire a company (rather than an asset deal), keep it as a separate legal entity so if all goes wrong you can put the company into administration and cut your losses without harming the core business.

Many purchasers claim the vendor has made a mammoth mess of managing the business, but they should not be surprised – it was probably poor management that provided the opportunity to buy the business.

You bought the company to gain more customers but the

last thing you need is the extra overheads that come with them. Don't waste any time: shut down their head office and hand over control to your own managers. The reorganisation will cost you some cash but you will soon reap the benefits by better profitability.

Meet your new customer-facing colleagues as soon as possible. It is important to win their confidence (they will assume you are as incompetent as the last lot). Among their ranks you will almost certainly discover some hidden superstars who have been held back by their previous boss.

Don't panic. It takes time to turn round a poor performer but one day you will almost certainly wake up and be delighted with your new acquisition.

Here is a final thought to cheer you up. It is a lot easier to make money from buying a basket case at a big discount compared with paying the full price for a successful company.

I've just had a call from a rival that I know well who has got himself into a bit of bother and has basically run out of cash. The business is sound, I think, and I've seen them win work that we would like to have done. He's offering to sell up if we can offer a decent price. What should we do? I know recessions are meant to throw up opportunities like this, but this would be our first acquisition and I know that making such things work is not easy.

Before talking to your bank manager, sign a confidentiality agreement, get hold of your rival's books and dig as deep as you can. Aim to know more about the target than your rival knows about his own business!

Find out the answers to some key questions: What has gone wrong? Why has the cash disappeared? How much do they owe to their creditors and where do they stand with their bank? Are there any lethal liabilities like long property leases or onerous contracts? How much extra profit could it add to your bottom line? Would anyone else want to buy it? How much would you be happy to pay?

If you decide to go ahead, look for a bargain. A business put up for sale during the recession has to be cheap. If your rival is asking for too much, hold back. The company could go into administration, giving you the chance of a much better deal without taking on any of their debt.

If you manage to agree a price and get a nod of approval from your bank manager, be prepared for a busy few months (deals always take longer than expected). The lawyers and accountants will soak up a lot of your time, so try hard to keep a close eye on your core business – it is easy to let things slip.

If you successfully complete this deal, be single-minded: integrate the new acquisition as quickly as possible and keep a tight control on the cash. Don't be tempted to leave their management in charge. Run the new business through your own people who you know and trust. You don't need two sets of overheads, so the sooner you close their head office the better.

I hope this checklist hasn't put you off, because this may be the opportunity to take your business to another level – but please be careful.

I have the opportunity to do a management buyout of my company. I am not sure whether I should proceed. Please can you give me some crucial tips before I start out on this exciting but risky venture?

This is probably the opportunity of your working lifetime. On top of your salary, a buyout gives you the chance to make a substantial capital gain on an equity stake. As long as you are reasonably optimistic about your company's prospects, go for it.

If you have never been involved in a big deal, be prepared to learn a lot in a short time. You will be surrounded by bankers, accountants and particularly lawyers who have done this many times before. The process can be frustrating – be patient and expect some surprises.

A buyout involves several transactions. You may think it is simply the purchase of your business from the owner or holding company, but there are several deals to be done with people who you think are on your side. The bank will negotiate new facilities, and you may need a mortgage to finance your investment. Your most important deal is with the venture capitalists. You will probably only have to put up a modest amount (the venture capitalists want your expertise, not your money). Try to get a significant equity share on terms that are not too draconian. Every extra percentage could one day be worth a lot of money.

You will need to produce a business plan. Be optimistic. The figures will be the subject of sensitivity analysis – bankers don't like taking risks. Your plan must be robust to get approval.

Don't be totally distracted by the deal. Through all the excitement you still have to run the business. The MBO gives you a stake but you must substantially increase profits to make your fortune.

My acquisition of a competitor has been a disaster. We were hit by a number of nasty surprises that a more thorough due diligence process would have revealed, but since the company we bought was a close competitor they wouldn't fully 'open the book' for us. Once bitten, twice shy – I think I'll stick to organic growth from now on. Would you buy a close competitor that wasn't prepared to be completely open with you?

Don't be put off acquiring more of your competitors, just learn a few lessons from this bitter experience.

Organic growth might involve less risk but if you want to grow quickly, buy some competitors, especially if you can increase their sales and eliminate their overheads.

Don't overpay. Well run companies tend to cost too much money. As I have noted above, in my experience it is much better to buy a business that is doing badly (we have purchased four companies that had gone into administration). You can turn a poor performer into profit simply by introducing your successful formula. It is much harder to improve a business that is already doing well.

Reluctance to share sensitive information is a typical negotiating ploy in the early stages of a deal, but if your competitor continues to keep you away from the detail, be wary. He has probably got something to hide.

Frankly, if you have done your homework, you should already know more about your target than they reveal in the information pack. Don't buy a business unless you feel you know as much about their trading as the current management. But no amount of market intelligence will reveal hidden liabilities and undisclosed onerous contracts.

You need a good lawyer who can winkle out the truth with a comprehensive list of warranties and indemnities.

In every transaction you have to use your instinct. A sixth sense should tell you when the other side has something to hide. But don't let this put you off doing another deal. My favourite definition of profit is 'the reward for taking risks'.

I've been offered a deal to sell up but it's subject to a three-year earn out and I only get 30% cash up front. I'm keen to sell and move on (even after three years) to other ideas but not at any price. Have you heard of similar deals – should I push for better terms?

If you are desperate to sell your business and this is the only offer you are likely to receive, go for it, but beware – this type of deal can end in tears.

At least you are assured of some cash up front, but while you wait for the rest of the money you will have to work with the buyer. Do you trust and respect each other enough to operate as a team? Three years is a long time if you are not having fun.

With most transactions, having fought clause by clause to resolve a draft full of worrying warranties and indemnities, the sale and purchase agreement is signed and you will never look at it again. This deal will be different. The earn out formula is critical, and is likely to be complicated – make sure you fully understand how the final price is calculated and be aware of any conditions that control your future conduct as the Chief Executive of this joint venture. But first, check how the 30% deposit is determined – are you going to collect as much cash as you expected?

You are entering a legal minefield that will require a lot of goodwill on both sides. For your own protection try to negotiate a minimum guaranteed price and make sure you have got a good lawyer.

I have started up a new business recently and it is going as well as I could hope for. A competitor has come up for sale and I feel I must go for it. Have you any guidance on the price I should pay, perhaps by the number of years to get a payback?

First let's get your thinking straight. You don't have to do anything! Sometimes what appears to be 'the opportunity of a lifetime' can become 'a step too far'. Before you even think about the price make sure it is a deal you really want to do.

Acquisitions can put the core business at risk. It is easy to take your eye off the ball when the deal is being done, and when it is over there is a danger that everyone falls in love with the new toy to the detriment of the main business. But the biggest danger is that a deal too far will saddle the company with an unaffordable level of debt. It is vital to forecast cash flow – the price will have a big influence on your future finances.

There is no magic formula. Forget about earn out ratios – simply decide the maximum you would be willing to pay, then negotiate. Hopefully, the vendor's minimum figure is within your price bracket.

Whatever the price, expect some surprises – very few acquisitions go according to plan. There are bound to be some hidden problems but some deals do far better than anticipated.

My best advice is to follow your instinct, only pay what you can afford to pay, and keep your fingers crossed.

Good luck.

Family Business

I wasn't surprised to get a lot of questions about how to hand over a business to the next generation. That's when a company can be properly called a family business.

If my great-grandfather hadn't opened a shoe shop, and developed lots more, I might well have been a lawyer or an accountant. But I've never needed to go through a job interview and, despite some desperately depressing times, I can't imagine any better career than working in a family business.

To my mind a family business is much more than a firm that provides jobs for the family, it is an enterprise that the family create together. But, although the family needs to work together, they must have a leader – not necessarily Dad or his eldest son or daughter but the family member who is the most talented entrepreneur, wants to do the job, works well with their relatives and has the courage to encourage unsuitable siblings to seek their happiness elsewhere. This family leader needs to go beyond the boundaries of the usual Chief Executive. As well as caring for the business they must also look after the interests of all the family shareholders, but, when necessary, stand up to the demands of an interfering relative. I am not a fan of family councils, a democratic way of satisfying far-flung family that runs the danger of upsetting both business and family in one move.

Like institutional shareholders, family members are similar to football supporters. With the benefit of hindsight they know exactly how the business should be run, but fail to think more than six months ahead. There should be a simple answer available to every dissatisfied shareholder (public and private) – sell up and get out. A family business should always be prepared to buy out any tricky relative.

It is not surprising, with such a key role for the family chief exec, that I get so many questions about succession. I'm amazed some academics claim that family businesses are bad news for the economy. These business school bookworms simply don't get it. Family businesses provide loads of growth by looking to the long term and caring for their employees.

There is every chance that, in a family business, your son or daughter will be well prepared, having been pretty close to the business before the age of ten. Despite such a long apprenticeship, junior will have to work hard to earn the respect of the workforce before being accepted as a proper boss.

Some find it impossible to find the right successor and decide it is time to sell, but I reckon I already have some very capable grandchildren.

It is always difficult to draw the line between business and family life. From a commercial viewpoint the business is more important than the family, but never forget that your family matters much more than the business.

*

I work in an established family business which has just hired a non-family Chief Executive for the first time. All well and good, but I can't stand the man's management style – he's so 'process-driven' I feel like we waste half

of our time on interminable meetings and bureaucracy. What's the best way to tell my new boss some awkward home truths?

You don't say why the family has brought in an outsider. If he has been recruited to rescue a struggling company his sharp shift in executive style may well be overdue. Perhaps your company has been too cosy for too long and a tough dose of hard-nosed management is just what is needed.

But maybe, on the other hand, one generation has retired and no descendants are ready or able to step into the hot seat. If they were hoping to continue the family tradition they've found the wrong man – every business is a reflection of its Chief Executive and the recent appointment will create a completely different company. I could send him a copy of my book on 'Upside Down Management' but don't expect it to make a difference – he will run things his way with lots of meetings and little delegation.

There is little doubt that he will upset plenty of people, you included, but a little bit of his medicine may be good for the business. He could be clearing out a number of long-ignored cobwebs.

On the other hand, he may be making short-term profit at the expense of the long-term good. If he is one of those people who flit up the ladder by changing jobs every three years, he might carve up your culture to cut costs and make quick profits. Look out for the warning signs: less training, cut in perks and bonus, a round of redundancies, and some of your best people jumping ship to join the opposition.

If this is the case, the family have made a big mistake. But if they don't get rid of him it is time for you to join the exodus and work for someone else.

A recent academic study suggests that family businesses would benefit from some more professional management and that it is often dangerous to hand over control to a son or daughter. Don't you think that at a certain size every family company needs the experience of a properly trained top team?

I wonder what criteria academics use to define a professional manager. I suspect they envisage an executive who follows best practice with a fair dose of good governance, risk assessment, appraisals and KPIs.

Business schools are bound to preach the importance of a proper process because it is impossible to teach someone how to be an entrepreneur – you don't acquire flair by going to university.

To suggest that family businesses are holding our economy back is bunkum. And to think it is dangerous to put your company into the care of a son or daughter is a sweeping generalisation that shows ignorance of the benefits a family business can bring.

Look down any high street and you will see names that had their halcyon days under family management – Marks and Spencer, Sainsbury's and Clarks are prime examples of businesses built by several generations.

In a family business most colleagues know the boss and enjoy a consistent style of management. Family managers tend to look after their staff and make long-term decisions.

It is now being suggested that caring companies are more successful – a family business is more likely to care for its colleagues and reward those that give a lifetime of service.

Business is not just about market research, ratios and best practice, it is primarily about people – 'professional managers' don't always seem to get that message.

I will never forget the man who told me he was good at buying family businesses and putting in professional management. He bought one of our competitors and managed to lose £120m in four years – we then bought it for £1!

So forget the academic study. Family businesses will continue to create a considerable amount of the country's wealth – they should be enthusiastically encouraged, not wrongly criticised.

I own a family business that I expect my daughter or son to one day run, but they are both still teenagers and I am in my late fifties now. Two of my closest senior managers have both said they want more of a stake in the business in the future in recognition of their efforts and the possibility that my offspring will not succeed me. I'm wondering what to do?

You are not alone. Many business owners face the same problem. Only last week I was talking to a man who had built up a very successful business, which is now causing a lot of sleepless nights. 'My son is only seventeen', he told me. 'I don't think I want to stick around for another ten to fifteen years.'

Don't make a rash decision. The recent tough economic climate can create loads of stress and may make the thought of retirement quite appealing. But after a lifetime building up your business this is unlikely to be the best time to hand over control to your management.

It is a personal decision that depends on how keen your children are to work with you, whether you think they have what it takes, and if you think your business will stand the test of time.

I have been lucky. My son James is only 28 years younger than me, so we have already enjoyed over a decade with me as Chairman, James as Chief Executive. To me, owning a family business is an enormous privilege and I will fight hard to keep our independence for future generations.

If you too want to keep it in the family, don't hand out any equity to your executives. Pay them a good salary and give them a generous bonus but keep the shares to yourself. The more diverse the shareholding, the more difficult it will be to keep control.

My daughter works for me and, one day, will become Chief Executive of my company. However, she wants the job now but I don't think she is ready for it just yet. I still have something to offer and, furthermore, why should I retire to suit her? I know you have a son in your business. How are you handling this situation? It is becoming an irritant for both my daughter and myself and we need to find a satisfactory solution before this problem gets out of hand.

You should be delighted that your daughter is so keen to get involved, thus ensuring that your enterprise will continue for another generation. This will make your job even more worthwhile and make sure you give priority to the long-term decisions.

But she should be a bit more sympathetic to her Dad's position. The business has been a large part of your life and although you do not reveal your age I can tell from the tone of your letter that you still have a vital role to play.

Don't retire! Just change roles. It's your daughter's turn now, so let her become the Chief Executive with you as her Executive Chairman. Hand her the day-to-day management while you continue to take a close interest. That way you can escape a lot of the detailed hassle while still enjoying a hands-on role. Show you can let go by taking a few extra holidays and playing more golf.

All this seems to have worked well for myself and son James, who became MD at the age of 31. Some saw it as a brave decision – they thought he was too young – but I had help from his mentor Patrick, an experienced non-exec director, whose advice was valued not only by me but also by my wife, Alex. (It is quite interesting being married to your Managing Director's mother.)

I believe James and I have a good working relationship based on mutual respect and trust. It certainly seems to have worked, with our business growing rapidly under his guidance. The last few years have been the most enjoyable of my career.

My daughter and I started a business together twelve years ago. It's gone from strength to strength, but I find myself handing over more and more responsibility to

Anne. How do I know when it's time to hand over the reins completely?

You're very fortunate to have been able to create such a successful business with your daughter.

I expect at the start you took the lead, but as you have been together every step along the way, you both know the business inside out. Your daughter has had the perfect preparation to take over as the Chief Executive and in doing so secure the continuity of family control.

It is wise to hand on the day-to-day responsibility sooner rather than later. Clearly your daughter has the talent and confidence to take over and, being blunt, youth is on her side. Much as you might think that you can do what you did ten years ago, as you get older it is hard to keep up with people who are half your age.

So the time has come for you to take a backward step, but don't disappear from the boardroom. Your daughter probably doesn't want you to be meddling with the detail, but she needs you to keep in touch so you are always available to provide advice whenever it is wanted.

At first you might find it difficult to let go, but it is the right thing to do for you, your daughter and the business.

My son really doesn't get our business and while I've given him every chance I am starting to think that he'll never be good enough to succeed me. Do you have any advice on how I should manage this?

You are facing a decision that will affect the rest of your life.

At stake are the future of your business and the relationship between you and your son.

Before giving firm advice I would need to know the answers to several key questions: Do you really want to retire? How old is your son, and how long has he been working in the business? How well do you and your son get on together? Do others agree with your assessment of your son's ability? Is it possible that your son has got it right and that you are out of touch? What does your son want to do?

If everything confirms your fear that he simply hasn't 'got it', the two of you urgently need to have a frank conversation. For the sake of your business and its employees your son must not be your successor. But you need a solution that keeps the family together.

A worthwhile job outside the boardroom could provide a short-term solution but once you retire and either sell the business or hand over to a new CEO, your son's position may be vulnerable.

I suspect your son needs a complete change of direction. Everything you say suggests that the family business is not for him. By trying to follow in your footsteps he is probably missing out on a vocation much better suited to his talents – do everything you can to help him find it.

Those of us who enjoy a fruitful father/son working partnership are extremely fortunate.

My grandson, who is still at school, wishes to join his father and myself in our family-owned group of car dealerships. We are delighted but that is the easy bit.

**My grandson wishes to join us immediately on leaving
school in two years' time; I want him to go to Australia
on a gap year, then go to university, then get a few years'
work experience elsewhere; his father is sitting on
the fence; his grandmother and mother are not shy in
offering their opinions. Adjudicate for us, please. What
do you think is best for the young man in preparing him
for life and running our business in the future?**

You have a good plan but it clearly needs to be communicated
cleverly to persuade the rest of your family.

It is great to hear your grandson is keen to join the business. He wants to start straight away so why wait? Give him
a taster with some serious work experience during the school
holidays. This will help you to answer two vital questions. 1)
Does he really like working in the business? 2) Has he 'got it'?

Gap years are good news. When my eldest son James
asked for the funds to set off round the world I thought it was
an extravagant way to spend time but I couldn't have been
more wrong.

But gap years don't need to be all backpacking. Get your
grandson to spend the first few months working in the business. It is important for the boss's son to spend some time on
the shop floor and it is much easier to get that vital experience
just after leaving school.

University isn't for everyone – you don't need to be an
academic to manage a business – but the student life is an
important part of growing up. If possible your grandson
should study for a degree but there are plenty of long holidays
when he could get his hands dirty in the business.

If someone else offers him a job after university, so much the better, but don't let him wait too long before entering the family firm. You don't want him to arrive with all the answers – no one likes a know-all.

You've got the plan but will you be able to persuade your wife and daughter-in-law to give it their backing? There is no rush. Bide your time until they come up with the same suggestion for themselves, then agree with them!

I have been in the flower business for twenty years. My father was in the business before me. These days, I can't stand the sight of the things. Do you ever get shoe/key fatigue? If so, do you have any advice to help me shake off this boredom-induced aversion?

I wonder whether you have ever loved the business. Perhaps you felt obliged to follow in your father's footsteps but secretly always wanted to be a barrister or a doctor, or pursue some other career outside business. If that's the case it's never too late to hand over to someone else, leaving you free to achieve your dream. Such a move could be good for you and great for your family business.

I'm lucky. I've never been bored since I served my first customer in a Timpson shoe shop in 1960. When I worked in our buying department, even shoe styles I didn't like the look of looked great if they became bestsellers, and I've never had any problem liking the colleagues who make us money. I can't cut a key and have never repaired a watch but that doesn't stop me loving the business. I've had plenty of stress, sometimes even wondered whether we would survive, but I've never experienced boredom.

It wouldn't have made any difference if my father had been a pharmacist, a cobbler or a florist. If flowers were the thing that made us money, I would love them to bits (even with a pollen allergy!).

Shortly after we got married, Alex observed: 'You never stop thinking about that business.' I originally thought this was a compliment but now realise it was constructive criticism. I hope I've taken more notice of another tip from Alex: 'Don't be complacent, you are only as good as last week.'

When things go well, it is good to celebrate success but the real fun about doing business is to work out what to do next. As long as the business keeps changing I will never find it boring.

For many years I ran a modest import/agency business dealing in modern furniture and accessories. My main customers were the department stores and specialist retail shops. Although I still have an interest it is now run by my son. Obviously turnover has recently suffered a downturn. I continually urge him to get off his 'dongle', out of the office and visit existing customers and potential new ones. He maintains that retail is dead in the water, the internet is all powerful, and prefers to concentrate his efforts on the contract side of the business where the eventual rewards can be interesting but the process is long drawn-out and quite complicated

with no guarantee of a result. I feel he is missing a trick and spending too much time at his desk.

I agree with you, but I guess it's going to be tough to get the message across to your son.

For young people setting out in business it is tempting to stick in the office and develop a website. With the internet still growing strongly, why bother to pursue retail sales?

We are seeing a hint of the lemming-like behaviour during the dot-com disaster over a decade ago. Some websites are a great success but many more make no money. Success shouldn't be measured by sales or the number of hits – what really matters is creating cash.

The internet is profitable for the service providers – those webmasters who design sites, get you higher up the Google listings and guarantee a quantum leap in traffic. But few website owners are heading for a fortune.

Retailing is hard work. We serve 400,000 customers a week, so it sounds a lot easier to have a few contracts with commercial buyers. But big deals take a long time to negotiate and have a habit of not happening.

Regardless of whether your son still sells to retailers or takes your company into new markets, he won't keep in touch if he sticks behind his desk.

I hope your son takes your advice but you might have to wait until he learns through experience.

How does your private, family-owned company take the really big decisions such as buying a company and raising the finance to do so, or diversifying, or entering a

foreign market? Public companies will have procedures involving consultations, professional advisors, committee meetings leading to board papers and decisions by the board. Is this your style? What happens if your wife and son disagree with your next proposed big decision?

I can understand why companies are so careful, but formal meetings, procedures and financial appraisals don't guarantee a good decision. I prefer the informal approach that allows fast decisions based on intuition rather than a strict procedure peppered with professional advisors.

Although we can move very quickly, our two biggest acquisitions both took over eight years from the first approach to completion. By the time we sealed the deals we knew the businesses we were buying better than the vendors. Whenever bidding for a competitor I find it better to spend my time travelling the country getting to know their shops instead of sitting in meetings poring over spreadsheets.

James and I have plenty of help from fellow directors and company colleagues. We occasionally consult outside experts who really understand our business and appreciate our management style. But in the end we make up our own minds – it makes a big difference when you are spending your own money. We would never let a merchant bank do a deal on our behalf.

We talk on the telephone several times a day and are happy to make instant decisions (our last major purchase, Max Spielmann, was concluded within eighteen days of coming on the market and we never had any formal meetings to discuss the deal).

Whatever system you use, expect a few mistakes – we have done much better buying businesses that are losing money. It is difficult to get a decent return when you pay a full price for a peak performer.

On the rare occasions we disagree, James wins the argument – first because, as Chief Executive, he has the job of making any deal work; and secondly because he is very like his mother.

I am a director of a small company, t/o £7m, manufacturing and selling a product through a type of vending machine. There are moves afoot to buy a smaller competitor, t/o £2m, who made a loss of £200k+ in each of the last two years. Their asking price is £2m which I think is miles too high? They also want to keep their, admittedly small, brand name. What is your advice?

It doesn't matter what he is asking for – decide on the price you are willing to pay and make that the maximum. I agree that, unless there is a hidden gem lurking among the assets, a business making a loss of £200k is desperately overvalued at £2m. In fact I would be worried that, if you purchase the company, the liabilities could make it worth next to nothing. If you go ahead with a deal it is probably better simply to buy the assets – much safer than purchasing the company.

I assume you plan to run the extra turnover through your existing overheads, thus turning all their top line contribution into profit. But don't calculate a price by applying a high multiple to this marginal increase in your revenue. The business may be worth more to you than anyone else but that does not mean that you should pay a premium.

Be hard-nosed. You don't have to do the deal, so offer a price equal to no more than a two-year payback (after deal and reorganisation costs) and see what he says. Include the brand name in your offer – you can always use it as a bargaining point at a later stage.

The seller will probably tell you to get lost but you never know, he might be so keen to sell you could pick up a bargain.

What's the best way to navigate through boardroom bust-ups in a family business? Have you ever had to do this at Timpson? I'm struggling to balance keeping harmony in the family and what's best for the direction of our company at the moment!

I got my big boardroom row at an early age and it nearly cut my career incredibly short. The experience taught me some fairly fundamental lessons, which luckily I was able to put into practice a few years later.

In 1972 I was caught up in a classic case of family rivalry. There were two other family directors: my father, the Chairman, and his cousin who had always been keen to take the chair. A poor set of results gave him the chance to get the five non-family directors on his side and father was ousted by six votes to two. As a result my father and I carried out our threat to sell our shareholding to a potential bidder and the 108-year-old business went out of family control.

Fortunately our new owners, UDS Group (John Collier, Richard Shops, Allders, etc.) kept me on the payroll. Two years later I replaced my uncle as the Timpson MD and in 1983 led a lucky management buyout – lucky because we got 80% for the management. Remembering the boardroom bust-up I made sure I got over 50%. It was a family business again, but now I was the only family member involved.

No family is the same and there isn't a single recipe for family business success. All I can do is provide a list of the tips I would pass on to my grandchildren. Perhaps they will help other families in similar circumstances.

1. Only employ those family members who are good enough at their job to gain the respect of the workforce.
2. Don't make any relation a director unless you are pretty sure he or she is a superstar.
3. Keep the rest of the family fully informed, make them feel part of the business, give them a dividend but don't let them interfere.
4. Some family firms set up a family council to keep everyone happy – we don't! Such 'annual general meetings' encourage criticism from those not involved in the business and create resentment from those who are. No happiness there – just discontent.
5. Keep a majority shareholding, preferably 100%.

My main aim is to help create a successful business that can stay in the family for generations to come. You can't expect everyone to agree all of the time, but most boardroom bust-ups occur in poor-performing companies where mediocre managers are made directors.

Big families with a big business have a tough task keeping

control. Our business was started by my great-grandfather. I have eight grandchildren who will have some interesting times to tackle if they are to keep today's business in the family in two generations' time.

I set up my business three years ago and last week, for the first time, I found myself thinking: 'I'm surplus to requirements. Everyone is busy but I have nothing to do.' It was unnerving. I'm too young for the golf course. What would you do?

You are not redundant, you have a new job. Call it whatever you like – Managing Director, Chief Executive or Chairman – but you are no longer a General Manager.

By picking a good team and delegating responsibility you can now leave them alone to deal with the day-to-day problems – your responsibility is strategy and communication. Your team might appear self-sufficient but they still need you. Expect constant calls for advice. You developed the business and they know that you instinctively understand the way it works better than anyone else.

You feel surplus to requirements because your business appears to have paused for breath. Don't stand still for long; every company needs to grow. It is your job to inspire the team to take up the challenge. They need your leadership to find the ways to get bigger.

If you don't want this new job, or have lost the will to develop the company, it is time to go and play golf. But be warned, you may find golf is not as much fun as running a business.

A year ago I employed a major shareholder's daughter. Recently, she's been performing badly, missing deadlines and producing sloppy work. How can I get rid of her without upsetting the shareholder?

If you're lucky, your shareholder's daughter will be poached by a competitor and you could be the one who pretends to be upset. But life seldom provides such good fortune, so prepare for the worst.

Don't ignore the problem – the girl has to go. You must follow the same disciplinary procedure laid down for all other employees. After all, you don't want this sorry saga to finish in an employment tribunal.

As soon as you issue an oral warning it is time to meet your shareholder. It will not be an easy conversation and much depends on how well you know each other. Although news of the girl's shortcomings may be unwelcome, be honest about her performance. Your shareholder probably knows his daughter only too well and, although he might be upset, will understand why you want her to go.

Don't make matters worse through bad management; follow employment legislation to the letter, insisting your top HR executive deals with the details at every stage. You probably think this whole thing is a pain in the neck but don't forget you did agree to employ the girl in the first place.

I've been running my own printing business now for three years. I'm 25 years old and while the idea of corporate life or a normal 9 to 5 job doesn't appeal, my current role is getting so stressful I'm losing sleep at

**night. I have two employees who depend on me and yet
the order book is drying up. Half of me wants to pull out
altogether and get a normal job, the other half tells me
to keep going and see it through. What's your advice for
staying calm, managing stress and keeping the business
afloat during tough trading conditions?**

You are not alone. I expect there are thousands of people,
running their own business, who are saying something very
similar.

I can understand your fear of becoming a 9 to 5 pawn
in another company, but it might be better for you and your
family. However, don't change direction until you have had
a big think and talked things through with a few level-headed
friends.

Your question is filled with negative thoughts and the
business appears to be providing little profit, less fun, and
no sense of achievement, but I wonder whether this is a
true assessment or simply a reflection of the way you feel
right now.

Stress can play some strange tricks that distort reality. I
speak from experience having been through several stressful
spells in my career. You will probably recognise the signs –
life switching from butterflies in the stomach to total misery
several times a day with no period of peace in between. You
can't concentrate, forget to do things, can't make decisions
and feel everyone else thinks you are a failure.

I have spent many days envying the relaxed faces of
passers-by who clearly could cope with an everyday life,
wishing I could change places. It doesn't help when they

ask the usual polite, 'How are you?' and you lie by replying, 'Absolutely fine thanks.'

You feel you won't recover, and will never be the same again. Fortunately stress usually disappears, often quickly, sometimes after months rather than days, but it is better not to fight it on your own. Tell your partner (Alex has been my perfect mentor) and the people you work with; they will already have noticed you are not your usual self. Then go to the doctor and follow their advice.

Having your own business is bound to put you under pressure. It is natural to want to show the world how well you can do, but be realistic. It is important to accept who you are. There is a dangerous temptation to think we must do everything to perfection. Most kids want to grow up to be a celebrity but few do. Many businessmen hope to emulate James Dyson or Richard Branson and create a multimillion empire – very few do. No one is perfect; accept that the talents that make up your personality are different from the skills of the guy next door (who may well be jealous of your successes). Don't beat yourself up for having a few failings – take a pride in who you are.

Avoid any major decisions about your future career or your business until you feel better. If, when you are back on top form, the company still looks to be becoming a basket case, then, whether you like it or not, it is time to become an employee working for someone else. But you may not need to work from 9 till 5 – more and more companies are seeing the benefits that come from flexible working.

Once you have decided what to do, don't look back. There is no point in mulling over a decision that has already been made. Whichever direction you choose – employer or employee – good luck.

I've reached that point in my small business where I'm doing too much and probably preventing growth. Some people are advising me to hire a non-executive to provide some guidance and to challenge me. Is that a good idea? Who did you call on for guidance earlier in your career?

It is always a good idea to have a guru, whether they are a friend, a partner or a non-executive, but whoever you talk to, they will almost certainly tell you it is time to delegate.

Your business would not have been created without your energy and determination but if you insist on sticking to all the day-to-day detail you will be the barrier that prevents the business getting any bigger.

All companies come across critical points as they develop. Multiple retailing has two tough barriers to growth: opening the second shop (you can't be in two places at once so need to appoint a shop manager) and getting beyond about fifteen shops (you can't cover them all yourself so have to appoint an area manager).

Some people find it difficult to delegate authority when they still have responsibility, but that is what you must do if your business is to grow. The secret is to pick people who you can respect and trust them to do the job.

As I was born into a family business a lot of my early lessons were learnt from my father and grandfather. I now have three non-execs to help, but regular readers of this column will know that a lot of the critical help has come from my wife, Alex. These days I also rely on younger advice, especially when it comes to computers – Bede, our fifteen-year-old grandson, and Beth, eighteen, a one-time foster child, both seem to be born with the instinct to immediately find the answer to my impossible IT problems.

When you start a new venture it is natural to think you need to know about everything and do a lot of it yourself. But it is now time to let go of some of the detail and allow your colleagues to take control. You can't build your business without them.

I run a successful, but small, recruitment business. A move into a new sector has meant we've had a great couple of years but I'm cautious about the future. I've always been pretty conservative about what I take out of the business but now we've hit a decent patch my husband thinks I should be taking out a little more to spend on things like a new house. How do I convince him that successful businesses make sure they save resources for a rainy day?

I'm on your husband's side. He's not asking to blow your success on a yacht or a sports car, he simply wants to move up the housing market.

I, like you, am paranoid about our cash flow forecast. Every day for twenty years I have monitored our company bank balance and am determined that our growth plans don't come with too much risk. But your family deserves to benefit from your success – I bet your husband has put up with plenty of traumas and bad moods while the business has grown.

By all means be careful with the company cash but don't include your husband in the cost-cutting. You could find yourself economising on a cheap week in a tent near Tenby while your top salesman is sunning himself in the Caribbean. Harmony at home is an important asset for a family business, as divorce can do untold harm to your bank balance and your confidence.

It sounds as if you and your husband are happy to build the business without any plans for a big payday exit. Hopefully, your company can provide an increasing income to improve your lifestyle, but there are bound to be a few blips along the way.

I'm thinking of releasing some of my company's shares to key members of staff to align my interests more closely with theirs. I imagine all the Timpson shares are held by the family but I'm keen to explore this further. What pitfalls have you heard about?

I did it once. Shortly after our management buyout of the Timpson shoe shop business in 1983 we issued shares to most of the management team. I didn't think it through. I wanted to share some of the benefits of ownership, but I didn't anticipate the legal complications.

By providing fellow colleagues with some equity we created a lot of new paperwork – our annual report and AGM took on a completely new significance. I am keen for all our people to know how the company is doing – every year I send a detailed company report to every colleague's home – but it is written by me, not by a lawyer or an accountant.

It was tough retailing footwear in the 1980s and before long we sold the shoe shops. Our employee shareholders got a slice of the proceeds, but I had hoped the scheme would create an incentive for success rather than provide compensation for failure.

Before signing up for an employee share scheme, be crystal-clear why you are doing it. There are plenty of easier ways to set up an incentive and reward loyal colleagues. You can have a bonus scheme based on profits without issuing shares.

Altruistic owners may want to follow in the footsteps of The John Lewis Partnership but it is a lot simpler to avoid the legal fees, spare the paperwork and keep total control of company strategy.

Company shares may eventually produce a big payout but most colleagues prefer the certainty of a generous annual bonus.

Why do you think British businesses have been so reticent about selling equity compared to our American neighbours? Do you think this is a bad thing? Many commentators suggest it is inhibiting the growth of some of our most promising businesses.

If growth is being stifled, the cause is more likely to be banks being reluctant to lend rather than businesses who are reticent about selling equity.

There are lots of differences between business here and

across the Atlantic. I welcome the way Americans applaud enterprise and celebrate entrepreneurs. In the UK it only seems OK to earn lots of money if you are a media celebrity or play football. Americans have some great ideas but there is no need to import every facet of the way they do business. I can understand why we are more reluctant to give away equity and risk our future in the hands of venture capitalists.

I will always be grateful that a highly leveraged management buyout enabled me to buy back our family business, but now we have regained our independence I'm not tempted to cash in a single percent of the equity.

Most months I am approached by a banker keen to 'take an equity stake' to 'help with our expansion plans' and 'provide a route to realise some capital' or 'give me an exit'. I take the old-fashioned view that it is a good discipline to fund expansion from cash flow and that a family business should be handed on to the next generation. I hope my exit is a long way away.

I know that some banks have been keen to convert equity into cash so entrepreneurs could live the life now and pay them back later (an entrepreneur's equivalent of a pay day loan or buying a new bedroom from BrightHouse). I prefer to keep the shares, forget the yacht, and keep control.

Bill Grimsey, in his recent book *Sold Out*, talks about troubles on the high street and points to the part high levels of debt have played in retail failures such as Peacocks.

Sizeable transactions, like the recent sale of a significant stake in B+M Bargains (whose owners were right to cash in at the height of the budget shopping bonanza), bring fabulous fees to big hitters in the City. The deals may put capital in the hands of shareholders and boost bankers' bank accounts but if the transaction lands the business with a mountain of debt, the ultimate price could be paid by an administration and the loss of jobs.

Perhaps it is wise to follow the more prudent British approach and expand within your means and keep a tight control on the equity.

Process and Professionals

We seem to have forgotten that management is an art, not a science. If you run a business by the book, you will create a healthy, safe and diverse workplace at the expense of the profit-making flair that is needed for success.

Obeying the rules costs money without guaranteeing anything other than a mediocre performance. Companies are throwing money down the drain in a national campaign for corporate conformity. I prefer to challenge every regulation in the cause of common sense.

There appears to be a blind assumption that if you put in a proper process it will produce the desired result. When the professional management team acquired our shoe repair competitor Mr Minit, consultants identified a new strategy based on multi-service shops (shoe repairs, key cutting, watch repairs, engraving, dry cleaning and photo processing all under one roof in a one-stop service shop). It was a good idea but on professional advice Mr Minit made some expensive mistakes. The new concept shop, called Minit Solutions, was designed on the back of market research that told them to separate dirty shoe repairs from the dry cleaning – as a result the cobbling was hidden behind a screen and sales fell dramatically. Things got worse when qualified cobblers were replaced as branch managers by graduates who couldn't cut a key. Four years of following their carefully crafted business plan produced losses of about £120m.

Reports, KPIs, market research, compliance, best

practice, strict guidelines and company policies all take time and cost money. It is a lot better to find someone with flair and trust them to do the job.

Have you wondered why it takes so long to get a reply from a big business and even longer to get a decision? It's probably because everyone has to follow the company procedure. Recently, Sheila, who works part-time for Alex at our home, was planning to move house but had problems with the mortgage. Sheila had paid off all but 10% and simply wanted to transfer the mortgage to her new property, but her bank wouldn't play ball until all the forms were completed. The local manager had no authority to short-circuit the system.

I know I am becoming a grumpy old man but I am right to complain when box-tickers tell me what I have to do. Several times a year I am told 'You can't do that!' or 'We have to follow the rules!' When I say, 'I'll run the business the way I want', I am told, 'But it's a legal requirement.' Often they are wrong – they are quoting gold-plated guidelines produced by cautious consultants and lawyers.

While I am on my grumpy soapbox (and we have introduced the subject of lawyers) let me name my number one irritant – salesmen on the street who ask: 'Have you had an accident at work?' I have been well served by many good lawyers but too many are looking for new ways to sue. This rule-creation and exploitation industry is earning big fees and we pay the bill through bigger and bigger insurance premiums.

If everyone employed a full set of advisors, followed all their rules and filled in every form we would all finish up with the same boring business. You create a successful company by standing out from the opposition. It's the mavericks that will make the money.

*

I recently sold some shares in my business and took on a new director, thinking it would be good to share responsibility and the input of someone with broader experience than my own would help grow my business. All he's done so far is put a whole load of big company process into the equation as far as I can see, the most irritating manifestation of which are endless meetings in which nothing gets decided. How do you make meetings actually achieve something in your business?

Sounds like you picked the wrong man, proving the point that plenty of professional managers spend loads of time on process that gets in the way of progress. I am willing to bet that as well as bringing in a mountain of meetings your team is now heavily engaged in appraisals, budgets and extra management training, and before you know it he will take everyone off on a retreat to draw up a forward plan and agree a mission statement.

I have a theory that the fewer meetings you have, the better you do. Certainly it is almost impossible to contact the CEO of a business in trouble because he is constantly 'in a meeting'.

I was delighted to discover that Asda have a meeting room with no chairs. With everyone standing they keep the chat to a minimum. In our office all meeting rooms have a glass front so I can see who is round the table. I am quite likely to barge in and ask what they are talking about.

I acknowledge the need to meet up to make sure everyone knows what is going on, but every meeting must have a purpose. It helps to have a Chairman who sticks to the agenda, with comprehensive papers issued well in advance – no meeting should take more than two hours and usually an hour is enough. But beware, meetings must never be so important that they stop managers getting out of the office to visit the business. And never let committees run the company. Meetings are for discussion and communication; they should never make decisions!

You already know you have made a poor appointment. Pay the price by buying back your shares at a big enough premium to persuade your process-driven director to take his talents elsewhere.

I am interested how you measure the financial performance of your private company. Presumably you have sales and profit targets for each of your 1,000-plus shops but do you have KPIs for the group as well as cash flow, profit and sales targets? And if so, why do you choose some indicators over others?

A long time ago I learnt that having a lot of figures doesn't mean you are better informed, it just makes life more complicated.

In the 1980s we set budget sales figures for every shop every week, our Finance Director insisting that individual shop numbers added up to his company budget. It was a tortuous process that took weeks of area management time, and although head office hoped the plan would provide the perfect incentive it made no difference to our performance. Sales never seemed to follow our forecast (our customers clearly didn't know how much they were expected to spend!). I scrapped the budgetary process and for the last twenty years we have compared branch performance with last year – it has saved us a lot of bother.

So life at Timpson has little to do with budgets and we don't have KPIs. We have bought several loss-making companies and found that every one of them was monitoring minute detail from head office. Sketchley were keen on keeping a count of their 'supercrease' sales, Max Spielmann (the photo chain) kept an eye on the average price of picture frames, and Mr Minit was controlling costs so closely that they recorded every shop's expenditure on postage stamps. While management concentrated on the detail, they seemed to miss out on the big picture. Instead of studying their computers they should have visited more shops to talk to the colleagues who met their customers.

Of the few figures I receive the most important is the bank balance, compared with the same day last year. It gives me a daily health check on our business. I get a daily report on all the new shops we have opened in the last three months and a weekly sales report for the company, in total, and by department (e.g. key cutting, watch repairs, photo ID etc.). We revise our profit forecast every week and produce management accounts every month (I seldom look beyond the front page summary).

The only time I ask for detail is when we are introducing a

new service – like our current growth in portraits, locksmith work and complicated car keys. If you know which shops are successful you can pass their secret round the rest of the business.

With little to look at, it is easy to see how the company is doing and I have plenty of time left to visit our branches and discover what is really going on.

I know my strengths and the discipline of setting year-ahead targets and then regularly monitoring progress against them is not one of them. Do you have any shortcuts to success?

You don't have anything to worry about. Comprehensive budgets and meticulous monitoring will probably have little influence on your annual profit. You will make much more money by picking the right people, creating a great culture and choosing a successful strategy. No one can guarantee a top performance by following a paper process. As I've said before, management is an art, not a science.

I have survived the last twenty years without bothering too much about budgets, KPIs or targets. Although we do produce a budget (the bank manager likes to see one) no one outside our Finance Department gets involved in the process. We save hours of management time and avoid plenty of business politics by ignoring the budget ritual that is standard practice on almost every corporate calendar.

I like comparing figures with last year – a figure based on fact instead of fantasy. I am amazed how many organisations only compare their performance with budget. In the 1960s when the buzz words were 'management by objectives' we had such a blind faith in targets that no one was allowed to quote comparisons against last year. The theory was that as long as everyone focused on the objective it was bound to be achieved! By simply chasing the company's optimistically created target we lost contact with common sense.

Recently I read a report that concluded most family businesses need more professional management – I totally disagree. Review meetings, personal appraisals, risk assessment and KPIs don't guarantee success.

Don't change your management style. Leave the budgeting to the Finance department and continue to rely on your flair and experience.

My sales manager has failed to achieve all the key goals that I set her last year but with the benefit of hindsight they weren't crucial to the business anyway. What do I do? If I don't take her up on this performance it undermines our performance assessment system.

It seems to me that the problem is not your team member, it is the assessment system.

I detect from the tone of your question that she is a bit of a superstar who has produced the sort of results that really matter. Be grateful that she didn't pursue your 'key goals' if in the end you found them irrelevant. She sounds to be ahead of the game!

Your story is further proof that targets, guidelines, goals and KPIs get in the way of good business. Forget all this micro-management. You will achieve much more by ignoring detailed objectives and giving your people the freedom to concentrate on delivering the end result in the way they know best.

In government and now in business there is a blind belief in process. But there is no magic formula; entrepreneurs win by following flair, not rules. Top-down management is an expensive and clumsy way to run any organisation.

Can I suggest that you give your 'direct report' a substantial pay rise and scrap the performance management system before it does any more damage?

Which specific indicators do you use to assess the health of a business that you're thinking of going into business with? There are a number of financial options: official credit score, cash in the bank, interest cover. Then there are the online ones: how often the company's website is updated, positive LinkedIn recommendations. And the physical ones: swanky offices and cars in the car park. But which are the most reliable in your view?

The accounts don't tell you everything but are a good place to start. I like figures that are easy to understand – a simple statement of affairs breeds confidence. Don't be fooled by lots of key ratios. I don't want to be blinded by analysis. I prefer historic performance to projections and find net profit more straightforward than EBITDA. The figures I most want to see are cash flow, borrowings and the bank balance.

To really find out about a company, go beyond the figures and visit the business. Get to know the product, talk to employees and chat to a few customers. People usually reveal the truth that is hidden by the figures.

There are some classic warning signs like a new head office with fountains in the foyer and a Directors' dining room. But I would be more wary of a Managing Director who puts his Maybach in an individually marked parking bay next to the office entrance. It could hint that he thinks he (it couldn't possibly be a woman!) is much more important than the business.

For me the most helpful questions are: 'Do I like the senior team, and do they "get it"?' I worry if they fail to reply quickly to letters or emails and don't return phone calls. A real bother is when they are always 'in a meeting' – companies in trouble spend a lot of time talking about the problem. I am also unlikely to like someone who is so busy they can't come to Manchester and when I make a special trip to meet them in London, keep me waiting and then ignore me to check out their text messages.

Mind you, if you are thinking of buying the business, all these bad signs are probably good news. The more problems you find, the bigger the chance of improvement. But if you plan to work together, follow your gut instinct. If it doesn't feel right, never mind what your advisors might say, stay clear.

It's budgeting madness here and I'm tearing my hair out trying to anticipate what our team can achieve next year as the outlook is so uncertain. I'm tempted to push for a lower target but I don't want to pitch too low for fear of being hauled up in front of our MD.

You have my sympathy. In a lot of organisations the annual budget round is a major waste of management time and an excuse for playing company politics.

Your question says it all – faced with putting in the budget bid, your main objectives are 'to push for a lower target'. You will be trying to keep the sales budget down and claim more than your fair share of capital expenditure while still being the boss's blue-eyed boy.

The process takes me back nearly 40 years to when our business was part of the UDS Group and I was competing against the other subsidiaries (John Collier, Richard Shops, Allders Department Stores, etc.). My main aim was survival – as long as another part of the group produced a worse performance than Timpson, my job was safe.

It is a pity that finance executives are obsessed with comparison with budget. Financial targets won't turn a mediocre team into superstars. In my experience it is nearly always better to give managers more freedom and pitch your performance against last year.

No one outside our Finance department gets involved in budgeting. No KPIs, no budget bids and no internal politics.

Sadly, you have no choice – you must follow the rules. Go to see your boss before he sees you. Give him your best estimate, then ask him what he wants. It might not be good business, but to win the budgeting game you are bound to play a bit of politics.

The received wisdom always tells small companies not to hold too much stock. The man running the wonderful little hardware shop around the corner from me seems to break the rules. His shop is piled high with weird and wonderful items: picture wire, a phone, a wedding card,

light bulbs, wall putty and a disposable barbecue are among the strange array of items I've bought from him. The approach seems to be working for him – the shop is always busy. Are there any other 'golden rules' that can be happily ignored by successful companies?

I also like ironmongers. They break the rules and provide a perfect example of customer service. They stock everything you need, with a shopkeeper who is always keen to find what you want. It is not surprising *The Two Ronnies'* 'Four Candles' sketch is so popular.

Twenty years ago I was shown round a competitor's warehouse. When we got to their key blank store I was proudly told how they had cut costs by eliminating all but the 60 most popular blanks. It was great news for us – key cutting customers expect you to be able to cut every type of key. As a service shop, at Timpson we try to tackle every job that comes our way. Accountants can count the stock but they can't measure the cost of lost sales.

You can't guarantee a golden rule will always work. Some retailers say location is everything – not true. Look at Richer Sounds. Julian Richer built a business in offbeat locations offering great service on a low rent. Another common phrase is 'retail is detail'. Only to a certain extent – first you need to get the strategy right. John Collier failed because they concentrated on made-to-measure suits. Granada Rental disappeared because people stopped renting televisions, and HMV have struggled as music has moved online. If you are in the wrong business, the detail is irrelevant.

Any golden rule can be broken. That is the beauty of

business – it is an art, not a science, that needs intuition rather than process. There will always be a place for mavericks who challenge the theory of management.

It's coming up to the cut-off point for holiday entitlements and, as usual, everybody has applied for a holiday in the same week. Usually HR sticks to a 'first come, first served' method for deciding who gets the favourite dates, but, this year, the three people first past the post are also the newest and, to be frank, least deserving. How can I decide this fairly, while also ensuring my long-standing staff get some much deserved time off?

Never forget who runs your business. You make the rules and can interpret them however you wish.

Your HR department are right to put people under pressure to book their holiday dates as soon as possible, but instead of promising 'first come, first served' they should simply set a deadline for applications. New employees and poor performers are not your priority. No manager should have favourites, but it is perfectly proper to let parents have the school holiday dates and look after your long-serving colleagues and star performers by giving them the slots they want.

Everyone is entitled to twenty days off plus bank holidays. Some stay at home and say they spend the time decorating (but many simply sit in front of the television). For others it is the chance to fulfil a long-held ambition.

Good employers are flexible. By bending the rules and carrying holidays over from one year to another we can help colleagues take an extended holiday to visit relatives in New Zealand or celebrate a silver wedding in South Africa.

Our managers are allowed to break all the rules, but they must give every colleague an extra paid day off on their birthday.

I know you train up many of your staff from scratch, in-house. Have we got the UK apprenticeship set up on the right lines? What do you think about planned changes which would see businesses taking charge?

A few weeks ago we advertised a job in Dundee and 531 people applied in one day. We picked Brian, who I rate 10/10. Brian applied because he knew we would teach him a trade.

This year we plan to take on over 750 apprentices who will all follow an in-house training programme, developed by our team over the last eighteen years. Nearly every colleague you see in our shops started as an apprentice.

By recruiting pleasant and positive personalities who are keen to learn, we can, within four months, teach the basics of all our skills including shoe repairs, key cutting and watch repairs. After a year they are ready to run a shop on their own.

There is no other UK training school for cobblers and key cutters, so without our apprentice scheme we wouldn't have the skills to provide a proper service.

I am delighted to hear, following ex-*Dragon* Doug Richard's report, the government are thinking about tax breaks to compensate for the cost of apprenticeship training. But I bet we will be thwarted by the little devils hiding in the detail.

A few years ago a lady who ran our training agency talked of giving us over £1m a year of state funding. We had two years of meetings but finished up with nothing. To get the money, our training had to change to comply with government guidelines, and we were expected to work with an approved training provider who knew nothing at all about cobbling, but was a dab hand at filling in forms and would pick up 50% of our grant for their trouble. We decided to do things our way and ignore the handout.

Perhaps the new scheme will trust us to train apprentices in our own way, but I can't help thinking the tax breaks will only come with a heavy dose of government guidelines, red tape and grants that will continue to be gathered by an army of training providers who know how to fill in the paperwork.

Whatever happens we will still take on the 750 apprentices, but we would welcome a scheme that hands out the money to people who create more jobs and train apprentices rather than giving grants to guys who are good at box-ticking.

The Apprentice is back on our screens again. What do you make of the way it portrays business? If you take it seriously, it suggests you've got to be a hyper-aggressive narcissist to succeed in business. Is this damaging or is it just a harmless gameshow that's completely divorced from reality?

I am not a regular viewer but have seen enough when channel-flicking to form an opinion. *The Apprentice* teaches no more about business than *Blind Date* and now *Take Me Out* tell you about building a relationship.

This is pure entertainment involving people who make good television rather than good business. I am keen on picking people for their personality but the producers of *The Apprentice* seem to specialise in finding intelligent, but eccentric, extroverts, making sure they pick a few pillocks. It is a mix that makes entertaining television but they are not all the sort of people I want running my business, and I can't imagine many of my existing colleagues would want to work alongside them.

It is not only the contestants that give a false impression. Lord Sugar is surely playing to the camera. Few executives will find success by sitting behind a desk making sarcastic comments to their young trainees.

But it is, remember, entertainment, and hopefully people realise you can still be a nice guy and run a good business.

Do business leaders have a duty to their employees to provide them with the best possible advice on the growing urgency to make the correct pension provisions for their retirement? How do you approach this problem in your company?

For the last 25 years I have fiercely tried to follow in my grandfather's footsteps by funding a generous final salary pension scheme. But a combination of short-term legislation and short-sighted accountancy standards have put me on the point of closing our scheme to new members.

When our colleagues retire I want to look them in the eye knowing we have done our best to help them provide for their financial security. But things have become progressively more difficult ever since Robert Maxwell jumped ship, Gordon Brown took away the tax breaks and we started to be ruled by The Regulator.

Twenty years ago pension funds were valued in line with investment income, thus avoiding the roller-coaster changes in share prices. We took a long-term view, happy in the knowledge that the fund's income was always sufficient to cover the pensions we paid out each year.

The Pensions Regulator sees things differently – the value of our fund goes up and down with the stock market, which would not be so bad if we hadn't been inflicted with 'technical provisions' (this is actuarial speak for the asset value they calculate is needed to safely pay all accrued pensions).

The calculation is unduly influenced by gilt yields, which have been so affected by quantitative easing that our 'technical provisions' have increased by 65% in nine months! Little has changed – our scheme has the same members on the same salaries with similar smoking habits – but because the Bank of England has been printing more money (which will eventually fuel inflation), interest rates have fallen and an actuarial computer says we need to find another £20m.

Pension accounting is bonkers. It is ridiculous to use short-term measures to calculate a long-term commitment, and then use the figures to ruin company balance sheets. But no one wants to listen to common sense. In a few years a combination of politicians, actuaries and accountants have ruined loads of fabulous final salary pension schemes, and sadly it is too late to undo the damage.

Although my instinct is to continue to follow my grandfather's example, the regulators have beaten me into submission and we will probably join the long list of final salary pension schemes that have shut up shop to new members.

But I still worry about our colleagues' pension plans. For a lot of our young people retirement is too far off to contemplate. They have been brought up in a live-now-pay-later world and their main concern is usually paying off debt rather than building up savings.

Shortly we will have to help them understand the complicated concept of auto enrolment (although we are not allowed to give financial advice), which, no doubt, will be succeeded by further initiatives inadequately designed to solve a massive problem.

It was a lot easier in my grandfather's day.

We are increasingly being asked to produce monthly management accounts by our banks, utilities and insurers and it's a real drag. What right do they have demanding access to this commercially sensitive information? Why can't they work off our annual accounts like everyone else? Do you have a limit on the sort of information you'll release about current trading?

We provide our bank manager with management accounts every month not because she asks for them but because we want her to know what is going on. Banking should be based on trust from both sides and we don't want her to have any surprises. We immediately make her aware whenever we change our profit forecast.

Utility companies are probably asking for financial details simply to tick one of their internal governance boxes. It might be irritating but you won't change their system, so for the sake of your blood pressure just go along with it.

Is your management information really that sensitive? Every year I have a lunch for all our main suppliers (bankers and insurers included). I use the opportunity to present our latest figures and talk about our future plans. It helps to build a better relationship and have more loyal suppliers.

Don't be surprised if you are being asked to supply details by people to whom you owe money. Your creditors hold the upper hand, so if you are not in a position to pay them off, be as helpful as you can.

If you were the bank manager for the Timpson Group, how would you describe your company in a report to the bank's head office?

If our bank manager writes the following report it will show she really understands the way we do business:

'I am sending this report on the strict understanding that you don't mention it to John Timpson. He firmly believes that all decisions on his account should be taken by me and my team at the Manchester office. I wouldn't want him to know that I ever have to talk to a credit committee.

'This retail business with a range of services including shoe repairs, key cutting, watch repairs and photo printing has a turnover of over £200m with profits of about £15m. It has over 1,000 shops, all in the UK, and is opening 75 new branches a year, mainly inside or in the car parks of out-of-town supermarkets. Despite the old-fashioned image of cobbling, this company keeps coming up with new ways to diversify. Current growth is coming from complicated car keys, mobile phone repairs and a rapidly increasing share of the dry cleaning market. It sounds a simple business but it took me some time to understand how they make it work.

'They call their method "Upside Down Management" – shop staff are trusted with almost total freedom to make the day-to day decisions. There are very few rules. Managers don't issue orders; their job is to help the people who serve the customers.

'Despite the lack of traditional discipline and regimented process, the business seems to perform remarkably well – perhaps because of their record of picking particularly good people. I get sent comprehensive management accounts every month, and Paresh their Finance Director keeps me fully informed so I never get any surprises.

'Sadly it is not all good news. They have an irritating habit of steering clear of overdrafts – their strong cash flow means that despite a hefty capital expenditure programme for most of the year, we are banking with them rather than them banking with us.

'One final point – this Upside Down Management seems so good, why don't we do a bit of it in the bank? Starting by giving me total authority to deal with the Timpson account without needing the approval of head office.'

I have been happily banking with NatWest for well over 30 years and our trading business as opticians (a family group of three practices) has always been very steady. Recently, however, my account has been given over to

the healthcare manager of the Royal Bank of Scotland, based some distance away. I am getting texts, telephone calls, emails, almost on a daily basis. Our account peaks and troughs throughout the month, and if the account comes within a whisker of the limits, I get a text. Now he may be doing his job, but the constant harassment makes me want to change my bank, although I was told not too long ago that I was a 'blue chip' customer. An independent financial advisor suggested it is better to be with the devil you know than the devil you don't. Is he right?

Computers, risk management and control from head office have changed the way a bank manager can operate. Today banking is less personal and more driven by process. Perhaps key performance indicators have become more important than customer service.

I don't agree with your financial advisor. If you are a gold-plated client you deserve help, not harassment.

Despite the difficulties during the credit crisis, people still live in fear of their bank and are nervous to criticise. But banks are in a competitive market like every other business and the main battleground is based on customer service. If your manager doesn't appreciate your business, take it to the competition.

Would it help me get preferential treatment if I get pally with my bank manager?

However much you suck up to your bank manager, you are

not going to secure much more than a sympathetic ear and an invitation to the bank's corporate golf day.

At a bank the big decisions are made by invisible members of the credit committee. Having said that, a good day-to-day relationship is important. Your local manager may not be able to authorise a big loan but he is the person who writes the report that will have a major influence on the decision.

If you don't like your manager or if you feel he doesn't like you, have the courage to contact a more senior suit at the bank and ask for a change. If they don't grant your request, change your bank.

There is no harm in becoming your bank manager's pal, but the best way to secure his support is to be honest in all your dealings, create a good business, provide him with all your latest figures, and don't give the bank any surprises.

In banking, however, nothing is for ever. As soon as you get comfortable with your bank manager and establish a strong bond he will be moved to Swindon or Edinburgh and you will have to start all over again.

If you had a magic wand, what would you do to improve the service that high street banks provide to their business customers?

My simple answer is to give more authority, trust and freedom to local bank managers. Today, too many decisions are referred to head office where faceless bean counters use inflexible ratios to decide the facilities they offer to customers they never meet face-to-face.

The safety of most loans depends on people, not

spreadsheets. It is more important for a banker to meet the management team than to apply sensitivity analysis to a computer-generated business plan. Sadly most of the big banks now see their bank managers as salesmen who are measured against KPIs and appraised on their ability to stick to a proper process. When it comes to approving loans they have to keep to company rules.

Someone has decided the way to cut out mistakes is to make all decisions at head office. They are wrong. Big mistakes will still be made, but by preventing the local man using his initiative, lots of good opportunities will be missed. Many highly competent customers will be starved of cash and clobbered by large arrangement fees because their balance sheet fails to fit theoretical financial guidelines.

I will never forget how my local bank manager made a decision that transformed our business.

In 1995 one of our main competitors went into receivership. We had been trying to buy the business for several years and at last had the opportunity. There was a lot of interest so we needed to offer a fair price – we decided that meant £3.5m but NatWest head office would only provide the cash to support a bid of £2.5m so I mortgaged our house for £1m to make up the difference. Alex, my wife, was not happy!

Our offer was only good enough to get us onto a shortlist and it quickly became clear that one of the contenders was our biggest competitor, Mr Minit, a well-funded global business run from Switzerland. Knowing I was outgunned, I rang the Minit UK Managing Director and suggested 'a half' – my idea was that following a joint bid we would toss a coin to decide who picked the first shop, then take it in turns to choose until every branch had been allocated. After fifteen minutes' thought he rang back to turn down my offer.

At 6.00pm that day we submitted sealed bids to decide the winner. We offered £4,019,024 (Richard Branson always suggests you add a little bit extra in case the opposition bids a round number). We won, but the vendor soon discovered we hadn't got the money. We were given until 10.00 the following morning to find the cash, while Mr Minit as under-bidder waited in the wings to sign the deal.

While we spent hours phoning everyone we knew who might plug the £500k gap, our bank manager, Brian Ferguson, back in Manchester, was working through the night on our behalf. We knew Brian well and he knew what a difference the deal would make. Brian rang at 9.30am to tell us he had authority to lend us the cash we needed. Thanks to Brian we did a deal that within two years had increased our annual profit from £400k to £2.5m. A result that showed the value of a real bank manager and helped me repay the mortgage within twelve months, which made a major contribution to the happiness of my marriage.

As your business expands, what has proved to be your wisest IT investment?

I put this question to Paul who heads our IT department. 'The BlackBerry', was his immediate thought. 'It helps Area Managers keep in touch and lets you spend more time visiting our branches.' He then made an interesting remark: 'Knowing how you run the business, I try to keep IT out of the way. You don't want me to interfere by producing projects that put a stranglehold around the people who run our shops.'

As a consequence, Paul steers clear of admin tasks that other IT departments regard as routine. He concentrates on ways to help increase sales.

Computers made a big difference to our engraving business. Computer engravers are quicker and produce better quality – they have doubled our personalised engraving sales. Paul is now helping us to develop a major advance in the world of complicated car keys, using internet access to help our branches copy electronic car key technology at a reasonable price.

'With broadband in branches', said Paul, 'we must be careful that internet access is not abused. We don't want to become a business controlled from head office. But', he continued, 'Broadband will bring more selling opportunities. I am already working on easier ways to sell our house signs.'

I am lucky to have an IT department that knows how to work within our culture.

My wisest IT investment was to hire Paul and the rest of his team.

What do you think of disaster planning – do managers take it seriously enough?

Even the most successful business can be brought down to earth by a stroke of bad luck, so don't think disasters can't happen to you.

Risk assessments and disaster planning are too important to be delegated to an in-house systems controller or an outside consultant.

Most boards of directors review risk by rating a matrix of major dangers on a scale from 1 to 5. This somewhat sterile exercise may demonstrate good governance but a bit of box-ticking won't make you take matters seriously enough.

Use your imagination to predict possible peril. I have written a list of Timpson nightmares. My catalogue of disaster includes a car crash that puts all the executive directors out of action and a European locksmith directive that ties up our key cutting service in paralysing red tape.

To ensure that everyone understands the need for 'Plan B', stage a realistic disaster recovery rehearsal. Take the company by surprise. Discover what would happen if your head office and warehouse were wiped out by fire. Suddenly shut everything down for 36 hours to see how your team can cope without a desk and with no stock to fulfil orders.

By taking a serious approach to risk you begin to realise that it pays to be as prepared as possible. But even with the most prudent approach you are still at the mercy of bad luck, so it is always worth keeping your fingers crossed.

Every week we get the release of statistics on some part of the economy, from one organisation or another. Do you think statistics and surveys are a help or a hindrance to good management?

We all need numbers to measure our performance. They tell us where we stand in the corporate pecking order and hopefully provide reassurance that we are doing OK. We get guilty satisfaction whenever a competitor produces a poor set of figures. Bad news for one business is often good news for another.

Most executives scan the business pages hoping to spot statistics that prove they are beating the market, but all figures should be viewed with a substantial slice of suspicion. You can't trust a competitor to tell you the truth when you ask 'How's business?' and it is unwise to believe every 'official' statistic.

A simple headline, 'Retail Sales Up 3%', may need interpretation. It isn't always clear whether the statistics are compared with last year or last month or whether they include the internet. Total sales are different from 'like for like' (a phrase that in itself can cover many different ways of calculation). You also may need to factor in the effect of the weather and when Easter falls before deciding what the figures really mean.

The recent double- and triple-dip debate shows that statistics about past performance, even if inaccurate, have a big influence on future thinking. Couple that with the British fascination with bad news and you can understand why it is taking us so long to realise the economy is already on the way to recovery.

Every day we wake up to another survey on *BBC Breakfast* – statistics about a better diet, global warming, hospital waiting times and poor customer service. Commentators usually concentrate on the bad news. When the recent benefit changes came into force, reporters only interviewed the minority who, statistically, were worse off.

Process-driven managers can become obsessed by targets. I recently met a man who is advising a part of the NHS where all performance targets are being beaten, but although they were described as outstanding, they have a lot of dissatisfied patients. His challenge was to get the management to understand that patients are not just a statistic.

Last week a consultant sent me an email offering to 'do some data capturing, advanced analytics and navigate our database which will bring a double digit increase to your bottom line'. I declined. Despite all the numbers at my disposal I always discover much more during a day visiting our shops.

One of our salespeople recently requested to go on a health and safety course. I let her, but she's now being ridiculously prescriptive and upsetting everyone. Last week, she removed everyone's desk and tower fans, saying they're a fire risk. Since our office isn't air-conditioned, that hasn't been a popular move. I want to intervene but am also scared of falling foul of regulations I don't understand. How do you cope?

This problem must be dealt with straight away. You probably think that your health and safety zealot is a troublemaker, but before jumping to conclusions check the facts – she might be right.

First find out if the fans are faulty. If they are, give her the credit for spotting a potential problem. But if she is just making sure you are following the regulations, check the legislation – she could be confusing someone's idea of best practice with a legal obligation.

Explain to her that health and safety is best achieved by observant colleagues using their common sense rather than an obsession with nit-picking rules. Make it plain that although initiative is to be encouraged, no one is going to tell you how to run your business.

If the fans are safe, put them back and with luck this enthusiastic colleague will return to reality. But if she insists on continuing with her campaign, lay down your own law.

You don't have to put up with a colleague who refuses to toe the management line. If she doesn't agree, it is time for her to go. But be careful – I sense trouble. Put a foot wrong and you could finish in a tribunal.

The golf club that told players that golf buggies were not health and safety authorised; a boots supplier claiming that it was banned from accepting dirty boots for return; cafes and restaurants refusing to heat up baby food. All supposed examples of 'elf and safety' that were in fact examples of firms erroneously using red tape as an excuse to refuse service. What's your view on this country's health and safety rules – any horror stories that have got in the way of you running your company, or is 'elf and safety' culture a bit of a myth?

We are mugs to put up with these people who inflict on us their barmy interpretation of the law.

I must take my fair share of the blame. I should have made a fuss when we weren't allowed to change a fuse in our tiny kiosk at London's Victoria station. We had to close the shop for over 24 hours until the station electrician and his mate were free to do the two-minute job.

Silly phantom rules keep cropping up. Some developers

insist that our experienced surveyors go on their half-day safety course before being allowed on site. Box-ticking stretched the shop fit of our tiny unit at Canary Wharf, which we could have done in a fortnight, into a job that took over a year.

It is still getting worse. The other week one of our Area Managers was stopped by a jobsworth in Ellesmere Port for carrying display material across the concourse to our new shop without permission.

If you wonder who is paying for this new unwelcome branch of the law, look no further than your soaring insurance premiums.

I don't like the American risk-averse world driven by best practice and a 'proper process'. Good customer service isn't created by making everyone stick to a set of rules.

To show I mean business I encourage our colleagues to let customers use our shop loo and look after their bags while they do some more shopping, and we are more than happy to repair dirty shoes.

If you ever get advice that doesn't seem sensible, check the statute and you will almost certainly discover it is not in the legislation. Lawyers, accountants, consultants and HR professionals are there to offer advice – they should not run your business. It is time for us to take a few more risks in the name of common sense.

Your recent column on safety raised a lot of interesting points. It is indeed outcomes that matter, not process. No amount of paperwork ever saved lives; it is the creation

of a genuine safety culture where everyone understands their role and takes responsibility which delivers real results. As a successful business leader, how do you think we can inject more common sense into health and safety? (Judith Hackitt, Chair, Health and Safety Executive)

Your letter has made me think. It was a very welcome surprise to discover that you share my view of the world of regulation.

I have now been in business for over 50 years. When I started, women were paid much less than men for doing the same job, our operatives were using unguarded machinery, and any vindictive manager could fire an unfortunate colleague simply because he didn't like the look of his face.

For 25 years things improved with the introduction of equal pay, safer working conditions and a fair deal for employees. But for the last 25 years business has suffered from the rapid growth of our fourth sector – the rule-creation and exploitation business.

Much has rightly been written about the growth of central and local government. In many areas of the country the majority of workers are public servants paid out of our taxes, with only a minority of the nation's workforce creating any wealth. While the last government was increasing the size of the civil service and introducing loads of new laws, the fourth sector found ways to exploit the legislation.

The 'no win no fee' industry is only the tip of a big and rapidly growing iceberg full of lawyers, consultants, insurers, training providers, accountants and even more civil servants. Laws produced to protect the individual are now being exploited to provide hugely profitable work for an enormous party of parasites.

The words 'best practice', 'governance', 'risk assessment' and 'due diligence' are music to the ears of this fast-growing fourth sector, and guess who pays the bill – we do. We pay in higher insurance premiums and legal fees, and by funding plenty of unproductive activities that we mistakenly have been persuaded are all legal requirements.

It is a relief to know that you, Judith, as Chair of the Health and Safety Executive, criticise the way advisors are creating pseudo-regulations that go well beyond the legislation. But it is not easy to see how you can reverse the stampede towards a totally risk-averse, rule-driven existence.

A good example is the PAT testing of electronic equipment. The law simply says that businesses are responsible for ensuring that the equipment is safe. The PAT test is put forward as 'best practice' by consultants who do the testing – it is not a legal requirement.

Like loads of other businesses we, for several years, have been paying a specialist to test our equipment. I checked how well it is working and discovered that we seldom if ever have a fault reported following a PAT test. Sara, on our helpline, tells me (and she should know) that every problem found in the last two years has been discovered by our own colleagues noticing something amiss. And that is the way it should be: a workplace kept safe by workers who take safety seriously and see it as a personal responsibility.

We have cancelled the PAT testing consultant's contract and saved over £25,000 a year. I have encouraged others to follow suit with little success. 'It's all right for you', they say, 'you run your own business and can take the risk, but I have a duty of care to follow best practice – what would happen if something went wrong?'

We have got so accustomed to living in a blame culture that life now revolves around running as little risk as possible. We are wimps, happily letting the fourth sector walk all over us.

Lawyers who chase business by text message – 'I understand you have been involved in an accident' – or by accosting people in the street – 'Have you had an accident at work?' – are in my view guilty of a new offence: 'irresponsible professional harassment'.

But I don't propose yet more legislation. It is up to business leaders to show some leadership by challenging best practice whenever it flies in the face of common sense and put the fourth sector back in its place.

I run a training company that shows public government organisations how money is wasted by the use of consultants. I then show these organisations what to look out for if the consultant's advice is bad. However there are times when these consultants' services are needed (guiding decision making, costing of large projects, project service management, getting short-term specialist staff). Would you agree, and if not, what is the alternative?

Of course you are right, there are times when it is best to bring in external expertise, but that should be the exception.

A few years ago, when I spent a week in what was then

the DTI, I was staggered to discover how most projects were handled by consultants. With third parties providing the analysis, the planning and the project management, I wondered what was left for the full-time team of civil servants to do. I was told: 'Our job is policy.'

The over-use of outsiders is a sign of weakness. As a foster carer I regularly came into contact with our local social services and saw their job gradually change. Much more time is now spent in front of a computer completing statutory reports and less time is left to meet the children who they are there to help. Social workers who want a career on the front line making a difference are disappointed to find the job is more about meeting other 'professionals' than meeting children. Unsurprisingly, recruitment is a problem and today over half the work is delivered by agency workers on short-term contracts – you can't create a proper team out of part-timers.

The use of outside advice is encouraged by the recent upsurge of corporate governance. To cover their backs, nervous executives are constantly seeking a second opinion. I see this as a pension scheme trustee – the box-ticking required by the Pensions Regulator provides plenty of fees for actuaries and accountants.

Our process-driven world has been a breeding ground for consultancy. Try to get a training grant and you won't be able to avoid using a training provider. Pitch for a government contract and you will need outside help to complete the Pre-Qualification Questionnaire.

Perhaps this is a good time for government to take a hard look at its use of outside resources. With costs being squeezed and public service jobs threatened, each department should publish the percentage of its budget that is spent on consultants.

We now live in a world where consultants find lots of work, but you can't create success just by following advice and sticking to a set of rules – it is important to trust the judgement of an entrepreneur. Experts can help but it's the individual flair within an organisation that makes the difference.

Can you divulge any interesting or amusing events in your company board meetings? I presume you do not just record the numbers of keys cut each month?

Board meetings aren't meant to be full of fun but I can understand why you asked your question. I still have nightmares about the tedious times I spent round various board tables. If my experience is anything to go by, millions of management hours must be wasted every month in nit-picking meetings that delve into the detail but fail to provide the inspiration and encouragement most companies need.

I plead guilty to presiding over plenty of pointless meetings myself. I have been Chairman of our business since 1985 and for twenty years fell into the trap of allowing past performance to dominate our discussion. We got so bogged down analysing figures below budget that there wasn't enough time to talk about the business. I hope our recent debates have been more useful and more fun.

Management accounts can ruin a meeting, especially if current performance is the first item on the agenda. Directors feel it's their duty to spot every shortfall against budget, often with an unhelpful suggestion ('If each shop repairs an extra shoe every day, we will beat our forecast!'). The discussion is repeated each month, with non-execs asking the same searching questions that put the resident team on the defensive.

The recent emphasis on governance and risk management hasn't helped. Boards must exercise some caution but they should also have the courage to take a few risks and back the forward-thinking ideas of their management team.

For the most part, we ignore the accounts. Instead of trying to control day-to-day management we concentrate on creating the company of tomorrow. The first item on our agenda is always 'growth and new development', which last month included expanding into supermarkets, more mobile locksmiths and a new shop that offers garment repairs and alterations.

This probably doesn't sound like a bundle of laughs but I can assure you it is more exciting than the standard risk assessment grid used by many boards, which measures the impact and likelihood of risk under 54 headings. We use a sharper way to highlight risk. I write a story about the ten worst things that can happen, like:

'After the accident James was out of action for twelve months and we made the mistake of hiring an outside "professional" manager. The hottest summer since records began brought a dramatic drop in shoe repair sales and the new man started cutting costs. He cancelled the branch bonus scheme, sold our holiday homes, and before reducing the field management team made everyone reapply for their job. It took us five years to recover from his dictatorial management ...'

By telling a story you bring the real dangers to life – it's much better than a sterile bit of box-ticking.

To make our meetings fresh we only have six a year, and to hold everyone's attention we aim to finish within two hours. We never take a decision! Our aim is to discuss, communicate and support the executive team, who then have the job of deciding what to do.

PLCs might have to run their meetings according to a proper process but running a family business is much more fun.

Politics and Economics

During the recession I got plenty of questions about the economy, some suggesting the government should have been doing more to kick-start demand. It made me wonder how much difference politicians and economists really make.

To suggest that politicians influence the economy assumes they know enough about economics, or at least have some competent economists ready to help. But I'm not convinced even the economists know enough to beat the market.

History shows that things go in cycles. Shoe fashion moves from round toes to points, politics swings from left to right and the economy goes from boom to bust and back again. The Chancellor's budget might bring a bit of benefit but the real key to recovery is confidence and that's where the media come in. By taking telling pictures and writing punchy headlines, journalists can do more to shift public opinion than the most charismatic Member of Parliament. But even *The Sun* will struggle to make much difference because most people are simply not bothered. Facebook, football and even *Strictly Come Dancing* are many times more interesting than Prime Minister's Question Time.

Fifteen years ago I spent a week in the Department for Trade and Industry (DTI) which is now named BIS. It was a culture shock. They didn't seem particularly bothered about what they achieved (as long as they could score points against the arrogant Treasury team). The important thing was to do it in accordance with government guidelines: 'We are an equal opportunity employer, with disabled access, that recycles and carries out 360-degree appraisals – we have a comprehensive set of policies and are investors in people.' That tells us a bit about how they operate but I am more interested in what they are trying to achieve.

While at the DTI, I couldn't stop wondering what every-one did. A lot of people worked there but were they doing a lot of worthwhile work? My acid test at Timpson is to check that everyone is doing a job that helps those colleagues who serve our customers. That would have been a tricky criterion for the DTI, where managers told me their main aim was to be a top civil servant.

The world of Timpson is poles apart from Whitehall, which leads me to conclude that business and government don't mix and have little in common. This is a good reason for the government to leave us alone to run our company the way we know best.

*

I believe we want a lot more positive thinking. I was hoping the Diamond Jubilee and the Olympics would kick-start the economy but we seem to be heading for another barrage of bad news and gloomy prognoses in this country. I know times are very hard for many people and many companies, but can you promote good news, optimism and a determination to succeed?

I support your plea to be more positive – we desperately need an upsurge of optimism. The Treasury can tinker with the tax system, interest rates, quantitative easing and government apprenticeship schemes but we won't see substantial growth until the country gets its confidence back. Things will only get better when enough people start to believe the upturn is under way.

Business leaders find it tough trying to be cheerful when sales are down, profits have disappeared and the bank manager charges a big arrangement fee for a small overdraft with onerous conditions. About the only cheerful news is when a close competitor goes bust.

But anyone as old as me has been there before. The early 90s were difficult and the start of the 70s was even worse with inflation over 25%, the stock market on its knees, and the fuel crisis causing a three-day working week. I got a bizarre reminder of those problems in April, when I went to Ladies' Day at Aintree and saw the girls parading in platform shoes with eight-inch heels. I had seen the same styles before – they were the height of fashion in 1973.

I can't remember what triggered revival. I have been through two significant downturns but can't single out any event or government decision that pepped up our confidence and put us back on the road to recovery.

It is unwise to expect the Olympics to create a feel-good factor, or to hope the Office of National Statistics will announce enough good news to start media talk about green shoots. The likelihood is that confidence will only be restored when today suddenly seems better than yesterday.

Both business and fashion follow a cycle. It takes twenty years for footwear to go from big, clompy shoes to winkle-pickers and back to clompers. Business also has its ups and downs. Platform shoes always seem to appear when trade is tough and the bigger they are the more dire the dip in our economic performance.

Things are bound to get better as the financial world continues on its inevitable roller-coaster ride. Sometime in the next five years, for no obvious reason, confidence will come back.

But beware, when big platforms return in 2032 we will once more be in a world full of doom and gloom!

My business has had a much better last quarter than we budgeted for. Am I getting ahead of myself or should I expect this trend to continue?

Sometime someone has to say it and that person might as well be me, so I will say it now. 'Business is getting better and things are on the move.'

I know I am taking the risk that trade will take a turn for the worse the moment this column goes to print, but it is about time the doom-mongers were put in their place by a positive piece about the economic upturn that has already started.

My comments are not based on statistics (although sales in our shops are comfortably ahead of last year). I go by gut instinct.

I know some of you will think that shoe repairers are hardly a reliable guide, and you could be right, but I am not alone in seeing some green shoots. In the last week I have spoken to five entrepreneurs who all had a smile on their face. Some were almost embarrassed to admit their success – perhaps they are so used to living in a world full of pessimists.

Wherever you look there are signs of economic activity. Since the Olympics, shopping centres have had more of a buzz, cranes and concrete mixers are starting new construction contracts and traffic is being disrupted by more roadworks.

It always was a question of when the recovery would commence, not whether things would ever get better. No doubt my remarks will be met with derision by the 'flatliners' and the 'shock waves from Europe' brigade.

Few people really think that the future looks bleak. Most agree that during the next twenty years businesses will grow, incomes will increase and equity prices will rise significantly. I am willing to bet the FTSE will reach 8,000 in the next ten years. In the short term we are collectively cautious. It is safer to say, 'I expect another tough year before we see any real improvement', but I am willing to be bold and repeat what I said: 'Business is getting better and things are on the move.'

Unemployment figures fell again last week – do you get a sense that the economy is turning a corner or is something else going on?

I made the mistake recently of confusing a couple of weeks of bumper business with the first green shoots of a growth market. I should have known better. As soon as my optimistic forecast was printed in this column, sales slipped back and since then business has been at the unexciting level we have seen since 2008.

But I remain confident and regard the triple dip as a technical term created by statistical anoraks and welcomed by media doom-mongers who love to latch on to the latest bit of bad news.

There isn't another big dip, we are simply bumping along at a similar level to four years ago. But with a lot of businesses building cash reserves and many households keeping clear of too much credit we are getting poised for an upturn.

As well as the better employment numbers, the stock market has suddenly realised that share prices have been held back for far too long and it suddenly seems fashionable to talk about good news.

I suppose we at Timpson are in a pretty good place to spot the improvement when it comes (despite my false hopes last autumn). Our weekly sales closely follow the footfall on the high street. There are a few quirks: shoe repairs are busier in the winter when wetter weather finds the holes in people's soles; we have a peak for taking passport photos in January when families turn their mind to their next holiday; key cutting has its biggest volume in the second week of September, with keys for kids going back to school. But our sales are steady enough for me to take a regular reading of the economic temperature.

I have never got a grip of macroeconomics (I am not sure anyone has!) so cannot claim to have a formula that forecasts our financial future. I am just as suspicious of analysts and expert stock pickers as I was of Horace Batchelor and his Infra Draw method that forecast the football pool results in the 1950s. But despite my scepticism and lack of expertise I remain an optimist.

I guarantee that however many dips are announced by the Office of National Statistics any business with a really good idea and great people will continue to flourish.

I own an upmarket ladies' dress shop selling outfits from Paris and Milan as well as from the UK. We are doing well with a huge customer base. As the Eurozone could break up in the future, should I be doing something now to protect my business?

I haven't a clue where the Euro crisis is heading, but it's probably better knowing you don't know than pretending to have the answer to a situation no one seems to understand.

Twenty years ago I said the EU would end in tears. I could see the point in Europeans being nice to each other rather than waging war, but once they started telling each other what to do there was bound to be trouble. Our different cultures aren't designed to play on the same team.

The Euro has distorted normal market forces. Individual currencies help to correct the balance of trade between one country and another. When weak countries devalue, lower-priced exports can help stimulate demand. It is not surprising the Euro has been such bad news for the poorer economies.

It hasn't been great for Greece but why should we be sucked in to the present doom and gloom? Recent talk of the lost decade followed by years of stagnation is almost certainly way off the mark. It was refreshing to listen to an economist saying recently that too many forecasters fail to look beyond this year – his prediction for the next 35 years is so optimistic that he has the UK top of the European league by 2050.

Whatever happens, one thing is certain: there is very little you or I can do about it, and Joe Public (while still complaining) will carry on filling his car with fuel, buying a television for the kid's bedroom and having a few beers every Friday night.

This might seem a long way away from your dress shop but I am getting to the point. I haven't a clue whether it will be easier and cheaper or tougher and more expensive for you to import from Paris and Milan, so don't double-guess what will happen to Euro-economics. Stick to what you know best.

In twenty years the Italians and French will still be producing great fashion clothing and there will continue to be a strong demand for their products in your type of shop.

Forget economic forecasting and simply concentrate on doing what you do best, making sure that you do it better than your competitors.

The Beecroft review has suggested changes to employment rules, such as reducing the consultancy period for 'collective redundancies' and relaxing employment tribunal rules. Would these changes really make you or any other employer more likely to take on staff, as the government is claiming?

Plenty of pressing problems are more likely to limit the level of employment, like the availability of finance and confidence in the economy. But a hint of red tape being reduced would help, and will indicate that government understands how business works.

I got a reality check a few weeks ago when I was showing a Norwegian party round a training workshop that covers all our skills from key cutting and watch repairs to dry cleaning and passport photos. 'If this was in Norway', said one of the group, 'you would be dealing with six different unions and each trade would have its own set of regulations.' Perhaps we should be grateful that we, in the UK, are not as tied up in red tape.

Most employment legislation is based on the belief that, given a free hand, managers will exploit their workforce. Some of us take a different view. Creating a great place to work is one of the best ways to build a successful business.

But some of the regulations make our job more difficult. They protect the poor performers at the expense of our best people. No one wants to work alongside a characterless clock-watcher but it takes a lot of management time to say goodbye to someone who is letting the side down. It is a lot simpler and much more honest to explain to the colleague that 'your best will never be good enough for us' and part company as quickly, pleasantly and generously as possible.

But we are stuck with the misguided idea that to be successful management should follow a process – so we live in a world where sticking to guidelines is seen as more important than making a profit.

We should be grateful that we are less regulated than many countries – I wouldn't like to run a chain of shops in France. Complex employment law is one of the main reasons why the Timpson business will stay exclusively in the British Isles. Perhaps this is proof that less regulation encourages managers like me to employ more people.

Do you think it's wrong to force unemployed people to work for free if they're to keep their state benefits?

I can understand the general reluctance to give benefit claimants 'something for nothing' and the desire to give everyone work experience but I wouldn't force anyone to take an unpaid job.

It is time to face up to the fact that people differ in their ability and attitude. Whether it is due to their genes or upbringing, some are not right for sitting behind a desk or stacking supermarket shelves and, indeed, some folk are simply not suited for the world of work.

We spend a fair slice of our management time saying goodbye to colleagues who discover they are not keen on cobbling or simply have a poor attitude to work. I am happy to give work experience to people who are keen to find a career but I only want to work with people who want to work.

The recent criticism of Poundland who opened their doors to the unemployed was grossly unfair. It was a case of providing free training rather than getting free labour.

Most strands of our welfare system bring unintended consequences. I know a young man whose partner recently got a place at college. He also enrolled. He didn't want to study but if they were both students they could claim free childcare for their baby. When the local benefits office insisted that he needed to make a few job applications to retain his jobseeker's allowance, the college gave him coaching on interview techniques that make sure you are not offered a role. (The college wanted to keep him on their books as the student count determines their income!)

The benefits system is so complicated that few people understand it, especially those who never have the need to make a claim. It would be fascinating to see how different families fund their lives. My guess is that, far from being fair, some play the system while others are in desperate need of more help.

For some time I have proposed my simple answer. Give everyone the same level of benefit. Under my dream system every British citizen – man, woman and child, in or out of work – would receive £400 a month and £200 on their birthday, an automatic benefit that gives each family basic cash in the same way that Monopoly players get £200 every time they pass Go. This universal payout would replace unemployment benefit, family support, pensions and most other welfare payments.

To keep things simple I would make all tax rates 20% (income tax, death duty, capital gains and VAT would all be the same).

My uncomplicated tax and benefit system would be easy to understand and much fairer; there would be little need to fill in a form. The workload of both the benefits offices and the Inland Revenue would reduce dramatically.

It would take a very brave politician to make such a radical change, which would produce some losers as well as winners and should substantially reduce the number of civil servants. My dream is unlikely to turn into reality.

I was intrigued by your suggestion concerning a simplified tax and social payments system. A 20% rate

for all taxes and a payment of £5,000 per annum for every person with no other social payments has a catching simplicity. I am, however, finding it difficult to do the maths. If the UK population is 60 million, then the bill just for the payment side comes out at £300 billion, which is just over half the total tax paid in to the Exchequer. Is this feasible? I like your idea very much, but could you flesh it out with a little more detail? For instance, what would the effect of a 20% tax rate have on revenue? What about all the other claims on revenue, e.g. defence/ pensions, etc.?

You are right, of course. If you assume that my dream of a simplified tax and benefit system is applied to the existing structure, my numbers don't add up. But in my dream, things do change – dramatically for the better.

With every UK citizen having the right to the universal benefit of £400 a month and £200 on their birthday, no forms need filling and there is no need for any benefit-based civil servants to check the red tape.

The flat 20% tax rate will eliminate a lot of tax avoidance and evasion. Businesses will be happy to be based in the UK and multi-millionaires will be just as pleased to live in Maidenhead as Monaco. As a result, despite much lower rates, tax revenues will rise.

After a few years we will really reap the benefits of my simplified system when the balance of our economy shifts dramatically in favour of the private sector.

A lot of public sector jobs will disappear and there will be false fears of a permanent jump in the number of people who are unemployed (at least every member of their family has the benefit of £400 a month and £200 on their birthday), but the jobs that go will be dead-end tasks – unnecessary administration, superfluous policy-making and boring box-ticking. As new jobs appear in the private sector these lifetime civil servants will find new roles that, for the first time in their lives, will create wealth and strengthen UK plc.

We will move towards a society that values work and is pleased to pour praise on the high achievers who make plenty of money. We employ a lot of colleagues who are proud to produce a decent pay packet by earning big bonuses. But many of their mates down the pub think they are mugs – by cleverly working the present benefit system their household has a bigger net income than their hard-working neighbour. No wonder we have a broken society.

A simple change in tax and benefits could do more than just balance the economy. It could, in the process, sort out a lot of the problems in our society – but I did say at the beginning it is only a dream!

We're getting calls from energy consultants saying that with energy prices rocketing again we should re-examine our ROI (return on investment) assumptions from investing in new energy-efficient lighting and insulation in our warehouses. What sort of approaches have you heard businesses adopting?

As I lack the patience to dig into the detail, I leave our cost-cutting to my colleagues, but I notice that every time they examine energy costs they manage to save some money.

There will be a mathematical formula to tell you whether to change light bulbs. You need to factor in the size of your warehouse, your working hours, the cost of the bulbs currently being used, and maybe a solar panel on the roof. But don't bother to do the sums yourself. This is the perfect time to call in a consultant. Use someone who has made the same calculations many times before – but don't pay up front, pay him by results.

Utility pricing doesn't seem to reward loyal customers. By switching suppliers and taking advantage of special tariffs or subsidies many a good deal can be done. But this is a specialist field, so use an expert.

The government commitment to renewable energy will lead to some dramatic increases in costs over the next few years, so energy efficiency makes a lot of sense. For most of us it isn't a question of saving the earth – it will simply be a vital way to save cash when we are forced to use expensive sources of power to meet the requirements of the Climate Change Act (2008) and the EU Renewables Directive (2008).

The appearance of more and more wind farms is proof that energy policy is dominated by a drive to cut greenhouse gases and increase renewable sources.

As a result business is going to face a bigger and bigger bill.

What's a reasonable debt-to-GDP ratio in a household, and should the same rule apply to nations?

I'm a fanatical follower of Mr Micawber, only happy when income exceeds expenditure and cash flow is positive. I check our cash position every weekday against the same day last year – a report that reveals at a glance the health of our business.

I don't like borrowing money and am paranoid about paying off my credit card balance quickly enough to avoid interest. You will have already guessed that I think the current levels of personal and government debt are far too high.

We have seen the banking sector bringing us big trouble by believing 'you have to speculate to accumulate' and I now wonder whether we can trust the Treasury, who believe 'we must spend our way out of trouble'. All these clever people, most of whom have never run a business, seem to fly in the face of historical wisdom. They wrap up their policy in grand-sounding gobbledygook like 'quantitative easing' but in truth they are simply spending money we haven't got. Unfortunately too many people are fooled by this modern version of the emperor's new clothes.

Cash control is one of the best management tools ever invented. As long as you live within your means you will stay in control of your business and your life. Satan is always sitting on the businessman's shoulder suggesting that a rash rush of investment is the route to real success.

Those who have the discipline to keep cash in the bank will reap the rewards in the next five years.

I see the government is considering bringing in the private sector to help it run some of its Small and Medium Enterprise schemes. Do you think people with commercial experience can really make a difference?

I feel like we've been here before and even well-meaning entrepreneurs can't influence the bureaucratic juggernaut of the state.

I am coming to the conclusion that the best way government can help business is to leave us all alone.

In the 1970s I was on the Footwear Economic Development Council, one of several sector committees created to help get British business back on track. Our job was to stop the decline in UK shoe making. For three years there were regular tripartite meetings between business, government and the unions. We produced plenty of reports but didn't do any good. When we started talking, over 100,000 people worked in British footwear factories; today there are fewer than 5,000.

Ten years ago I spent a week in the Department for Trade and Industry (the bit of Whitehall that has become BIS) and was impressed with the intelligence and friendliness of their senior civil servants. But I was amazed how much time they spent developing support schemes and planning conferences that business didn't need. A lot of their time was taken up with joined-up thinking, which often meant scoring points against other government departments. I asked one of the clever mandarins whether he knew they were chasing shadows. 'Of course', he replied, 'but I love my job.'

I spent a morning with the Director of Training to find out how much of their training scheme was to do with trade and industry. The answer was 'None! We train our people to be civil servants.'

I expect BIS has developed a more commercial focus than

the DTI I saw a decade ago. But it is still bound to be difficult, even for streetwise business people like James Caan and Lord Sugar, to tune in to the ways of Whitehall. The structured life of a government department is a long way away from the competitive world of profit and loss.

If BIS has a role, it should be to help and support business by taking away any obstacles that get in the way of success. We don't need free advice from a consultant or training grants that come with complicated strings attached, and we don't want to attend another free 'New Way Forward' conference. We would rather save the money and use it to cut taxes.

As I never tire of pointing out, management is not a process. It is an art, not a science. Successful companies ignore the rules and use their initiative. Such *laissez-faire* thinking is unfamiliar ground in Whitehall, where it will be difficult to resist the temptation to interfere.

There is no need to search for a formula for success when a near-perfect system already exists. BIS should leave us alone and simply let the market economy do all the planning and joined-up thinking on their behalf.

The government has repeatedly stated that business must create more jobs to get the country out of this patchy economic recovery. Are there any realistic incentives that would encourage you to create jobs? For instance, if companies received directly from a government agency, the unemployment benefit of an individual for the first three months of his or her employment with them, do you think it would encourage

them to take on extra people to train and usefully employ them?

I have yet to find a government subsidy that is provided without strings attached.

Three years ago we spent a lot of time and attended a series of meetings searching for a formula that would allow us to receive support for our apprenticeship training. We discovered that funds could only be offered if we changed our training to conform with government guidelines, and the subsidy could only be claimed through a training agency who took a substantial slice of the money for ticking the boxes on our behalf.

After eighteen months it was clear that the training agencies didn't understand the way we do business and that their process was more important than our apprentices. So we filed all the papers and forgot all about it. Although we were promised up to £1m a year I would rather pay for the privilege of doing things our way.

So would we employ more people if a subsidy came with no onerous conditions? Probably not. We will only take on the people we need. I have seen what happens when you are overstaffed – the business loses its buzz. It may sound strange but we have often found that by increasing the number of colleagues in a shop we reduce the turnover.

Your ingenious suggestion to divert unemployment pay to a new employer may appeal to politicians but it suffers from the same problem shown by most government schemes – it costs money that has to come from the taxpayer. I am pretty sure the best way to create more real jobs is through less intervention and lower taxes.

With banks being reluctant to lend, there's a lot of talk about online marketplaces that allow companies to raise debt or equity finance from consumers – sometimes their own customers. What do you make of them – and, if you ever needed to, would you ever turn to your customers to raise growth capital? Doesn't the 'Timpson bond' have a certain ring about it?

The idea of borrowing money from customers fills me with horror. Our lawyers would have a field day drawing up the documentation and making sure we carry out all the corporate governance needed to protect these minority shareholders.

For years we have tried to avoid borrowing. Before the recession I was accused of being irresponsible: others said we should leverage the company assets to borrow money and invest in growth. No one is saying that now.

I once conjured up a cunning plan to create cash inspired by the Bank of England's programme of quantitative easing, but instead of printing money I would issue Timpson discount vouchers.

We already sell vouchers at our Anglesey pubs, The Oyster Catcher and The White Eagle. They work well – people pay for the food weeks before they or their friends come for dinner, and some vouchers are never used.

As well as extending the scheme to all our shops, I planned to pay our suppliers with Timpson vouchers (carrying a redemption value after six months). With a decent 15% discount I could see Timpson vouchers become an alternative form of currency. Once the idea caught on I would use them to pay landlords, utilities, local authorities and the tax man, and all of them would flock to our shops to get their shoes repaired.

I feel there must be a flaw in my voucher scheme but haven't spotted it yet. Mind you, I am still trying to work out what will go wrong with quantitative easing.

What do you make of George Osborne's shares for rights idea? A good way for small businesses to grow with the help of staff, or a fudge of two very different issues – employment regulations and shared ownership?

Once, when I had nothing better to do, I compiled a list of irritating business phrases, which included: 'Let's run this up the flagpole and see if anyone salutes it.' (Translation: 'Here is my latest idea, which I won't take seriously unless people say they like it.')

This idea is in the flagpole category.

It may be wise to wait and see if there is any more detail before jumping to a conclusion, but I already reckon the idea combines two misconceptions:

1. Employee shares are a magic wand.
   It is, quite rightly, fashionable to admire The John Lewis Partnership, but their success isn't just due to the share structure. Share ownership doesn't in itself create a more committed workforce. In many small businesses, like ours, it is much better to award a significant bonus based on profits than create the complications that come with issuing equity.

2. Employment legislation gets in the way of good business. Why should anyone want to give up their employment rights? The law only covers things that a reasonable boss would take for granted. The regulations are fine, it's the lawyers and consultants who cause problems by adding another layer of rules labelled 'best practice'.

The exchange of employment rights for company shares isn't a great deal for either employer or employee, so if someone tries to run it up the Timpson flagpole I wouldn't salute it.

You've said that twenty years ago you predicted the EU would 'end in tears'. What do you make of the current talk of Britain eventually having a more informal free trade relationship with Europe?

I did indeed suggest the EU would have an unhappy ending and see no reason to change my mind. The Common Market was established for the right reasons. In a world stifled by tariff barriers, a free trade area was a welcome boost for exporters and importers, and the spirit of cooperation has brought an unprecedented period of peace in Europe.

If it had simply remained a trading arrangement all would have been fine, but Euro-politicians were bound to bring in Euro-rules including working time directives and compulsory use of the kilo. Once they agreed on a common currency there was no turning back – the Euro had to lead to a unified finance policy, which is a short step from the Federation of Europe.

We didn't sign up to losing our identity. We want the

freedom to be different and to decide for ourselves if prisoners should be entitled to vote or whether there should be a quota of women in the boardroom. Every year we find a further slice of our life is being dictated from Brussels in a parliament we seldom see by politicians few of us know (can you name your MEP?). There are 27 Commissioners, one for each country. Check out which ones are responsible for Finance and Economic Affairs, Industry and Entrepreneurship – the Commissioners from Italy and Spain.

The prospect of becoming an associate member has considerable appeal, but I doubt whether we can retain the trade benefits without keeping to most of the rules. Swiss traders have to comply with Euro-regulations if they want to do business in the EU, and we will have to do the same, but at least Brussels won't be setting our interest rates or telling us when we have to take bank holidays or change the clocks.

We wouldn't want to miss out on the European market, but relegation to associate status may make us pay even more attention to business in the fastest-growing markets around the world – not a bad strategy.

We are more likely to remain as friends if we keep clear of full membership. A centrally governed United States of Europe will either quickly split into the 'haves' and 'have nots' or the rich countries will have to pay penal taxes to bail out their poorer partners. I still think it will end in tears.

I expect the recent spell of extreme weather will feature later this year in a few Chairmen's Reports as an excuse

for poor results. Does the weather make a difference to your sales, and will climate change be good or bad for your business?

Of course, the weather influences our business, especially when breakfast TV presenters wake up the country with talk of treacherous conditions causing schools to close for health and safety reasons and motorists not risking a short drive to the shops.

But bad news for one business can be good news for another. We like lots of rain – it shows the holes in your soles and helps sell umbrellas. Sun is good for our photo shops – people go out and take more pictures. A heatwave is perfect for the ice cream vans and I am told that Talk Talk think heavy snow is 'magic dust' because people make more phone calls when they are trapped at home.

We never do well during a big freeze, when only a handful of people go shopping (and those that do wear boots that don't need repairing). I wouldn't have wanted to be a cobbler in the Ice Age.

The media seem delighted whenever they discover a climate fact that is the highest, lowest, wettest or coldest figure since records began. They see this as evidence that global warming is becoming a reality. Anyone under 30 probably thinks they are the first generation to experience hurricanes, high water and heatwaves but those who are much older should know better. I was pictured by my father in 1947 playing in a deep snow drift near Alderley Edge. I clearly remember 1962/63 when the big freeze started on Boxing Day and continued for over three months – there was no chance of playing golf until April. Our shops suffered a severe sales drop in 1976 when the ten-week heatwave made it too hot to shop. The hot spell only ended when Denis Howell, the Sports Minister, was appointed Minister for Drought (it rained within days of him picking up his new portfolio). Perhaps Maria Miller is poised to be appointed Minister for Weather.

I am happy to accept whatever weather comes my way and regard it as arrogant for man to think he can control the climate. I cringe whenever I spot a wind farm and think of the tax I am paying to provide a politically unsustainable eyesore that doesn't solve a problem that may never exist.

The problem with the British weather is that it comes when you least expect it. Fashion retailers often suffer at the start of each new season. In March shop windows are full of summer dresses but sunny days seldom start until well into June. By then the dresses are in the sale. There is a similar problem in the autumn. At the beginning of September shops display bags of boots and rails full of coats just in time for an Indian summer. The snow they need often doesn't fall until February. Late seasons cause lower sales and higher mark-downs.

I have the solution: simply change the calendar by six weeks, so, for example, the beginning of March turns into the middle of January and 8 November becomes 27 September. Following my date change a July heatwave will come in May, helping to sell loads of sandals at full price. The Indian summer will arrive in time to ensure a good clearance in the July sale, and winter will start well before Christmas, a big boost for shops selling boots.

There is a snag. My idea poses a political problem – to change the calendar we would have to stick on the same date for 42 days. I thought of picking my birthday, but by the time the calendar resumes its progress I would be aged 112. I considered 25 December so that, for six weeks, every day could be Christmas Day. But as it is a quarter day our landlords might try to collect rent 42 times over. Eventually I found the perfect date, just before the end of the financial year to give us more time to pay the tax man.

The date I have picked is 1 April.

A Personal View

During the last few years I have seized on questions that give me an excuse to bang on about my pet topics and talk about the lighter side of life. The answers give a clue to what floats my boat – a mixture of Mustique, tennis, horseracing, golf, writing, the business, and life with Alex who claims I am turning into a grumpy old man.

To be fair, I have found plenty of things to be grumpy about. I hate filling in forms, most meetings, long words when little ones will do, being kept waiting by a call centre, and jobsworth administrators who insist that I stick to their rules. I also have an aversion to poor customer service, political correctness and people whose priority is to stick to a proper process.

Being someone who doesn't like detail or sticking to rules (unless they are laid down by Alex) I am well suited to Upside Down Management. I used to be worried that I can't cut a key but now know the boss doesn't need to be an expert at every job in the business, he just needs to be good at being a boss.

Kit Green, James's predecessor as Timpson Managing Director, once told me: 'You will never understand how your employees live their lives.' He has a point. I have had plenty of personal privileges and precious little hardship, but 90 foster children and their families have widened my education. I have learnt a lot by living with Alex.

I've been lucky – with so many interesting things to do, it

is difficult to know when work stops and leisure begins, but if the business is your number one hobby, time management can be a major challenge. I can't say anything has been planned. The business has given me the opportunity and Alex has given me permission to spend a large chunk of my time doing things I thoroughly enjoy.

Some parts of this collection from the column might not appear to have much to do with business, but what happens at home can have a big influence on what goes on at the office.

*

How do you cope when your staff do a better job than you could – turn to the happy pills?

I am delighted to report that everyone working in our shops is better than me when it comes to shoe repairs, watch repairs, and all the other jobs we do. I am so hopelessly ham-fisted that Alex declared me a definite dunce at DIY 40 years ago and I haven't been allowed to do any decorating since – and no one lets me cut a key.

It gets worse. With my lack of discipline and attention to detail I'd make a useless Area Manager, would be a woeful Warehouse Manager and pathetic in Personnel.

Thankfully my role is to help create a culture that helps our experts flourish, by setting the strategy and clearing away any obstacles that get in the way of progress. I don't need to be a good cobbler – I simply need to know when the good cobblers need help.

But my job is changing. At 67, day-to-day operations have less appeal and there are plenty of people who relish the tasks I am now happy to avoid, but I can still offer the advantage of experience.

Since James took over day-to-day control I have become more of a mentor than a manager. Eventually the business will move on to the point that my experience becomes irrelevant. When everyone knows more than me it will be time to play more golf.

In the meantime I'm staying on the payroll.

Do you suffer from stress? What do you do about it?

I've had periodic bouts of stress for over 35 years. It is an affliction I would not wish on anyone but it is comforting to know I am not alone – I understand 20% of us suffer from time to time.

Those that never experience these 'black periods' in their life find it difficult to understand; some suggest you should 'get a grip' or 'snap out of it'. They don't realise there is nothing more you want than a relaxed day full of purpose, clear thinking, and achievement. Instead you constantly turn things through your mind without coming to any conclusions. Your mood moves from depressed misery to nervous apprehension. Every morning you hope it has gone, but before breakfast you know it will be another difficult day.

Many years ago a doctor explained to me that stress is nature's way of 'saying enough is enough'. I'm thankful that early on I realised I needed his help and wasn't ashamed of popping pills.

He told me to think of it in the same way as a common cold. You don't know how you got it or how long it will last, but at least you know it will definitely disappear.

I started my own business three years ago. For the first two years I worked twelve-hour days and weekends and after a few months, friends drifted away and I got used to being on my own. Now I am finally in a position where I can delegate to my staff and start having a life outside of my business but I'm having trouble letting go. How do you draw a line between work and your personal life? I'm worried I'll never get my friends back.

I know how you feel. In 1987 I finally took notice of Alex, who had been telling me for years that my life was full of nothing but work. It isn't surprising friends disappear if you don't give them any of your time. I never got to the bottom of my 'to do' list, so I always had an urgent task on my agenda and felt guilty whenever I wasn't working – which, like you, included weekends.

A couple of things got me out of the rut. One day each week I started having a tennis lesson or played a game of golf with Gordon, one of the few friends I had left. I was still behind my desk by 10.30am but, although it wasn't quite what Alex had in mind, it was a move in the right direction. More popular was my decision to take Tuesdays off, a plan that only lasted a year but was enough to prove I was not indispensable. To be honest, the business did much better without my undivided attention.

If you do everything yourself, your company can't grow.

A bit of time off and a lot of delegation are essential parts of getting bigger.

For the last three years you must have turned down loads of invitations (although after a time people stop asking). To change your life, start saying 'Yes'. Meet mates for a pub night, take weekend breaks, go to the football or a game of golf – and before saying goodbye, put another date in your diary.

I no longer feel guilty about taking time off. Last week, as well as having a snooker evening, I played tennis twice, plus two games of golf. The business is benefiting from my absence but Alex now thinks I play too much sport. Perhaps I should start taking Tuesdays off.

Would you ever go into business with your wife, Alex? I once worked for a small firm run by a husband and wife team where they ended up working completely different shifts on purpose so they barely had to see each other: a day shift for her, and a self-imposed night shift for him!

I was asked a similar question a couple of years ago, which I boldly answered without consulting Alex. This time I asked for her views. 'Certainly not', was her immediate reply, 'it would be a nightmare.' I agree. Alex hates meetings, couldn't be keen on cash control and would always put people ahead of profit. If we worked together I would have to appoint Alex as the Chief Executive because I can't imagine her ever taking instructions from someone else.

There isn't a golden rule. Some couples make the perfect

business partnership, especially those who met through their business relationship and got married later. For many it becomes the perfect way to start a family business.

But it is important to draw a dividing line between the office, home life, and leisure. Both need to escape from day-to-day business problems – it won't help if the sales budget is still being discussed over Sunday lunch.

People who live above the shop running a pub or a post office can put a lot of pressure on their marriage, especially if they are also bringing up a young family. With each new arrival it is important that one takes maternity or paternity leave. During pre-school years parental attachment is a vital part of growing up. If you both look after the business, who is looking after the children?

Years ago, when Alex was stopped for speeding, the policeman asked: 'Have you a job or are you a housewife?' In fact Alex has found more than a full-time job as a housewife who looked after loads of children and still supports several foster families.

Our arrangement works well. When I have a business problem Alex acts as my perfect sounding board, and I have given a little bit of support to help her be a full-time parent and foster parent.

We never contemplated working together and I know exactly what role I play at home. A few years ago, when I was our golf club Captain, one of the members rang me up at home. Alex answered the phone. 'Can I speak to the Captain?' he asked. Alex replied: 'You're speaking to her.'

I know you're a big Man City fan. That club is an anomaly now in that it has one, uber-rich owner. For the majority of English Premier League clubs, however, it's increasingly looking as if the game is up. In essence, their revenues aren't great enough to support the debts/ wages they've incurred. What would you do to sort out the flawed finances of the beautiful game?

I wish I had a magic formula to put football on a firm financial footing but I don't. Thankfully, when they get the chance to invest in a football club, most successful businessmen lose contact with their commercial instinct, giving the rest of us the chance to enjoy what is indeed a beautiful game.

I can't get my mind round a business where weekly wages are often considerably more than weekly turnover, with some employees paid £100,000 for a week in which they don't turn up for work due to a niggling injury.

And I don't understand why their bank manager happily backs the purchase of even more players at over £10 million each to strengthen the squad of an already cash-strapped club.

Funding a football club can't be compared with controlling a cobbling company, but I do have a couple of ideas to encourage cost-cutting and make the Premiership more competitive.

1. To create a 'level playing field', the width of the opposition's goal posts will be reduced by six inches for every £1 million invested in the players declared on the team sheet.
2. Instead of docking points for going into administration,

the troubled club will be entitled to acquire any player of their choice on a free transfer.

My ideas probably won't work, so I am happy to remain a pure spectator and continue to use my City season tickets (whenever Sky TV's fixture changes fit in with my diary).

Do you sit on other boards as a non-executive? If you could sit on any business's board, which would it be?

A few years ago a head-hunter approached me about one non-executive directorship but I clearly failed to make a great impression and was never called to a proper interview.

If asked to join another board today I would almost certainly say 'No', but I could be tempted by one of our big retailers like Next, John Lewis, Tesco or Marks and Spencer. Not that they could learn much from me, but I am sure I would learn a lot from them.

However, I am well aware that being Chairman of the board of a private business with no outside shareholders is very different from the demands of a public company. My maverick approach and enthusiasm for entrepreneurial freedom would not be compatible with the plc preference for best practice and a proper process. If the non-exec is needed to tick the governance box, I am not your man.

Over the last twenty years my involvement outside Timpson has been partly with charities but mostly with schools – I am currently a Governor of our local primary, which educated many of our foster children, and I am a Trustee of Uppingham School, the senior school where our own children went. I have thoroughly enjoyed watching the highly successful development of both schools at close hand.

Although Alex thinks I am a workaholic, I would prefer another two weeks away with her on Mustique than be at a meeting every month round someone else's board table.

Setting aside your existing directors, who seem to be doing an excellent job, if you had the chance, who would you appoint as your perfect board and would it include Angelina Jolie?

This must be one of the trickiest questions I have tackled. Picking people is the most difficult part of the job.

My first choice is Simon Cowell, someone who seems to make a lot of money almost by instinct. The thought of this media magnate getting mixed up with a collection of cobblers is bound to bring us plenty of publicity.

Next I have chosen Bill Gates, not for his IT expertise or his money – I just admire the way he has given his wealth away. We like getting involved in the charitable causes we support. Bill Gates will be able to tell us how The Big Society can work in practice.

My third pick is Terry Leahy, probably the best retailer in the UK. He has given us all a masterclass in how to continually reinvent a business, and will be an ideal mentor to James, who is keen to keep our company growing. Family businesses gain a lot from the stability provided by family management, so James stays on the board, as does Paresh, my FD. It is a joy to work with an accountant who understands Upside Down Management.

I am including my wife Alex, who has been advising me for over 40 years. It is about time her contribution is recognised. Alex doesn't like meetings but may be tempted to attend when she hears the name of my next choice.

Mick Jagger has a good business brain with an innate ability to keep costs below budget. His mean streak will help to keep us all under control.

That, finally, brings me to Angelina Jolie. James points out that we have a common interest in adoption and reckons she would be a good addition to the team.

I didn't need any more persuading.

What do you regard as your biggest single business mistake? And would you change it if you could, or was it a good learning experience?

I have made so many errors it is difficult to pick which one to confess in this column. I have chosen a mistake made many years ago – in the passage of time, personal failings become less embarrassing, and anyway, I was a young man at the time.

Most of my mistakes involved people – failing to recruit the ideal candidate, picking the wrong man for the job, and hanging on to key colleagues doing desperate damage to the company. Too often I hoped they would get better. I was desperately keen to avoid having to tell them to leave. My delay in tackling problem people cost a lot of money.

Sometimes I failed to recognise my own weaknesses. In 1983 I was given a cartoon in which I was depicted holding a crystal ball – a reference to my reputation for making intuitive decisions and failing to follow up the detail. This side to my character was revealed in 1969 when I started a new chain of shops called Shoetique.

It was a good idea, ahead of its time. The high street was full of shoe shops and fashion retailers, but very few stores sold women's shoes alongside clothing. That was what Shoetique did, several years before Next was founded or Top Shop set up shoe concessions.

It failed because I didn't delegate. I knew how to buy and sell shoes but that didn't give me the experience to tackle the rag trade. I didn't know what styles or sizes to buy in what quantity, and how to do the display.

By the time we brought in a manager with fashion experience it was too late. We persevered for three years and opened four shops but they all lost money.

The whole episode taught me a few lessons.

1. A good idea in theory doesn't always work out in practice.
2. Being successful in one business doesn't mean you can transfer your skills in another.
3. I don't have the patience to deal with the detail.
4. Find an expert and delegate.

It was an expensive way to gain experience, which I have never forgotten. It cost £75,000 to shut up shop at Shoetique. I have kept clear of fashion retailing ever since.

I haven't taken a break for eighteen months now because of the tough trading conditions my company finds itself

in. I could do with getting away to clear my head but I can see the next three to six months will be crucial again for us. Have you found yourself in a similar situation and what have you done?

Life is too short to spend all your time at the office. Your obsession with work means you are missing out on your hobbies, losing touch with friends and most of all failing to stay close to your family. If you have children, spend as much time with them as you can – they grow up very quickly.

My wife, Alex, would never have let me miss a holiday. Even at my most critical time, in the middle of our management buyout, I still managed a three-week family break. Although I have no intention of retiring, I plan to add an extra week of holiday every year. The scheme is working well this year – I am already booked to be away nine weeks.

Your reluctance to take time off suggests a lack of trust in your colleagues and a serious shortage of delegation. If you haven't got a good number two you can trust, get one. I am pretty sure there will be someone on your team who is quite capable of handling things in your absence. They can always contact you if there is a crisis.

A couple of weeks away will almost certainly do you, and your business, a lot of good.

Don't delay, book a holiday immediately. Once you are sitting on the beach thinking about things from a distance, your business might not seem so bad. But if on reflection you still find future prospects pretty impossible, perhaps it is time to sell up.

Do you have a personal motto in business or a creed that you live your business life by?

I don't go in for personal mottoes or mission statements, but have found several things that work so well I intend to always keep doing them.

Here are my top ten:

1. Pick personalities – when you recruit, look at the person not the CV.
2. Look after your best people – find lots of tangible ways to praise your star performers.
3. Discriminate against drongos – if you employ Mr Lazy, Miss Dishonest, Mrs Late or Mr Grumpy, they will get in the way of good business. Don't dither, get them to leave as soon as you can.
4. Don't issue orders – trust your people to run the business on your behalf.
5. Visit every shop – relentlessly keep meeting your colleagues, seeing every part of the business.
6. Praise ten times as much as you criticise – you do much more good by saying and writing 'well done' than telling people off.
7. Keep investing in training – if you keep helping your people to get better, they will make you more money.
8. Take plenty of holidays – workaholics seldom work miracles. Book regular vacations, take a break from the office and give your colleagues a bit of a break from you.
9. Check the bank balance every day. Compare your cash

with the same day last year – it is the best way to measure company performance.

10. Make easy decisions. Don't make life difficult – concentrate on the no-brainers.

What's the worst-selling product line that you have personally championed at Timpson, and have you thought about why it didn't work?

At the height of the dot-com boom I backed a brave scheme devised by my son James, then a few years out of university and an enthusiastic young manager full of funky ideas – he called this one 'CityCobbler.com'.

The plan was simple. City customers could get their shoes repaired without even leaving their desk. An email would bring young Timpson colleague Keith, a keen motorbiker, speeding to your office to take your shoes to our nearest shop. While you wear a pair of loan shoes the job is done, and within an hour your footwear is returned as good as new.

Initial results were excellent. Two customers on Monday, three on Tuesday and five on Wednesday. I was dreaming of dot-com success and owning a new business with a multi-million stock market value. And Keith was happy spending much of the day on his bike.

On Thursday a journalist from the *Evening Standard* was due to test the service for a feature in Friday's paper. Sadly, on Thursday Keith fell off his bike on the way to work and broke his collar bone. The new service was suspended. The newspaper saw the funny side of our embarrassment but their article proved that not all publicity is good news.

City Cobbler was a one-week wonder. By the time Keith returned to work our little bit of goodwill had evaporated. Like a lot of the dot-com ideas it relied on people power for success.

I am pleased to report that Keith still works for Timpson. You will find him in one of our City branches, but these days you have to take your shoes to him.

I'm constantly being frustrated by little things in my business. They niggle and irritate and get me down. What are the things that annoy you most in your daily business life?

Things don't irritate me – it's people who don't pick up their telephone.

I hate office voicemail. Some people expect every caller to leave a message.

'You are through to the voicemail of Geoffrey Jones. I am not available at the moment. Try my PA Sally Smart on 020 7XXX XXXX.'

I ring Sally's number and guess what? Her telephone goes straight to voicemail!

I leave a message: 'Please ask Geoffrey to call me. I am around until 5.00pm.'

Having heard nothing, I ring again at 4.30pm. Geoffrey is still on voicemail but I get through to Sally. 'He has been in back-to-back meetings all day. If I can't get hold of him by 5.00pm I'll make sure he rings in the morning.' He didn't.

When you track down these elusive people they always

have an excuse. 'It's our year end.' 'I never got your message.' Or the most irritating: 'I was just about to ring you.'

Voicemail is banned in our office. When you contact Timpson House you speak to Dorys. If the person you want is unavailable Dorys does all she can to help.

'What's the topic this week?' asked Alex when she saw me writing this column. 'Voicemail', I replied.

'That reminds me', continued Alex, 'last Friday I tried your mobile three times and you completely ignored me.'

'Sorry', I said, 'I never got your message.'

What is the worst piece of advice you have ever had?

I wish no one had ever suggested that it was worth opening a shoe repair shop on Wardour Street, right in the middle of Soho. But I only have myself to blame. I looked at the site three times before giving the go-ahead, and on every occasion the area was buzzing with people. I saw them all as potential customers – especially for the repair of stilettos (the slimmer the heel, the quicker it wears out).

When the shop opened I quickly discovered my mistake. Our kind of multi-service shop wasn't providing the sort of service shoppers were seeking in Soho.

That was an expensive mistake but not as bad as KeyCall.

In the early 1990s I was given what seemed a ground-breaking idea – a car key rescue service. If you subscribed to our KeyCall club there was no need to worry about losing your car key. We would log the details of your car key code on a clever computer that could cut a duplicate, which our on-call biker delivered to your car within two hours.

It was an eccentric scheme that showed an unbelievable faith in logistics and technology, but I would not have lost as much money if I had ignored the advice of our direct marketing consultant, who, after what he called 'amazingly encouraging market research', persuaded me to spend 10% of Wayne Rooney's weekly wage (£300,000) on leaflets stuffed in the middle of several Sunday papers.

I started to worry on the first Sunday morning when I saw a man standing over the garbage bin outside our local Delamere Stores shaking out unwelcome flyers so he could concentrate on the bits he wanted to read.

I feared the worst but had no idea how catastrophic our failure would be. Following the £40,000 campaign we only signed up nine customers, of whom two worked in our office and another was my aunt.

It was an expensive experience I will never forget.

Sir Winston Churchill is replacing Elizabeth Fry on a new £5 note, which will be issued from 2016. If you were in charge of the Bank of England, who would you make sure got their face on banknotes?

Your excellent question led me to a lively discussion with Alex during most of a drive from Tarporley to Uppingham.

We ruled out early favourites Alexander Graham Bell, Arthur Conan Doyle and Alexander Fleming because they are all Scots and we can't be sure that Scotland will still be part of our economy in 2016.

We considered a long list of dead and famous candidates who could qualify, but Alex noticed the lack of women. I pointed out there will be plenty to choose from in 50 years' time but for now we decided it was appropriate to pick Emmeline Pankhurst, the pioneer of such dramatic changes, who just got the women's vote ahead of Marie Stopes, it being too soon to select Margaret Thatcher.

Alex had good reason for suggesting John Charnley, who developed hip replacement surgery, but keen to find some-one with a more universal appeal, we thought about sport. To encourage future British superstars our list included Fred Perry, Bobby Moore, and W.G. Grace.

We thought we ought to recognise the dramatic influ-ence of television and computers but had to rule out John Logie Baird (another Scot) so our technology candidate is Alan Turing.

Edward Elgar set a musical precedent by appearing on a £20 note, so to represent the arts we considered Gilbert and Sullivan but finally opted for John Lennon.

Passing Uttoxeter on the A50 we started to think about candidates who made a major difference to people's lives and discussed Lord Baden-Powell, Dr Barnardo (until we discov-ered he was born in Dublin) and William Wilberforce.

It was only then that I realised that, as this column appears in the Business Section, we should concentrate on the world of commerce. The City has already been repre-sented on a £50 note by John Houblon, the first Governor of the Bank of England, and one banker is probably enough. I wondered whether we could commemorate a retail champion – someone who founded a format that still survives on the high street. My candidates were Jesse Boot (Lord Trent), who not only developed Boots the Chemist but also masterminded

Nottingham University (for which I am personally grateful), and Simon Marks and Thomas Spencer who created M&S.

Although he wasn't a businessman we nearly gave the prize to the explorer Ernest Shackleton, who has often been used as the prime example of great leadership.

In the end we chose a man who created an amazingly strong company culture. We considered Joseph Rowntree for his philanthropy, we talked about the way the Lever Brothers, William and James, looked after their employees, but our ultimate choice to appear on a bank note is the man who created an employee-centred organisation that is stronger now than ever before.

Our nomination is John Spedan Lewis, who formed The John Lewis Partnership.

Jane Austen is to be the new face on the £10 note. A good decision, although I liked your choice of John Lewis. Who or what would be your choice for the fourth plinth in Trafalgar Square? The current masterpiece, an enormous Blue Cockerel, unveiled by Boris Johnson this week, is debatably interesting. Perhaps it will unite Tottenham and Chelsea supporters.

I thought of several fanciful ideas like picking a big pigeon, a bulldog or even a statue of Boris, but eventually decided that the perfect person to put on the plinth is C. Northcote Parkinson.

It is time we recognised the man whose *Parkinson's Law* contains more common-sense comments than a library full of modern management books. He didn't just recognise that

'Work expands to fill the time available for its completion' but also spotted why a bureaucracy steadily gets bigger, as do committees, where he pointed out: 'Time spent on any agenda item will be in inverse proportion to the sum involved.'

If Parkinson had written his book today he would have found enough material to fill many more than its original 120 pages. He would have spotted how governance, risk management, employment legislation and the fashion for joined-up thinking have added a few more layers of administration. He would have learned even more by looking at how things work in Brussels.

Like *Yes, Minister*, too many people see the funny side without learning from the main message. Taking action to avoid the consequences of 'Parkinson's Law' could cut red tape and overheads, accelerate the switch from public sector to private and encourage managers to concentrate more on the main task and less on their internal politics. The result would be a significant improvement in our economy!

The lessons of *Parkinson's Law* are even more relevant now than when it was written in 1956. I hope that every business school and management college has the book at the top of its recommended reading list.

Putting a statue of C. Northcote Parkinson on the plinth would pay attention to some of the most important management principles that so often get forgotten.

There are hundreds of business awards out there, but many seem to honour the same people, particularly entrepreneurs, over and over. If you were to launch a

John Timpson Business of the Year award, who would win it and why?

Many years ago, I optimistically competed for a number of awards. It was a familiar routine: fill in the entry form, appear before the judges' panel, then, pleased to be short-listed, proudly purchase a ticket or even a table for the awards dinner, only to discover that cobblers seldom win the cup. We no longer enter, but I can see the appeal of being a sponsor so I can pick the winner instead of waiting to be picked.

Your question gives me the excuse to nominate my favourites. I am bound to select a lot of retailers – it's the world I know.

While there's been a lot of whingeing about the woes of the high street, some of the smarter traders have shown the way simply by providing what people want today. These companies are creating the future of shopping while others complain life is too difficult.

My first candidate, Primark, have proved that teenage pocket money can purchase a wardrobe full of the latest fashion – good taste at amazing prices.

Analysts enjoy pinpointing the problems of the squeezed middle but two companies keep making good money in the centre ground. Next kept a clear head and keeps making more money in the clothing market (have they ever thought of acquiring M&S?) and John Lewis consistently succeeds by looking after the colleagues who look after their customers. Both these businesses have made the link between online and physical shopping.

I have plenty of candidates in the food category. Aldi, Lidl and Iceland all realised the benefits of selling a limited range at low prices, while Waitrose is winning with a completely different formula. These big companies will pick up plenty of other prizes so I have selected a relatively unknown food retailer – Cook, who (mainly in the south-east) have put real quality into ready meals.

My family business nomination is also in the food sector. It goes to breakfast food manufacturer Morning Foods, now being managed by the fifteenth generation of the Lea family. It was founded when William Lea started milling in 1675.

My list has to include Pret a Manger, which provides the UK's quickest fast food with great service. I would also make a special Women in Business Award to EasyJet's CEO, Carolyn McCall, who has used common sense and customer care to increase market share and create shareholder value.

Your question rightly suggests that most awards go to well-known companies whose CEO has a big team to deal with the detail. I prefer to recognise entrepreneurs who do it all themselves. I am amazed whenever I talk to owner-managers like Michael who runs Percy Granthams in Alderley Edge, the best deli in the north-west, and Annie who manages Smarties, an exemplary day nursery near Chester. As well as being the Chief Executive, they also look after sales, personnel and finance. They deal with all the detail and have to fill in all the forms. Our authorities need to think of the burden their rules and regulations create for small businesses that abhor bureaucracy.

To represent these superstars I have chosen a real niche business. If invited to a fancy dress party and the theme is anything from 'Dead Famous' to 'The Sixties', you will find the answer at Party Place in Ellesmere Port. They have three floors full of costumes for hire and, even better, helpful colleagues all with a welcoming smile who make shopping fun. I always leave with exactly what I want and a broad grin, which is what will be on my face next time I call to present them with my Business of the Year Award.

I have read how you manage and measure the success of your business. Cash is king and performance is compared to last year on a weekly basis. Does your wife Alex manage and measure the success of her racehorses in the same way?

Owning racehorses isn't a business, it's a hobby, but at least it is cheaper than buying a football club.

Winning the Grand National is highly lucrative; coming first in a weekday meeting at Wetherby doesn't win enough money to show a profit.

The sums are simple. Training fees, the vet, transport, the jockey's fee and other bits like tipping the stable lads total about £24,000 a year per horse. On average horses run six races a season so you need £4,000 per race to break even. The first prize is usually under £3,000 and only one horse wins each race.

It can get much worse. Alex bought The Crafty Cobbler at the Doncaster sales and paid training fees for a year without getting a penny back on my investment. He died from a heart attack on the gallops and never went near a racecourse. Another, King of Keys, had only run 300 yards on his first outing when he broke a leg and had to be destroyed.

Some horses race much fewer than six times a year. Alex keeps in constant contact with her trainers, who sometimes suggest it would be wise to avoid next week's race. 'Going too soft', 'Doesn't like left-handed courses', 'Race is too hot', or, worst of all, 'He's got a bit of a leg', which means some expensive visits from the vet with several weeks to recover.

If you can't make money, why own a racehorse? Like all sports there is more to it than meets the inexperienced eye.

Despite the setbacks, we always arrive at the racecourse full of optimism (even if bookies are quoting 33/1).

It's fun getting free access through the owners' entrance, seeing our horse saddled up and meeting the jockey in the paddock for a final briefing – 'We're up against four handy horses that will make the running, I'll settle midfield and see how it goes' – code for: 'He's far from the best horse in the race so don't blame me if he is soundly beaten.'

We get nervous at the start and feel a surge of adrenaline that lasts until our horse is tailed off. Excitement turns to disappointment, but the jockey's debrief, well away from the winners' enclosure, usually provides some encouragement: 'He's still a bit green but there's plenty of promise. He's got the character to be a good chaser next season.' So, despite finishing 50 lengths behind the winner we happily keep paying the trainer. Sometimes we win and Alex is photographed receiving a trophy (one was a plaque that our shops sell for £15).

The occasional win helps us ignore the negative cash flow and keep on racing. Pastimes don't have to make a profit. Investment in a project that makes Alex happy is money well spent.

I recently had a meal at The White Eagle in Rhoscolyn and I was extremely impressed with the efficiency with which it is run. The food was excellent and quick to arrive, the staff were friendly and took an interest, the premises were clean, well cared-for and comfortable and it was clear that Timpson's were held in great affection by the staff. Later I saw the quote from Gordon Ramsay advising you to stick to cobbling and key cutting and avoid running a restaurant. As you ignored that advice and went on to create by far the best pub on Anglesey, would you like to comment on the business ideas you used to make it such a success in a field where you were a novice? The White Eagle is well run, good value and a model of good hospitality. Please share your thoughts on how to approach a new business in an area where you are not an expert.

Gordon Ramsay was probably right when he colourfully told my son James: 'You must be mad to open a pub, stick to cutting keys.' However, if we'd taken his advice we would have missed a fascinating venture and a lot of fun.

We got involved on a whim after Alex 'persuaded' me to buy a holiday cottage in Rhoscolyn. Alex hates cooking and likes to eat out but wasn't impressed with the food on offer nearby. Her answer was to buy The White Eagle and make it her sort of pub. Alex's determination to turn her vision into reality is probably the original secret of success but it didn't happen without many unexpected problems and lots of help from some fantastic people.

The first few months were a nightmare. We passed our

licensee course but it didn't tell us how to deal with a dirty kitchen, which, on the day we took over, stored only two frozen burgers, six fish fingers and a limp lettuce. We spent hours sitting quietly at a corner table just watching. Some days we had fewer than ten customers. We decorated, changed the menu, produced a regular newsletter, provided toys, books and a menu for children, a changing specials board for their parents, we took barrels of my favourite beer, Weetwood, from a brewery near our home in Cheshire, in the back of our car and we went through seven head chefs in the first twelve months.

Steadily things got better, sales doubled and we started making money. I was happy but Alex was far from satisfied. 'It's OK but not great. If you do something you should do it properly.' To show she meant business, The White Eagle was closed for nine months and mostly demolished to build the pub Alex really wanted, with a little bit of the Timpson culture added in.

It worked, not just because of the building but mainly thanks to the people who made it happen. We took the team to see lots of pubs we liked and got generous advice from successful publicans Gary and Woody, who saved us from making several silly mistakes. Rupert, our interior decorator, designed the pub to feel like home. We were lucky to have Stuart and Kirsty, our first experienced managers who understood what we wanted. The standards are maintained by Adrienne, who is in charge today. We didn't just want pub grub and were fortunate to find Roger, who must be the best head chef ever to come to Anglesey, and Dave who produces puddings to die for.

We were naive to think that it is simple to turn round a rundown pub. It was going to be a hobby but soon became pretty serious. There wasn't a secret formula. The White Eagle has been created by people, not a process. Alex had a vision and was determined that nothing would stand in her way. But she could not have done it without trusting lots of talented people (all those I have mentioned and many more) with the freedom to help turn her dream into reality.

It worked well enough for us to open another pub down the road at Rhosneigr, The Oyster Catcher, which includes a training kitchen to help young people on Anglesey. They are both busy but we now know that running a pub is hard work and have no plans to expand our catering division. We will stop at two pubs and enjoy them. A cobbler should stick to his last.

This is not a business question but, as the festive season approaches, I am planning parties for my teenaged children and their friends. As you must have done this in the past for your children and foster children, have you any tips to pass on, as I am dreading the task?

Office and teenage parties have similar pitfalls but there is a subtle difference. Your team expects you to turn up at the office do (but make sure you leave before the dancing starts and drink gives colleagues the courage to criticise their boss). By contrast, your child will hope you won't attend their party. Ignore that advice, especially if they plan to invade your home. Stay around until every guest has disappeared or fallen asleep.

Following mistakes made when our children were teenagers, I wrote a 'Guide to Teenage Parties', which I'll send to any reader who emails their address to askjohn@telegraph.com.

Here is a flavour of things in that guide.

Send a formal invitation – it discourages gatecrashers. Less than 65% will reply but don't assume the rest have refused. Never let your child issue invitations by word of mouth because their message will be passed on to many more friends than you bargained for.

Your child may have 'really nice chums' but will probably invite at least one tearaway and one is enough to create mayhem.

If possible, push the idea of hiring a local hall. Whatever the price, it could be a big money-saver. You will want to protect your property and safety precautions for a party at home can come at a considerable cost.

If you can afford it, hire a marquee and make the house out of bounds. Portaloos are expensive but should stop guests roaming round your home. Most guests will be staying the night so designate a community sleeping area or, even better, buy a couple of tents. Make as much of the house as possible out of bounds. Lock internal doors, lock your car and any outbuildings and, if you have one, lock your wine cellar. I don't want to be alarmist but consider hiring a security guard and check that you have a well-stocked first aid kit.

Hire a disco. Guests may take little notice of the music but the disc jockey creates a friendly atmosphere and comes with a wealth of experience. He can tell you how the party is going, where and who the problems are, and what to do next.

If your child goes to a boarding school, expect some guests to arrive two days early and use your house as a hotel while they visit other friends in your area. Most guests that come from a distance will expect you to pick them up from the train.

Initially the guests will appear more mature than we were at their age, but don't be fooled. For the first two hours a lot will drink and some will drink a lot. Girls talk to girls and boys to boys, at first it appears like an adult drinks party; then one by one they start to enjoy themselves, and the party will spread as far through your house as possible.

You can't supervise while standing in one place. Find an excuse to wander about – collect empty glasses or pick up litter. Stay on patrol until everyone is docile and you think it is safe to go to your bed (but don't say 'Goodnight').

Your guests won't be so cheerful when they wake up in the morning but you will be only too willing to give them a lift back to the railway station. Don't expect many to write a thank you letter, although a couple of emails thanking you for an awesome party will make it all feel well worthwhile.

How to Be Nice and Make Money

Occasionally I am asked (but so far not by a *Telegraph* reader), 'Why do you keep working? What do you do it all for?' The inference is that having made a fair amount of money, anyone with any sense would cash in and spend the funds on a fabulous retirement. It is assumed that successful businessmen have an exit strategy. I don't – I plan to hand over the family business to future generations. In the meantime I will continue to enjoy following the fortunes of the company that has been such a big part of my life; and, thanks to prompting from Alex, we are finding ways to use our success to put a bit back into the community.

The usual phrase is 'to make a difference', but on the charity front I start with a disadvantage. I'm pretty poor at fundraising, I don't like sitting on charity committees and when it comes to charity balls I would happily pay twice the ticket price to stay at home. The Timpson Foundation doesn't simply distribute donations, we concentrate on causes close to our heart where we give time as well as money.

I would much rather be a mentor than a committee member. I like to think the £2m we have given After Adoption has mattered much more because we keep close to their team. Our investment in people leaving prison works because we give them a job and become their life coach.

Without having a business, few entrepreneurs could 'make

a difference', but many more than the public appreciate use part of their profits to 'put something back' and in the process discover that doing good is good for business. Both customers and colleagues like companies that care – and what, unfortunately, is now called 'corporate social responsibility' pushes companies up the pecking order of public respect.

The charity you support is a personal choice but the priority before any other worthy cause must always be to look after those company colleagues who need your help. Before the business starts to look after others, make sure it looks after the colleagues who look after the business.

*

What do you consider is the best idea that you have introduced?

The best ideas are so simple they last a long time.

Thirteen years ago, my wife Alex and I were invited by the Duke of Westminster to a small dinner at his Cheshire home to launch a campaign on behalf of the NSPCC. On the way back in the car Alex gave me a clear message: 'We had a great evening but we never had to hand over any money', she said. 'You ought to do something really special to help.'

I had a sleepless night worrying what to do, but over an early cup of tea the following morning I gave Alex my answer: 'Little bits of stitching and holes in belts.'

'You'll have to explain', said Alex, looking slightly irritated. I went on: 'We do a lot of quick and simple jobs in our shops for which we charge nominal amounts like 50p and

£1.50. My idea is to do the jobs for free and simply ask the customer to put £1 in a charity box.'

It worked. In the first week we collected over £2,000 and customers have continued to put £1 in the box in return for free jobs ever since. While collecting money for charity we are also impressing customers with our service. A typical compliment came from a man who had a stitching job in Bath: 'I was amazed, I wasn't sure he would even bother to do the job, but he did it for nothing and just asked me to pop a £1 in the box.'

Since the scheme started we have collected over £4m! First for the NSPCC, then ChildLine, and now we are helping to finance SafeBase, a programme developed by After Adoption to help adoptive families cope with the profound problems that can occur when caring for children whose difficult start in life has caused Attachment Disorder.

We are now using our customers' donations to leverage an even bigger pot of money. To encourage local authority social service departments to run the SafeBase support courses, we offer to pay half if they will match our funding. It is working – this year we hope to help well over 200 families, but with at least 2,000 children being adopted each year we need to do much more.

SafeBase costs £2,000 for each family we help, but the financial benefits are much greater than that. 20% of adoptive placements break down, leading to an average annual cost of keeping a child in care of about £50,000. So potentially every £2,000 spent on SafeBase is saving £10,000 every year – a 500% return on investment.

SafeBase is the perfect candidate for government support

through a social impact bond, a way of investing in social projects that give a real return on capital.

If we could attract central support of £2m we would be able to offer the SafeBase programme to every new adoptive family and achieve a brilliant benefit on behalf of our customers who put £1 in the box.

Many years ago we started to hear the phrase 'unacceptable face of capitalism'. But does business still deserve such a damning reputation?

I wish to do something fairly unfashionable. I want to talk about good news.

Recently, while in the USA, I met Jeremiah and Paula, young relatives who have just moved to live and work in San Francisco. 'It's great', said Jeremiah. 'What a difference', added Paula, 'everyone is so full of positivity.'

I returned home to find another barrage of negative news about business – media complaints about bankers, bonuses, fraudulent practice and fat cat bosses that give employees a rough deal.

When running a business you can't be nice to everyone all the time, but it's possible to do lots of good along the way, and many bosses do. I am not just talking about the sustainable stuff – being a good business isn't simply about cutting out carrier bags and creating a smaller carbon footprint. Doing good goes much deeper than ticking boxes under the heading 'corporate social responsibility'. By creating a caring culture companies can make a big difference to people's lives.

Businesses all include 'charitable giving' statistics in their annual reports but they are often the tip of a very big iceberg. I checked the Timpson return for last year: it declared donations of £136,000. Not bad, I thought, until I started to dig deeper.

During the year we recruited 93 people from prison. It is a sobering fact that 61% of ex-offenders return to prison within two years. For those with a job, the re-offending rate falls to 19% and the Timpson experience is down at 3%. The annual cost of keeping someone in prison stands at over £50,000. As well as putting 93 lives back on track we probably saved the taxpayer about £5m.

£50,000 of our reported donations go to After Adoption, our company charity. That only tells part of the story. In addition, we collect nearly £6,000 a week by doing free jobs for customers who then put money in our charity box. Our colleagues raise a further £40,000 a year through a range of exploits like running marathons and jumping out of aircraft. The total we give to After Adoption of nearly £400,000 a year is used to match-fund local authority expenditure on support for adoptive families, providing an estimated benefit of at least £4m.

We train 400 apprentices a year. Many companies receive around £1,250 of government funding for every apprentice – we get nothing, saving the state £5m.

I could include the contributions that colleagues make to other causes (with our support), and the free counselling our managers provide to employees and their families. But I have already shown benefits that total £14m – more than our annual profit. I plead guilty to using some rough and ready accounting but however you work the figures, it is bound to be a large number.

We are not alone. Loads of other businesses do their big bit for society – indeed, I am willing to bet that the social good being done by the private sector is worth more than £20 billion a year!

A lot of us have discovered that doing good is good for business. People like working for a company with a conscience, especially if they are involved themselves. Enlightened entrepreneurs go beyond their company's charity policy by helping colleagues who want to support a special personal cause or launch a long-cherished project.

Customers are also keen on companies that make a major contribution to their community. Altruistic organisations, with an awareness of the outside world and a caring culture, attract colleagues and customers alike.

But all this goodness is hidden by the continual media attention given to corporate greed, deceit and incompetence. So I was delighted to meet Kay Allen, who is working with the Prime Minister's advisor on corporate social responsibility, Philip Green, on an initiative called 'Trading for Good'. This is a scheme that plans to tell the stories of inspirational businesses and help others to join the club.

At a time when we are bombarded by bad news about bankers, the rest of business is being tarred with the same brush. We are not all selfish and greedy – a lot of companies have a social conscience that they passionately put into practice.

I hope the 'Trading for Good' message will receive plenty of exposure and, for a change, we read some good news and celebrate all that is great about Britain's businesses.

**Our local Scout hall is under threat of closure and I'm
thinking seriously about stepping in. Several of our staff
send their kids there and I know it will be missed. We can
spare some cash for now but I want to feel that over time
it can get back on a self-financing footing. Has Timpson
had any experience of making such social investments
and are there any pitfalls to avoid?**

It is better to support a local cause that you know well rather
than put money into a big charity pot. The scouts, along with
cubs and beavers, play a positive part in helping to develop
young people. It is a good cause, but find out as much as you
can before signing a cheque.

Are you aware of the real reasons why it is under the
threat of closure? How well do you know the people running
the Scout group? Although they are volunteers, be satisfied
that the organisers are doing a good job and have a viable
plan for the future.

For the last four years we have supported Delamere
Primary School, a local school where a number of foster children went while they were living with Alex and myself.

Five years ago the school was threatened with closure. We
decided to help by offering to fund a significant extension to
the regular curriculum designed to turn Delamere School into
a true centre of excellence. We gave time as well as money – I
became Chairman of the Governors for a year and did what I
could to support Steve, the head teacher. I tried to ensure he
was left on his own to run the school and encouraged him to
spend as little time as possible ticking government-designed

boxes so he could spend lots more of his time looking after the kids.

It worked. The extra lessons included art, music, theatre, cooking, nature studies in nearby Delamere Forest, and the chance to go canoeing and orienteering. When children arrived in the morning they started to say, 'What are we doing in school today?'

Within three years we had an outstanding inspection report. The number of pupils doubled and on 1 April 2011 we became Delamere Primary Academy, probably the first and certainly the smallest Primary Academy in the country.

I learnt a lot along the way. Working with an organisation that relies on government or charitable funding bears little resemblance to a business, but on the most important aspect it is exactly the same. Success depends on having talented people with good ideas and the determination to succeed.

I wish you well with your Scout hall. I hope you can get closely involved and take pride in its success.

I have read that you have recently completed the London Marathon, which is a magnificent achievement. Presumably you raised money for charity. However, at your age and with your responsibilities, is it sensible to put your business and family at risk by undertaking such an activity?

You're right, I did take part in this year's London Marathon. I am not particularly proud of my time (over 33,000 runners finished in front of me) so you may well wonder why I bothered to enter.

In March I was installed as Master of the Worshipful Company of Pattenmakers. Alongside delightful invitations which have included dinner with The Basketmakers and lunch with The Apothecaries, the Livery Company has a charitable fund and our main money-raising event is the London Marathon. A significant sum from the £55,000+ we have raised will help to provide specialist orthopaedic footwear for injured servicemen at Headley Court through an initiative established by our Patron, HRH The Duke of Gloucester.

That was my excuse, but it was also a selfish move. My last marathon was in 1984 and I wanted to prove that at 68 I was not too old to do it again. As soon as I tried a bit of training I discovered that I can only run slowly, very slowly. But while I padded round the roads near home I started to feel fitter (a medical proved this was true), and jogging gave me lots of uninterrupted time to think about the business.

We made it a family affair. Sons Edward and Oliver plus my daughter Victoria and her husband all entered to run with me. In truth they all ran off and finished way ahead of me, apart from Edward who gallantly helped Dad get his dodgy knee round the course.

So no harm done – but having seen pictures of me at the finish, Alex has told me I will definitely not do it again.

I work in corporate finance for a large professional services firm. Recently when contacting a prospective client, I was asked to donate £200 to a specific charity, which would entitle me to an appointment. I have not

experienced this before and have yet to agree as I do not want to set a precedent. What should I do?

When something doesn't feel right, your suspicions are usually well founded. Not everyone raising money for charity is Mr Nice Guy. Blackmailing potential suppliers who ask for an appointment is probably the sign of an arrogant operator.

If you are tempted by his offer, you may find he changes the date of the appointment a few times before you eventually get to his office. He will probably keep you waiting in reception for 45 minutes, and if you do a deal he could come back weeks later demanding an extra 20% discount and 30 days' credit.

Keep well clear!

I have read that Timpson employs more prison leavers than any other company in the UK and that you select them on their personalities. This sounds admirable but rather risky. Would you recommend other employers to follow your lead?

Our involvement with ex-offenders started eleven years ago when my son James was helping to organise a conference in Thorn Cross, a prison near Warrington. James was so impressed with Matt, the guy who showed him round, he handed over his business card, saying, 'Get in touch when you get out and I will find you a job'. Matt now manages one of our highly successful shops and is happily married with two children.

Having helped Matt we decided to see if we could do it again, especially having seen some disturbing statistics. 61% of people leaving prison re-offend within two years, but if they get a job that figure drops to 19%.

There are about 88,000 people in prison and they come in all shapes and sizes. Among the bad and the tricky are plenty that are fantastic. When interviewing inside prison we use exactly the same standards that we use when recruiting on the outside, in the knowledge that so few other companies are willing to give them a job we have the pick of a talented bunch.

We had so much success, four years ago we opened a training workshop in Liverpool prison, fitted out like a Timpson shop with our own trainers going in every day, teaching prisoners who wear the Timpson uniform. All trainees who pass their skill tests are offered a job on release.

Some recruits from other prisons started working in our shops while still serving their sentence. This 'day release' scheme has been staggeringly successful – 90% of these ex-offenders have stayed with us for more than a year.

We have learnt a lot during the last nine years. In particular we now know that everyone needs a Dennis. Dennis Phillips, a burly amateur football referee who works in our People Support department, took on the role of mentor from day one. James had the courage to make employing ex-prisoners a priority, but Dennis turned the policy into reality by dealing with the detail and helping these new colleagues with the big range of problems they face outside work. People leaving prison find it tough to get back on their feet.

We have seen some real success. We are about to open our fifth prison workshop and sixteen of our shops are now managed by people recruited from prison. Out of nearly 300 men and women who have joined us over the last four years we only know of seven who have re-offended. But it isn't just the statistics that tell me we are making a difference. I receive regular evidence during my shop visits whenever one of our recruits from prison talks about their life-changing experience.

The scheme has worked better than I ever imagined but we still face a major challenge. So far we have only persuaded a very small number of companies to follow our example.

Do ex-Army soldiers make good employees? I should imagine their discipline, time-keeping, energy and getting things done are positives for many jobs. Has your company employed any ex-military men?

We employ colleagues from a variety of backgrounds.

I don't know why, but we seem to attract a lot of chefs and publicans, and I am pleased to say we are now seeing a lot more women, keen to do key cutting and shoe repairs. I think it is well known that we recruit a significant number of people from prison, and we have started to receive applications from a few veterans of the armed forces – if at all possible we give them all an interview.

Wherever they come from, success is determined by their personality rather than experience.

Military service certainly gives a strong level of discipline – most ex-servicemen turn up on time and look the part. But for some the freedom of Civvy Street can come as a shock. We want our people to use their initiative, and the lack of rules can make a few of them nervous.

The first few weeks are critical. It doesn't take long to see whether they can make the transition from the parade ground to commerce.

At the start of my career, business had a strong military base. Many of the management positions were filled by men who had served during the Second World War. As a result our company had 'standing orders' which were implemented with strict discipline.

Today we value trust and respect ahead of command and control, so working at Timpson is very different from being in the Army. A military background can help but it is vital to have the right personality.

Dear John, you've had incredible business success in your life. I'm curious to know: what things are left that you still want to achieve?

Every year Timpson faces a new challenge. In the 1960s the shops simply sold shoe repairs, shoe polish and laces. During the next 50 years 90% of the cobbling market disappeared, so we diversified – into keys, engraving, watch repairs and recently dry cleaning.

In the next twelve months another service will be introduced: mobile phone repairs – the latest move to make our sales grow in a declining market, on a difficult high street.

Before there was any talk of green shoots we embarked on a major investment programme. This year, we will open at least 100 new outlets (mainly supermarket sites). This brings another challenge. Can we keep our small company culture in a business that is getting a lot bigger?

But these days it isn't my job to tackle these problems. It is up to the CEO, James, and his team to make the running and take the credit for success.

Like many Chairmen, my personal challenge is beyond the business.

Alex and I had been foster carers and adoptive parents for fourteen years before we were told about the attachment problems that so often affect looked-after children. A shortage of love and security in early childhood can create lack of trust later in life, leading to behaviour that can test the most patient of parents.

Over 30% of young people in prison come from the care system, and attachment problems are at the heart of their behaviour. It is about time more people found out about attachment.

Fortunately help is at hand. As I mentioned in an earlier column, the charity After Adoption has developed a support programme called SafeBase that not only explains the significance of attachment problems but also gives parents the right strategies to care for their children. To quote one parent whom I met recently after she had completed a SafeBase course: 'It is amazing. We were an unhappy family at our wits' end, but SafeBase put our life back on track.'

My challenge is to spread the word about attachment and make SafeBase available to every adoptive family in the UK. As well as match-funding any local authority that signs up to SafeBase, we at Timpson have produced a couple of little picture books (*A Guide to Attachment* and *How to Create a Positive Future*) to get the message across to adoptive families and business colleagues with attachment difficulties.

If you think this is all soppy social service talk, let me tell you the business case. 20% of adoptions fail – for SafeBase families that drops to less than 2%. But the benefits go well beyond a crude return on investment. Poor early parenting and attachment problems have created a social time bomb that could cause more trouble in the classroom, undermine law and order, make more people unemployable. I estimate that the £2,000 it costs to provide each family with SafeBase support will on average save social services at least £20,000 every year.

Conclusion

When I'm visiting our shops many colleagues mention they have been quizzed by *Telegraph* readers who want to know whether I make it all up or if they really do have their birthday off and get free use of our holiday homes. It is good to know my column brings a few extra customers to our shops, where I hope they discover our colleagues turning my words into action.

In writing 'Ask John', hopefully I have shown that there is a light-hearted side to management, but I have also tried to make a case for a few important concepts in the cause of better business.

I'm keen to convince the world that management is an art, not a science. We are progressively being surrounded by a world that is run by process. I hope my column has persuaded more managers to have the courage to use their flair and initiative and to challenge the establishment who rely on governance and best practice. I am always happy to champion the cause of a maverick.

I'm pleased that readers often describe the column as common sense. Running a business doesn't need to be complicated – the simplest solutions tend to create the most success.

Our biggest simple idea is Upside Down Management. I reckon a lot of other businesses would benefit from adopting our upside down way of working. The transformation I've seen in the pleasure our colleagues now get out of their life at work, and the success they have created, can't just be something that can only happen to a cobbler. I hope my column has helped others to pick people on personality, do more delegation, and stop blindly running their business according to the modern management book.

I make a strong case for discrimination. I've seen the difference it makes when you fill your business with positive personalities who deserve to be rated 9 and 10 out of 10. As a result of recent employment law, management teams now spend the lion's share of their time dealing with the problem people who get in the way of success. Too few managers have the courage to tell their passengers: 'Your best will never be good enough for us, so it is time for you to seek your happiness elsewhere.'

We might be tough on the poor performers but I believe in finding as many ways as possible to praise and reward our superstars. We don't give everyone the same benefits. I am proud to say that we discriminate in favour of the people who make us the most money.

I hope we have proved that you can still be nice and create a successful business. I am amazed how many true superstars we have found by actively recruiting from prison. While other companies come up with a raft of reasons why they can't employ anyone with a criminal record, we continue to get the pick of a potentially talented bunch. I hope that by continuing to talk about the success of our ex-offenders we will persuade others to follow our example.

Over the years, the experience Alex and I have had with fostering and adoption has naturally led to the company supporting children's charities – NSPCC, then ChildLine, and now After Adoption. We have established a chefs' training scheme at our pub, The Oyster Catcher, for young people on Anglesey, and we have supported our local school, Delamere Primary Academy, with a bursary.

At Delamere I encouraged the head teacher, Steve Docking, to ignore a lot of the usual policies and guidelines and use his initiative to give the children a memorable education. Steve has created a true centre of excellence and in doing so has proved that Upside Down Management can work in organisations well away from the world of business. The Delamere success also shows the benefits that business can bring by spending some money and a fair amount of time in the local community.

The work we do with people leaving prison, the support we give to children's charities, the Chefs' Academy on Anglesey, and our link with Delamere School have become an important part of the Timpson culture. We found that doing good is good for business.

Observant readers will have noticed the number of times my wife, Alex, appears in the column to provide the straightforward thinking that so often seems to be missing from the boardroom. With the help of Alex I hope I have shown that good management should be based on common sense.

Please keep sending in your questions and comments to askjohn@telegraph.com. I will do my best to answer your problems, but to find out more, go and chat to one of our colleagues in a branch of Timpson or Max Spielmann. To help you on the way, you will find a discount voucher in this book in the form of a bookmark.

Index

financial performance,
measurement 218–20
Financial Times 119–20
Fleming, Alexander 293
flexible working 31–4, 207
fly on the wall
being 105–6
documentary 116–18
football 164–5, 283–4
Footwear Economic
Development Council 266
Foster Care Fortnight 126
foster caring 247, 277, 282, 324
'four-hour week' 108–9
France 259
franchisees, choosing 94
FTSE index 255
future
challenges 319–20
preparing for 112

Game 122
gap years 196
Garstang 70
Gates, Bill 285
General Electric 27
Gilbert, W.S. 294
Glasgow 149, 157
Gloucester, Duke of 315
golden rules 225–6
golf clubs 160
good performers
discriminating in favour of
87–8, 324
rewarding 66–7
government, business and 252,
266–7

government contracts 247
Grace, W.G. 294
graduates, hiring 12–13
grammar 16
Granada Rental 225
Greece 257
Green, Kit 277
Green, Philip 312
Greggs 125
Grimsey, Bill 212
growth
barriers to 208
future 63
and new development 249
organic 183
grumpiness 277
'Guide to Teenage Parties' 304–5
gurus 208
gyms 157

Hackitt, Judith 244
Hale 127
Hamilton-Fisher, Gouy 7–8, 29, 48
Handforth 95
Hanson Trust 171, 178
'Happy Index' 92
Hardship Fund 24
Harrods 54
Hawkin's Bazaar 122
Headley Court 315
heads of terms 171, 175
health questionnaires 15
health and safety 241–5
high street
and e-commerce 127–9
names disappearing from 122
neighbours 125–6

Index